# Creating Dynamic
# MULTIMEDIA
# Presentations

## Using Microsoft PowerPoint® 2003

### 3e

## Carol M. Lehman
*Mississippi State University*

THOMSON

SOUTH-WESTERN

Australia · Brazil · Canada · Mexico · Singapore · Spain · United Kingdom · United States

**THOMSON**

**SOUTH-WESTERN**

Creating Dynamic Multimedia Presentations Using Microsoft PowerPoint 2003, Third Edition
Carol M. Lehman

**VP/Editorial Director:**
Jack W. Calhoun

**VP/Editor-in-Chief:**
Dave Shaut

**Acquisitions Editor:**
Neil Marquardt

**Developmental Editor:**
Erin Berger

**Marketing Manager:**
Larry Qualls

**Production Project Manager:**
Heather Mann

**Manager of Technology, Editorial:**
Vicky True

**Manufacturing Coordinator:**
Diane Lohman

**Production House:**
Graphic World Publishing Services

**Compositor:**
International Typesetting & Composition

**Printer:**
Thomson West
Eagan, MN

**Art Director:**
Stacy Jenkins Shirley

**Internal Designer:**
Joseph Pagliaro Graphic Design

**Cover Designer:**
Joseph Pagliaro Graphic Design

**Cover Illustration:**
© Getty Images

Library of Congress Control Number:
2005929221

For more information about our products,
contact us at:
**Thomson Learning Academic
Resource Center
1-800-423-0563**

**Thomson Higher Education**
5191 Natorp Boulevard
Mason, OH 45040
USA

# BRIEF CONTENTS

# CONTENTS

Contents

# PREFACE

Throughout your career, you will be judged by the effectiveness with which you communicate in your daily activities. You might make a presentation to your peers in committee work, to subordinates as a part of a training or information program, or to senior management or a client in a formal presentation. In each case, your reputation is on the line. When you are effective, you gain status and earn respect. You find managing others easier, and you become promotable to increasingly higher levels.

Today's speakers are required to develop media-rich interactive presentations to be delivered in conference rooms or board meetings as well as Web-based presentations that may be delivered in different time zones. Yet, the basics of preparing an effective presentation have not changed. No innovative technological tool can substitute for the ability to determine a purpose that focuses on an audience's needs, to relate ideas clearly and effectively, and to be sincere and responsive to the audience. Instead, your effectiveness depends on your ability to focus on fundamental communication skills while using technology to enhance each phase of the presentation process: (1) developing crisp, well-organized content; (2) designing top-notch support tools appropriate for the delivery method (overhead transparencies, electronic or Web presentations, and audience handouts); and (3) delivering the presentation smoothly and professionally.

For these reasons, *Creating Dynamic Multimedia Presentations,* Third Edition, goes beyond the simple how-to manual for learning how to create simple PowerPoint presentations using standard presentation designs and consisting of dense, countless bulleted lists and other bland, dull designs. In 10 short projects, you will:

- Master the full functionality of Microsoft PowerPoint 2003.

- Apply presentation design guidelines that will empower you to build presentations that enrich the primary message and keep the focus of the audience's attention on you without stealing precious preparation time. Your efficiency will allow you more time to determine exactly what your audience needs and wants to know; develop logical, compelling content; and rehearse for a smooth delivery.

- Refine skillful delivery techniques that will reduce the distance technology often places between the speaker and the audience.

*Creating Dynamic Multimedia Presentations,* Third Edition, expedites your mastery of these powerful communication skills by minimizing the time you spend creating basic slides. Instead, you will critique "original" slides that a novice might design and then build enhanced slides that correct violations in basic slide design principles and focus on precise, strong visual content. This strategy is illustrated in the following slides.

### Greatest Fears

| Speaking | 41% |
|---|---|
| Heights | 32 |
| Insects & bugs | 22 |
| Financial | 22 |
| Deep water | 22 |
| Sickness | 19 |
| Death | 19 |

**Source:** Books of Lists, 2002

Original slide

### Public Speaking Tops List of People's Greatest Fears

| Speaking | 41% |
|---|---|
| Heights | 32% |
| Insects & bugs | 22% |
| Financial | 22% |
| Deep water | 22% |
| Sickness | 19% |
| Death | 19% |

Enhanced slide

Completing these 10 brief projects and the Reinforcement Activities will lead to proficiency in the following techniques:

- Creating a basic presentation that includes a title and bulleted lists with simple clip art, slide transitions, and custom animation.

- Adding impact and appeal with (1) dynamic and relevant images and sound, (2) creative animation techniques that target the audience's attention for higher impact, (3) compelling tables and graphs that clarify and reinforce potentially overwhelming numerical data, and (4) hidden slides and hyperlinks that add flexibility and interaction to the delivery of the slide show.

- Showcasing your organizational structure and cinching seamless delivery by:
  - Incorporating agenda and divider slides that transition the audience smoothly through the sections of the presentation.
  - Recording and analyzing rehearsal timings to identify a variety of content and delivery improvements.
  - Using the speller and style checker to eliminate embarrassing errors.
  - Creating useful speaker's notes and professional audience handouts that enhance your credibility and extend the usefulness of the presentation.

- Designing a custom template that fits the needs of a specific audience or topic and reflects your company's professional image and unique corporate identity.

- Taking your presentation design and delivery expertise to the next level by adapting PowerPoint content for a variety of remote audiences: (1) a live presentation delivered by videoconference; (2) a PowerPoint presentation published and posted to the Web; and (3) a media presentation produced using Microsoft Producer, a free add-on to PowerPoint 2002 and higher.

While mastering these creative design techniques, you will encounter feature boxes containing bonus information related to three presentation skill sets:

**◄ Designer's Pointer**—basic slide design principles that will allow you to escape the "Death by PowerPoint" verdict being handed down in corporate America today.

**► Presenter's Strategy**— suggestions for using a specific PowerPoint feature or design technique to enhance content or delivery style.

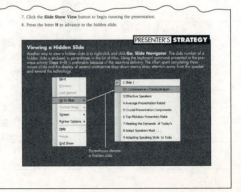

◄ **Technology Tip**—assistance with PowerPoint or Windows-related operations that the author anticipates will challenge readers. Also look for nuggets of useful information related to multimedia development.

The time devoted to completing this textbook will yield positive results as you seek to become an effective speaker in today's highly competitive workplace. You will gain expertise in designing dynamic PowerPoint presentations that focus on time-less communication skills that allow you to connect with your audience and achieve the goals you have established for that group—regardless of the delivery method you choose. You will be able to design and deliver a slide show in an effortless, seamless manner and recognize the importance of practicing until the technology is virtually transparent, positioned in the background to serve as your supporting cast. Assume your important role as the presentation star and you will reap the benefits gained from honing your presentation skills to meet the high expectations of today's audiences—live, remote, or connected in cyberspace!

# ■ ACKNOWLEDGMENTS

A special thanks to three professors who reviewed the previous edition of this book and provided useful comments and suggestions for the revision: Marjorie L. Icenogle, University of South Alabama; Professor Thomas A. Marshall II, Robert Morris University; and Susan Strack Vargo, Indiana University, Kelley School of Business.

# ■ ABOUT THE AUTHOR

Dr. Lehman is a professor of management in the Management & Information Systems Department at Mississippi State University, an AACSB-accredited school. She has more than 20 years of experience teaching business communication. Dr. Lehman earned her bachelor's and master's degrees in business education from the University of Southern Mississippi and her Ed.D. from the University of Arkansas.

Dr. Lehman teaches organizational communication, a core requirement for all business majors, and an MBA-level multimedia presentations course. Whether traditional or distance, her classroom instruction is supplemented with Web-accessible materials that enrich and enliven the learning experience for the students. Her multimedia presentation students perfect design and delivery of media-rich, dynamic presentations delivered through a variety of distribution points—live audience and remote audiences through e-mail, CD/DVD, and the Web.

Together with Dr. Debbie DuFrene from Stephen F. Austin State University, Dr. Lehman authors *Business Communication,* fourteenth edition, one of the leading introductory business communication texts. She is actively engaged in research and a frequent presenter at the national and regional meetings of the Association for Business Communication, for which she and Dr. DuFrene sponsor the Meada Gibbs Outstanding Teacher Award. Her consulting and training activities for industry have focused on multimedia development, business presentations, and written communication.

# Getting Started with PowerPoint

## ■ UNDERSTANDING POWERPOINT

PowerPoint, a graphics software program that is part of Microsoft Office 2003, has become the standard tool for building presentation visuals for the workplace. A PowerPoint presentation is developed by adding individual slides related to the same topic to a single file. The slides can be projected as a presentation to a live audience, printed as transparencies or handouts, or posted to a Web page or broadcast for viewing by a broad audience in diverse locations.

### *Starting PowerPoint*

1. Double-click the PowerPoint icon (or click **Start, Programs, Microsoft Office, PowerPoint 2003**). The startup dialog box appears.

2. Click **Create a new presentation . . .** to start PowerPoint.

3. Take the time to become familiar with the PowerPoint screen and presentation window before creating the first slide.

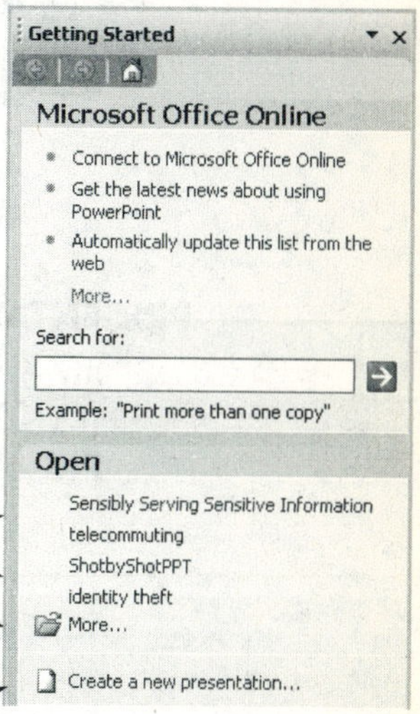

Click to list recently used presentation files

Browse to open another presentation file

Create a new presentation

## ■ UNDERSTANDING THE POWERPOINT WINDOW

Study the following diagram and terms that identify and explain the various elements of the PowerPoint screen and presentation window.

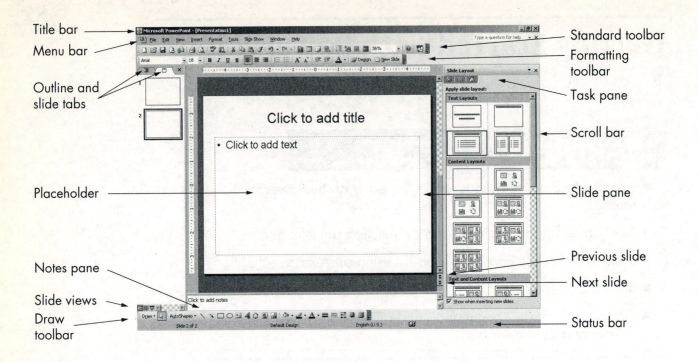

## SCREEN PARTS

| | |
|---|---|
| **Title bar** | Identifies that PowerPoint is running and displays the file name. |
| **Menu bar** | Provides menus from which features can be accessed. |
| **Standard toolbar** | Gives quick access to the most frequently used file functions. |
| **Formatting toolbar** | Provides buttons for changing font types, sizes, attributes, and color. |
| **Draw toolbar** | Provides buttons for inserting text or quick graphics. |
| **Task pane** | Provides commonly used commands that can be accessed while working on the slide. Navigation buttons allow easy movement between task panes. |

## PRESENTATION WINDOW

| | |
|---|---|
| **Slide pane** | Displays placeholders for text and graphics to be inserted. |
| **Placeholder** | Dotted-line boxes that designate the location on a slide in which titles, text, art, graphics, charts, and other objects can be placed. |
| **Text object** | A term used to describe text in a text box (often a graphic object). |
| **View buttons** | Control the number of slides displayed and the display layout (normal, slide sorter, and slide show). |
| **Status bar** | Contains the slide number and the template selected. |
| **Previous slide** | Displays the previous slide. |
| **Next slide** | Displays the next slide. |

| | |
|---|---|
| **Horizontal and vertical scroll buttons** | Moves the text in the window up, down, left, or right. |
| **Outline pane** | Displays the title and body text for slides or a slide thumbnail. |
| **Notes pane** | Provides space where text and graphics can be inserted to support the speaker. |

## ■ UNDERSTANDING DESIGN TEMPLATES

PowerPoint provides an extensive library of predesigned templates created by professional graphic artists. A variety of templates are available: (1) a blank slide with no color and minimal design; (2) a design template with predesigned formats; (3) AutoContent wizard with sample content; and (4) convenient access to presentations you've already created, template designs you've used previously, and other designs from a Web site. Template designs that include designs for color, fonts, bullets, graphics, and other formatting simplify the process of creating a basic presentation.

### *Selecting a Design Template*

1. Click **Create a new presentation...** from the startup menu. Review the various options displayed in the New Presentation task pane.

2. Click the **From design template** option. Scroll to view available options displayed at the right. Click a thumbnail to apply a design template of your choice.

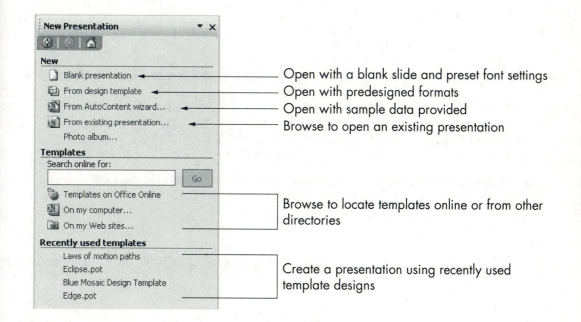

3. Click the **Color Schemes** task pane. Scroll to view the color variations in the design template you selected. Click a thumbnail to choose a color scheme for the presentation you will be building in this project.

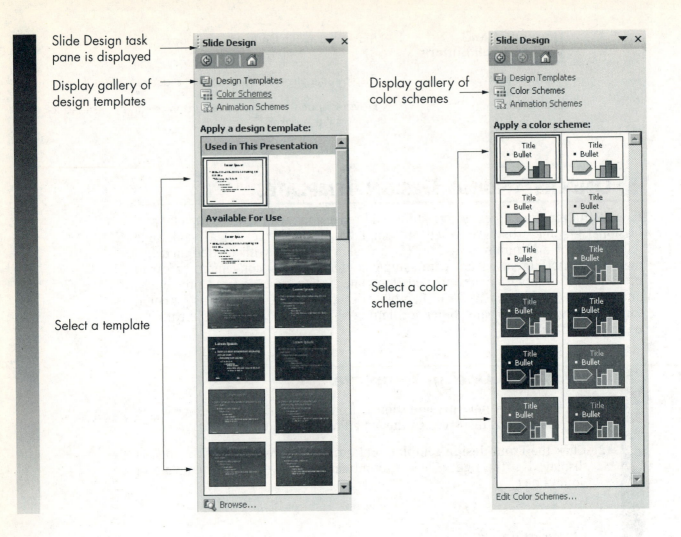

Slide Design task pane is displayed

Display gallery of design templates

Select a template

Display gallery of color schemes

Select a color scheme

## *Applying a Design Template to an Existing Presentation*

After you've opened a presentation, you may apply a different presentation design template for all the slides or selected slides in your presentation. Limiting design choices and applying them consistently throughout a presentation will produce an uncluttered, appealing design.

1. Click **Format, Slide Design** (or click the **Design** button on the Formatting toolbar and select **Design Templates**). Scroll to view the design templates displayed at the right of the slide.

Design button

2. Click a thumbnail to apply a template to all slides in your presentation.

*Note:* Pointing the cursor over the thumbnail will display an arrow indicating a drop-down menu. Click the arrow and then select **Apply to Selected Slides** if you wish to apply a design template to a specific slide(s).

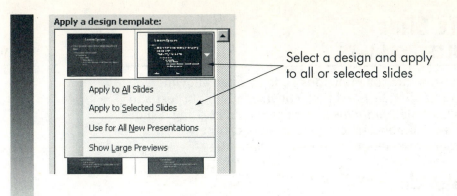

Select a design and apply
to all or selected slides

3. Proceed to the next section.

---

TECHNOLOGY **TIP**

## Enlivening Your Message with Creative Presentation Templates

Because media-rich, dynamic presentations have become the expectation for information distribution and training in the workplace, presentation designers must incorporate well-chosen digital elements that connect thematically to the presentation purpose or brand identity. These powerful images make an experience real or information more understandable or credible to your audience.

Static, overused templates and images must be replaced with lively, original choices. For efficiency and optimal selection, a presenter's toolbox must include a well-stocked professional library of digital media, including templates, backgrounds, photos, sound, and video clips. Recommendation sources for tools that will give your presentation a creative boost include the following:

- Search Microsoft Office Online for new presentation designs. New templates are added to this site regularly, including some developed by third-party providers to support PowerPoint.

- Create a presentation using AutoContent wizard. You simply edit a content template that includes a design template, a suggested outline, and text suggestions for your presentation.

Sample content template created with an AutoContent wizard

- Search online for quality templates available from third-party providers. After evaluating the free templates available, you can purchase the multimedia tools that work best for you. Online subscriptions allow you to conveniently search and download templates and images without the hassle of locating CDs. Here are a few resources to help you get started: Presentations Pro (http://presentationspro.com), Digital Juice (http://digitaljuice.com), and CrystalGraphics (http://crystalgraphics.com).

Enlivening your presentation with well-chosen images will increase the communication power of presentations you deliver in a traditional live-audience presentation setup. Dynamic PowerPoint slides are also the central content for more sophisticated multimedia presentations that you will design in Project 10.

## ◼ CREATING A TITLE SLIDE AND SIMPLE BULLETED LISTS

PowerPoint provides the basic structure for numerous slide layouts, allowing you to click in the designated area (placeholder) and then conveniently input text and graphics. These standard layouts, called *AutoLayouts,* guide you in creating a slide show with a consistent, professional appearance. AutoLayouts can be easily customized when needed to fit your presentation purpose and content.

### *Creating a Title Slide*

*Directions:* Follow the instructions to build the title slide as shown in the model.

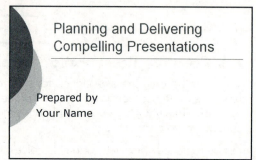

1. Click **Insert**, **New Slide** (or click the **New Slide** button on the Formatting toolbar). Available slide layouts that depict the way text and other contents are arranged are shown on the slide. A layout includes placeholders that will contain text and other contents such as images, charts, and so forth. Pointing the cursor to a layout in the task pane displays a brief description of the layout. The placeholders provide visual cues to the nature of each layout. Scroll down to reveal all layout categories.

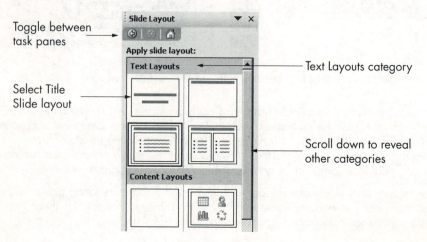

New Slide button

2. Select the Title Slide layout from the Text Layouts category. The selected layout is surrounded by a border; the shaded lines depict positions for a title and a subtitle.

Toggle between task panes

Select Title Slide layout

Text Layouts category

Scroll down to reveal other categories

3. Click in the title placeholder. Note that a selection rectangle surrounds the placeholder with the cursor positioned ready for text to be input.

4. Key the title.

5. Click in the subtitle placeholder and key the subtitle.

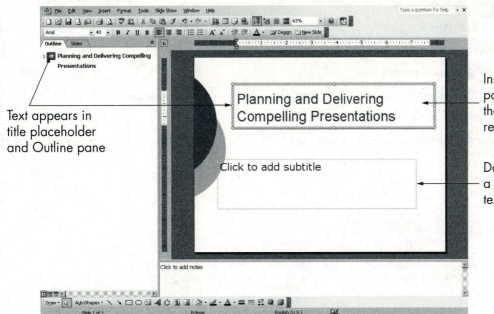

Text appears in title placeholder and Outline pane

Insertion point is positioned within the selection rectangle

Dashed lines denote a placeholder where text can be added

## *Creating a Simple Bulleted List*

*Directions:* Follow the instructions to build the slide shown in the model.

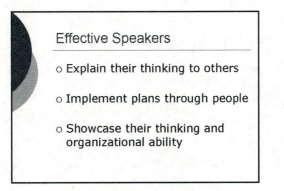

1. Click **Insert**, **New Slide** (or click the **New Slide** button on the Formatting toolbar).

2. Select the Title and Text layout from the Text Layouts category.

3. Click the title placeholder and key the slide title.

4. Click the bulleted list placeholder and key the text for the first bulleted item.

5. Press **Enter**.

6. Key the remaining bulleted items.

## Task Panes at Your Service

Task panes in Microsoft Office 2003 open automatically when you perform certain tasks, such as starting a new document, selecting a layout, inserting clip art, asking for help, and so on. To increase your productivity, learn to use this tool efficiently.

- **Open the task pane:**

  Click **View**, **Task Pane** or press **F1** if the pane doesn't appear automatically.

- **Select another task pane:**

  Click **Other Task Panes** or press **Ctrl+Spacebar** to open a list of task panes.

- **Navigate within task panes:**

  Click **Forward** or **Back** to navigate forward or back through the panes you have been working with.

  Click **Home** to open the Getting Started task pane.

Click Backward and Forward to move between task panes

Display a list of task panes

Clip Art task pane opens

Getting Started

Other Task Panes

### Microsoft Office Online

- Connect to Microsoft Office Online
- Get the latest news about using PowerPoint
- Automatically update this list from the web

  More...

Search for:

Example: "Print more than one copy"

### Open

Sensibly Serving Sensitive Information
telecommuting
ShotbyShotPPT
identity theft
More...

Create a new presentation...

Getting Started

- Getting Started
- Help
- Search Results
- Clip Art
- Research
- Clipboard
- New Presentation
- Template Help
- Shared Workspace
- Document Updates
- Slide Layout
- Slide Design
- Slide Design - Color Schemes
- Slide Design - Animation Schemes
- Custom Animation
- Slide Transition

Clip Art

Search for:

Search in:

All collections

Results should be:

Selected media file types

Organize clips...
Clip art on Office Online
Tips for finding clips

## *Creating a Bulleted List from the Outline Pane*

*Directions:* Follow the instructions to build the slide shown in the model.

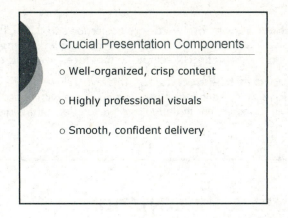

1. Be certain the Outline tab is selected.

2. Insert a new slide from the Outline tab:

   a) Click to the right of the last icon for Slide 2 or after the last word of the slide.

   b) Click **Insert**, **New Slide** (or press **Ctrl+D**).

   c) Select the Title and Text layout from the Text Layouts category. If the slide layout task pane doesn't appear, click **Format**, **Slide Layout**.

   d) Key the title to the right of the new icon designating a new slide and press **Enter**. Press the **Tab** key to begin the bulleted list and press **Enter** to continue to the next bulleted item.

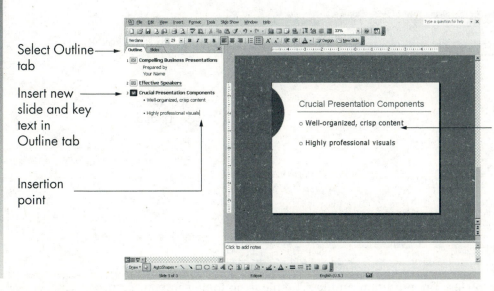

Select Outline tab

Insert new slide and key text in Outline tab

Insertion point

Text appears in the bulleted list area as it is keyed in the Outline tab

### Using Capitalization Guides to Maximize Readability

To allow your audience to grasp your message with minimal effort, follow these simple capitalization rules for text on your slides:

1. **Use initial caps in slide titles.**   Lowercase words are easier to read than UPPERCASE WORDS. Uppercase was used to emphasize ideas in the age of the typewriter, but today emphasis is added with a variety of techniques—bold and shadow effects; changes to font face, size, and color; and so forth.

2. **Capitalize only the first word in bulleted lists.**   This style allows viewers to scan a line of text and comprehend ideas quickly. A viewer's eyes move up and down with initial caps (first word and important words capitalized), a movement that creates a wave effect that is distracting and decreases readability.

# ■ SAVING AND CLOSING A PRESENTATION AND EXITING POWERPOINT

Save your presentation to the hard drive or a secondary storage device so that you can open and edit the file at a later time. Plan to save after you have created each slide to avoid losing data should your computer malfunction. Save more often when building slides that require a great deal of time and effort.

1. Click **File, Save As**.

2. Click in the **Save in** box and key a drive designation. Select a folder where you wish to save this file (e.g., Multimedia Presentations folder on the c: drive). Click the **Create New Folder** button and provide a name for the folder if necessary.

3. Click in the **File name** box and key **Present** as the file name.

4. Click **Save**.

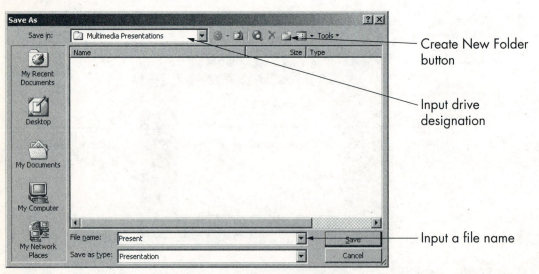

5. Click **File, Close** to close the presentation file. The file is no longer in your computer's memory but can be reopened for later use.

6. Click **File, Exit** to exit PowerPoint.

TECHNOLOGY **TIP**

### Managing Large File Sizes

The huge size of PowerPoint files containing graphics, sound, and animation has posed a challenge to users needing to transport files between computers. Trading in our floppy disks for ZIP disks, writable CD-ROMs, and USB drives (also call *pen* or *flash drives*) has certainly simplified this process.

In the event you get that dreaded "insufficient disk space" message, PowerPoint's Pack and Go Wizard could be a handy option for compressing the file to fit your secondary storage media or even your hard drive. Simply click **File**, **Pack and Go**, and the wizard will walk you through the process of compressing the files and fonts used in the presentation on as many disks as necessary. Later, when you wish to view the packaged file in its new location, click on the packaged file in Windows Explorer to execute the unpacking process that reassembles the files. If you plan to run the packaged presentation on a computer that does not have Microsoft PowerPoint installed, be sure to include the Microsoft PowerPoint Viewer in the package.

# ■ OPENING AN EXISTING PRESENTATION

You can open and revise a presentation that has been saved previously.

1. Launch PowerPoint (click **Start**, **Programs**, **Microsoft Office**, **PowerPoint 2003**).

2. Click **Create a new presentation . . .** from the startup dialog box and then click **From existing presentation . . . ;** the File, Open dialog box is displayed automatically, allowing you to browse to locate a file.

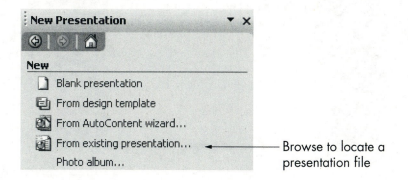

Browse to locate a presentation file

3. Open the file **Present** and continue to the next section.

# ■ VIEWING A PRESENTATION

View buttons control the number of slides displayed and the display layout. The View buttons (normal, slide sorter, and slide show) are located on the status bar at the bottom of the screen.

## Normal View

The Normal view displays the outline, slide, and notes panes all at once. You can conveniently click inside the pane where you wish to work. Adjust the size of different panes by clicking on and then dragging the borders.

- **Outline pane:** Displays (1) the title and body text for slides or (2) a thumbnail (miniature version) of the complete slide. This view facilitates organizing ideas in a presentation and is the most efficient view for entering text for numerous slides.

- **Slide pane:** Displays a single slide with text and graphics and is useful for entering text and graphics.

- **Notes pane:** Provides space below the slide pane where text and graphics can be inserted. The pane can be used for (1) inputting notes to prompt the speaker's next point, (2) inputting cues to aid a projectionist advancing the slide show for a speaker, and (3) recording ideas for further slide design. Project 8 focuses on creating useful notes pages using this pane.

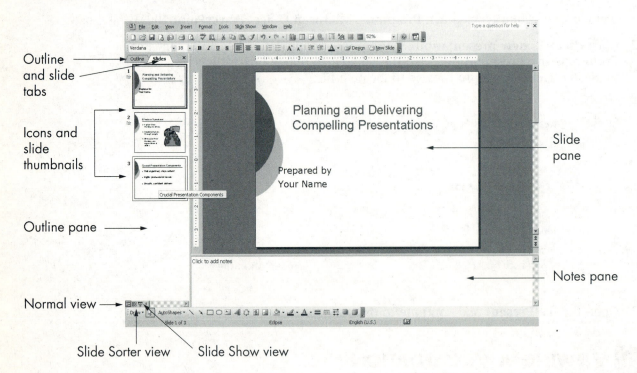

## Slide Sorter View

The Slide Sorter view displays a thumbnail of each slide in the presentation file similar to the way 35-mm slides are arranged on a light table. This view is convenient for adding, deleting, and moving slides and for adding transition effects between slides.

To switch to the Slide Sorter view:

1. Click the **Slide Sorter view** button (or click **View, Slide Sorter**).

2. Click **Zoom** (far right of the Standard toolbar) and select **33%**. This zoom level allows you to view slides without excessive scrolling. As you become familiar with PowerPoint, select a Zoom setting of your choice. The screen should be zoomed in large enough to recognize the content of the slides but small enough to minimize scrolling to locate a specific slide.

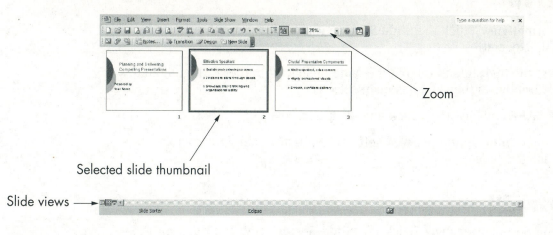

Zoom

Selected slide thumbnail

Slide views

## Slide Show View

The Slide Show view is used to run a full-screen presentation for preview on your monitor or to project the slide show while a speaker is presenting.

To switch to Slide Show view:

1. Click **View**, **Slide Show** or click the **Slide Show view** button. The slide selected when the command is executed is displayed.

2. Press the **Esc** key to return to the presentation window. Alternatively, right-click and click **End Show**.

# ■ MANIPULATING SLIDES AND INPUTTING TEXT

Learning to navigate within a presentation and to copy, delete, and change the sequence of slides will increase your efficiency in designing an effective slide show. Explore the various methods for completing these functions and adopt the ones you think work best for you.

### *Navigating Within a Presentation*

Explore various methods for navigating between slides in a presentation:

1. Be certain the file is open in Normal view (click the **Normal view** button from the status bar at the bottom of the screen or click **View**, **Normal**).

2. Choose a method for moving within the presentation:

   • **Slide pane:** Use the next slide and previous slide buttons, the arrow keys, or the scroll bar at the far right of the screen to move from one slide to another.

   • **Outline pane:** Click the numbered icon in the outline pane to move to a specific slide (displays the slide in the slide pane for editing). Scroll to reveal all slides in the outline pane.

## *Deleting Slides*

Slides can be deleted from Normal or Slide Sorter views.

## Normal View

1. Switch to Normal view (click the **Slide Sorter view** button from the status bar or click **View, Normal**).

2. Click to select the title slide in the outline pane (a shaded border or highlighted text appears to indicate the slide has been selected).

3. Press **Delete**. Alternatively, right-click and click **Cut**.

   *Note:* Click the **Undo** button (curved left arrow on the Standard toolbar) to restore the deleted slide.

## Slide Sorter View

1. Switch to the Slide Sorter view (click the **Slide Sorter view** button from the status bar or click **View, Slide Sorter**).

2. Select the title slide by pointing to the slide and clicking (a shaded border surrounds the selected slide).

3. Press **Delete**.

*Note:* Click the **Undo** button (curved left arrow on the Standard toolbar) to restore the deleted slide.

To select multiple slides to be moved or deleted, select the first slide and hold down the **Shift** key as you click additional slides. A border will surround each selected slide. If you click without holding down the **Shift** key, only the last slide clicked is selected.

## *Changing Slide Order*

The order of slides can be changed in the Normal or Slide Sorter views.

## Normal View

1. Click the numbered icon or thumbnail of any slide in the outline pane.

2. Hold down the left mouse button as you drag this slide to a position of your choice.

3. Release the mouse to drop the slide when a vertical line marker appears indicating that the slide can be dropped. This procedure is referred to as *drag and drop*.

## Slide Sorter View

1. Click a thumbnail of any slide.

2. Hold down the left mouse button as you drag this slide to a position of your choice.

3. When a vertical line marker appears indicating that the slide can be dropped, release the mouse to drop the slide. This process is illustrated in the following figure.

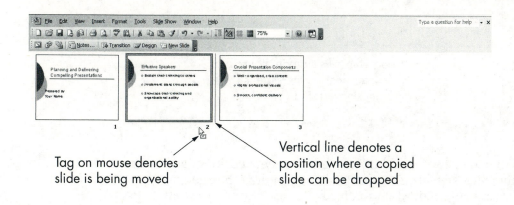

Tag on mouse denotes slide is being moved

Vertical line denotes a position where a copied slide can be dropped

## Copying (or Duplicating) a Slide

Slides can be copied in the Normal or Slide Sorter views. The Copy or Duplicate command not only saves precious design time but also ensures consistency in your presentation design. Duplicate a slide to create a model for slides that will follow a similar format. When experimenting with a design on a slide you've almost completed, edit a duplicate rather than the original. If your experiment proves unsatisfactory, you can delete the duplicate and revert to the original design with no time lost reformatting the slide.

## Normal View

1. Click the numbered icon of the title slide in the outline pane and click **Copy**.

2. Move the cursor to the point where you wish to insert the copied slide. A vertical line marker appears to indicate a position where a slide can be inserted.

3. Click **Paste**. Alternatively, click **Edit**, **Duplicate** (or **Ctrl+D**). A slide appears below the original slide and can then be moved to the desired position.

## Slide Sorter View

1. Select the slide thumbnail of the title slide and click **Copy**.

2. Move the cursor to the point where you wish to insert the copied slide. A vertical line marker appears to indicate a position where a slide can be inserted.

3. Click **Paste**. Alternatively, click **Edit**, **Duplicate** (or **Ctrl+D**). A slide appears to the right of the original slide and can then be moved to the desired position.

## Copying and Moving a Slide

1. Select a slide in either Normal or Slide Sorter view.

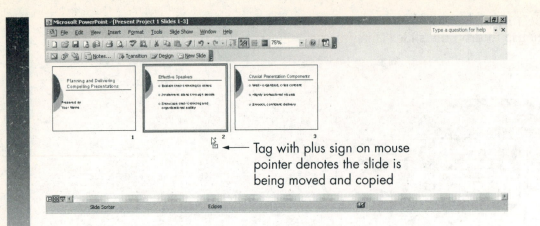

Tag with plus sign on mouse pointer denotes the slide is being moved and copied

2. Hold down the **Ctrl** key as you drag the slide to a new position. Note that an icon with a plus sign at the top appears as you drag the slide, indicating an object is being moved and copied. Release the mouse button to drop the copied slide into its desired location.

## Moving Slides Between Presentation Files

Often you will find it useful to copy slides from a presentation you developed previously into a presentation you are currently developing.

1. Open the file **Present**.

2. Click **File**, **New** to create a second presentation file. Apply a design template different from the one you used in the Present file. Insert a title slide and provide a title of your choice. Save the file as **Presentation 2**.

3. Click **Window** from the Menu bar and select **Present** to make the Present file the active presentation on your desktop.

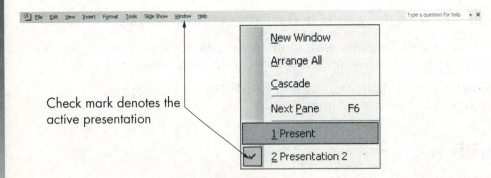

Check mark denotes the active presentation

4. Select Slides 2–3 and click **Copy**.

5. Click **Window** and **Presentation 2** to make this new file the active presentation.

6. Click below the title slide in the outline pane and click **Paste**. Slides 2–3 are inserted and reformatted using the design template of Presentation 2. You can also paste slides from the Slide Sorter view.

## ■ REINFORCEMENT ACTIVITIES

Add the following slides to the file Present for added reinforcement of the PowerPoint features you learned in this project.

### Activity 1

Build the slide as shown in the model using the Title and Text layout.

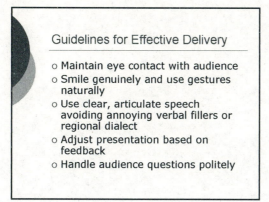

### Activity 2

Build the slide as shown in the model using the Title and Text layout.

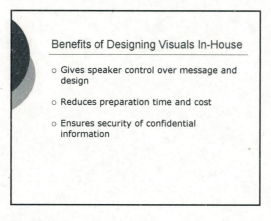

### Slide Order

Sequence slides in the file Present according to the table on page 209. Print and submit the slides as directed by your instructor.

# Creating a Basic Presentation

- Create bulleted lists with multiple levels and two columns.

- Add relevant, engaging clip art to bulleted lists by searching the Microsoft Clip Organizer and Microsoft Office Online.

- Customize an AutoLayout by adding and repositioning place-holders.

- Add slide transitions and custom animation effects to direct the audience's attention to the desired content.

- Print a presentation as slides, handouts, notes pages, or outlines.

- Run a presentation in a seamless, professional manner.

## ■ CREATING BULLETED LISTS WITH MULTIPLE LEVELS

Increasing or decreasing indention of text in a bullet list allows the speaker to show the relative importance of major and minor points within a bulleted list. Although PowerPoint allows up to five levels of bullet points, overdividing fragments the ideas, which increases the mental effort your audience must exert to follow your discussion or argument. In most cases, limiting bulleted lists to two levels will lead to a smooth, coherent flow of information that your audience can follow easily.

### *Changing the Indent in a Bulleted List*

*Directions:* Follow the instructions to build the slide shown in the model.

Adept Speakers Must . . .

o Meet audience's expectations of high-quality visual support
   • Flexible, non-linear designs
   • Alternative delivery methods
o Adapt to faster pace and shorter attention spans
o Face diversity challenges

1. Create a new slide using the Title and Text layout from the Text Layouts category.

2. Key the slide title and the first-level point ("Meet audience's..."). Press **Enter**.

3. Click the **Increase Indent** button (right arrow on the Formatting toolbar) or press **Tab** to begin the second-level point ("Flexible..."). Press **Enter**.

4. Key the next second-level point. Press **Enter**.

5. Click the **Decrease Indent** button (left arrow on the Formatting toolbar) or press **Shift+Tab** to move the text left to key a first-level point.

| Verdana | ▾ | 25 | ▾ | **B** *I* U S | ≡ ≡ ≡ | ≟ ≣ | A˄ A˅ | ≟ ≟ | **A** ▾ | 🖉 Design | 🗐 New Slide |

Click increase indent and decrease indent buttons to denote the level of points in a bulleted list

6. Complete the bulleted list.

## Creating a Two-Column Bulleted List

*Directions:* Follow the instructions to build the slide shown in the model.

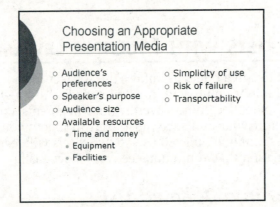

Choosing an Appropriate
Presentation Media

○ Audience's                ○ Simplicity of use
  preferences              ○ Risk of failure
○ Speaker's purpose        ○ Transportability
○ Audience size
○ Available resources
  • Time and money
  • Equipment
  • Facilities

1. Create a new slide with the Title and 2-Column Text layout from the Text Layouts category.

2. Key the slide title.

3. Click the left column bulleted list placeholder. Key the text using the **Increase Indent** and **Decrease Indent** buttons to create the list that includes major and minor points.

4. Click the right column bulleted list placeholder and key the text.

## ◼ ADDING CLIP ART TO A SLIDE

Today's audiences have come to expect media-rich, entertaining, and dynamic presentations. Including media clips on a slide can engage the audience's attention, reinforce an important point, and help the audience visualize a complex idea.

## Balancing Text and White Space

An audience will ignore an image perceived to be complicated or will concentrate on deciphering the slide and not listen to the speaker. Therefore, to keep your audience's attention, your slides must limit text and include only meaningful images. To create clean, uncluttered slides,

- Leave 60 to 70 percent of the slide blank.
- Follow the 7 × 7 rule: Limit text to 7 lines per slide and 7 words per line.

Positioning images strategically on the slide will enhance the impact of your message. Research shows that people notice graphics second only to headings. With this in mind, the optimal placement of an image supporting text is the lower right quadrant of the slide. Your graphic acts as a "draw" to pull the viewer's eye from the title area, through the text area, to focus on the graphic.

Media clips including clip art, photographs, video segments, and sound files can be conveniently accessed from the Microsoft Clip Organizer, Microsoft Office Online, and/or numerous third-party sources that contribute to PowerPoint's capabilities. Once inserted on the slide, the media clips can be sized, positioned, and animated to achieve a desired effect.

## *Selecting Clip Art from the Microsoft Clip Organizer*

This project will demonstrate the ease with which clip art (and other media) can be selected and inserted directly from the Microsoft Clip Organizer.

*Directions:* Follow the instructions to revise the "Effective Speakers" slide in the file Present.

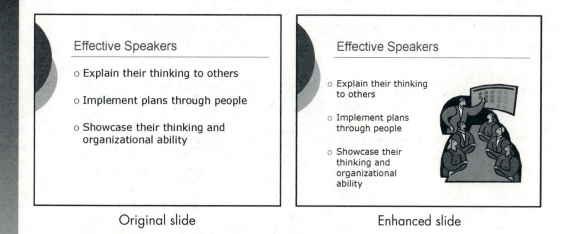

Original slide                                Enhanced slide

1. Display the "Effective Speakers" slide in Normal view.

2. Click **Format**, **Slide Layout** to display the Slide Layout task pane. Remember you can toggle between task panes you've been working with or press the Home icon to return to the opening menu.

3. Scroll to display the Other Layouts category and select Title, Text, and Clip Art. Note that the bulleted list reformats automatically and a placeholder for clip art is added.

Toggle between task panes or press the home icon to return to the opening menu

Select Title, Text, and Clip Art from Other Layouts category

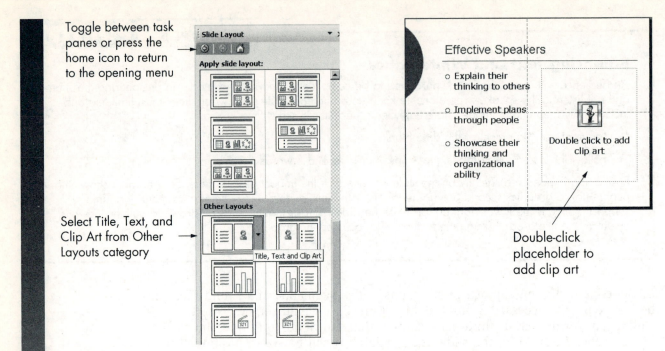

Double-click placeholder to add clip art

4. Double-click the placeholder to add clip art. The Clip Art task pane appears.

5. Input a keyword in the search box that describes the clip you wish to insert (e.g., "presenter").

6. Click **Go** to display a collection of clips matching your keyword.

7. Select a clip and click **OK**.

8. Click to add clip art to the slide. Point to a corner sizing handle and hold down the **Shift** key as you drag outward to enlarge the clip art until it is balanced with the text at the left. This technique allows you to change the width and height proportionally with no unappealing distortion of the image.

Clip art task pane appears

Input a keyword

Select desired clip art

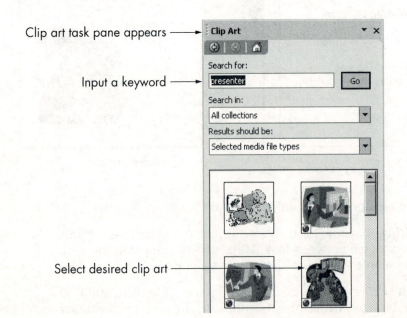

9. Point to the center of the clip art and drag it until it is balanced with the text at the left. Positioning should provide a realistic perspective that avoids the impression that the presenter is floating on the slide.

*Hint:* Use the arrow keys to nudge the object up, down, left, or right when you need to move the object a small increment. Often a nudge is all that's needed to position an object for appropriate perspective.

## *Importing Clips from Microsoft Office Online*

This project will demonstrate the ease with which clip art (and other media) can be selected and inserted directly from the clip art and media link at Microsoft Office Online.

***Directions:*** Follow the instructions to build the slide shown in the model.

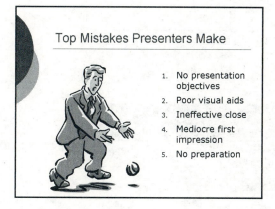

1. Create a new slide using the Title and Text layout from the Text Layouts category.

2. Key the slide title and the bulleted list.

3. Click **Insert**, **Picture**, **Clip Art** (or click the **Clip Art** button on the Draw toolbar). A search dialog box appears.

Clip art button

4. Click **Clip art on Office Online**. Wait while your browser connects to the Microsoft Office Online Web site.

5. Input a keyword in the search box (e.g., "mistakes") and click **Go**. A collection of clips matching your keyword appears.

Clip art task pane
displayed

Click Clip art on
Office Online

Input keyword

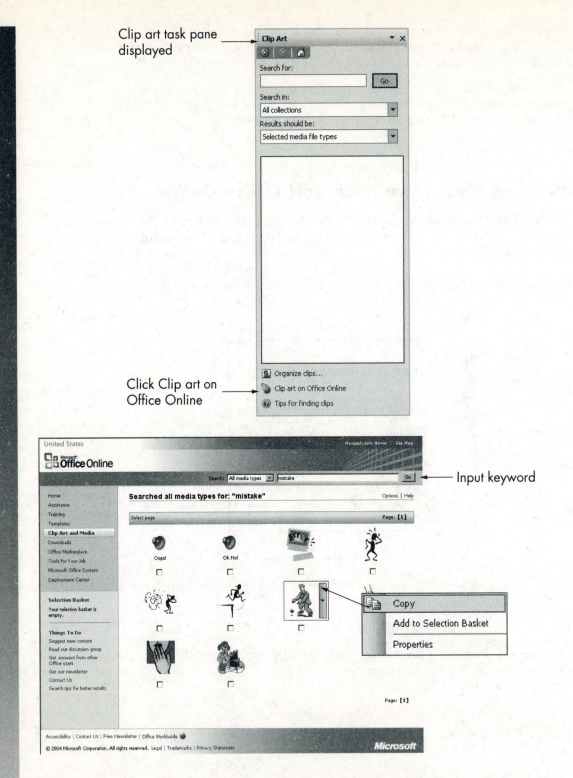

6. Click the down arrow to the right of the image and click **Copy**.

7. Return to your PowerPoint slide and click **Paste**.

8. Select the clip art to make the sizing handles appear. Point to a corner handle and hold down the **Shift** key as you drag outward to enlarge the image slightly. Point to the center of the clip art to move it into the desired position at the left of the slide and adjust the bulleted list for balance with the clip art.

# ■ WORKING WITH NEW PLACEHOLDERS

Any AutoLayout can be modified to fit the specific content of a presentation. In this project you will add a placeholder for displaying a source note for the list of mistakes included in the bulleted list. To ensure consistency and efficiency throughout the presentation, the format applied to this source note should appear on other slides in the presentation that contain source notes. *Specimen treatment* is a term used to describe formatting not included as a standard design element (e.g., slide titles, bullet lists).

*Directions:* Follow the instructions for revising the slide shown in the model.

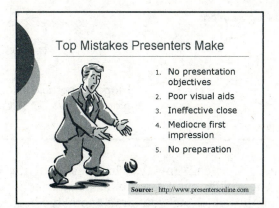

## *Creating a New Placeholder*

1. Click the **Text box** button on the Draw toolbar.

2. Position the mouse pointer anywhere on the slide. Click and hold the left mouse button as you drag down and to the right. A selection rectangle with diagonal lines and a series of sizing boxes (handles) surround the placeholder. The insertion point indicates that text can be keyed.

3. Key the text in the placeholder: Source: **http://www.presentersonline.com**

## *Repositioning a Placeholder*

4. Select the placeholder by clicking the placeholder once to display the selection rectangle with diagonal lines and then clicking a second time to display a shaded border between the sizing handles.

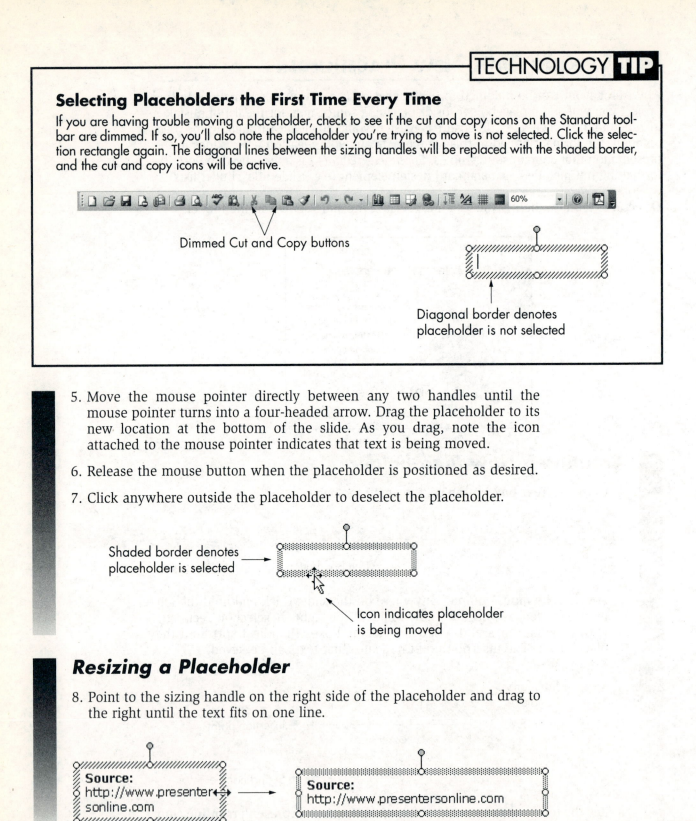

## Selecting Placeholders the First Time Every Time

If you are having trouble moving a placeholder, check to see if the cut and copy icons on the Standard toolbar are dimmed. If so, you'll also note the placeholder you're trying to move is not selected. Click the selection rectangle again. The diagonal lines between the sizing handles will be replaced with the shaded border, and the cut and copy icons will be active.

Dimmed Cut and Copy buttons

Diagonal border denotes placeholder is not selected

5. Move the mouse pointer directly between any two handles until the mouse pointer turns into a four-headed arrow. Drag the placeholder to its new location at the bottom of the slide. As you drag, note the icon attached to the mouse pointer indicates that text is being moved.

6. Release the mouse button when the placeholder is positioned as desired.

7. Click anywhere outside the placeholder to deselect the placeholder.

Shaded border denotes placeholder is selected

Icon indicates placeholder is being moved

## *Resizing a Placeholder*

8. Point to the sizing handle on the right side of the placeholder and drag to the right until the text fits on one line.

**Source:**
http://www.presentersonline.com

**Source:**
http://www.presentersonline.com

## *Deleting a Placeholder*

9. Select the placeholder containing the source note you just created.

10. Press **Delete**.

11. Click the **Undo** button (curved left arrow on the Standard toolbar) to restore the placeholder.

Undo button

## Editing Text in a Placeholder

As you edit the appearance of the text in this specimen placeholder, you will explore the numerous ways text can be enhanced to produce a creative design. However, do not make changes to standard design elements (slide title and bulleted lists) on individual slides. Edits that affect the appearance of all slides are made on the Master Slide to increase your efficiency and to ensure consistency among the slides in your presentation. Editing the Master Slide is covered in Project 4.

12. Highlight the text to be edited (**http://www.presentersonline.com**). Click the **Bold** button on the Formatting toolbar.

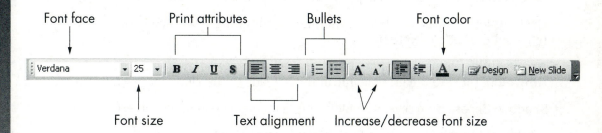

Font face          Print attributes          Bullets          Font color

Font size          Text alignment          Increase/decrease font size

13. Highlight the text to be edited. Click **Format, Font**.

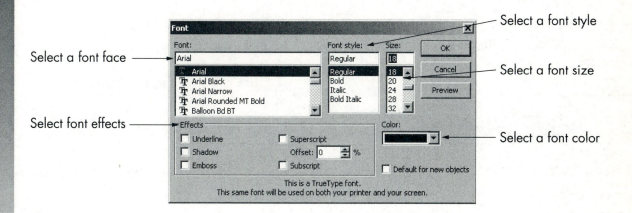

Select a font face

Select a font style

Select a font size

Select font effects

Select a font color

14. Select a new font from the Font box.

15. Change the font size to 14 points by selecting or keying a number in the Size box.

16. Change the text color by clicking the down arrow in the Color box and selecting a color from the menu.

Select a color that complements your template background and that can be easily read by your audience. For easy readability, choose a font color that has high contrast with the background color. For example:

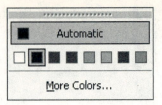

- *High contrast:* dark blue background with yellow text

- *Low contrast:* light blue background with white text

17. Study other changes that can be made from the Font dialog box (e.g., shadow, emboss, superscript, subscript). Note that changes in the font face, size, and style can be made from the font dialog box or the Formatting toolbar.

18. Study enhancements you can make to the source note placeholder from the Draw toolbar.

   - **Font color:** Choose from an assortment of colors complementary to the template or click **More Fill Colors** to select from a palette of colors.

   - **Fill color:** Add a solid color behind the placeholder.

   - **Line color:** Add a line around the placeholder.

   - **Line style:** Choose the width of the line surrounding the placeholder.

   - **Dash style:** Choose the style of the line surrounding the placeholder (e.g., solid, dashed, dotted).

   - **Arrow style:** Choose the style and direction of arrows drawn with the Arrow tool (next to the graphic line at the left side of the Draw toolbar).

   - **Shadow:** Choose from several shadow effects that add depth to the object.

   - **3D effect:** Choose from several 3D effects that add impact and depth to the object.

19. Select the source note placeholder and format it using the icons on the Draw toolbar:

   a) Add a 1-point-wide border around the placeholder that is a dashed line.

   b) Select a line color complementary to your design template background.

Line color   Line style   Arrow style   3D

Draw ▾ | AutoShapes ▾

Fill color   Font color   Dash style   Shadow

## ADDING SLIDE TRANSITIONS

Slide transitions add impact to the way one slide replaces another when the presentation is projected. Transition effects include blinds, horizontal or vertical; box in or out; cover or uncover; push; split; shapes (circle, diamond, wheel, plus); wipe; and so forth. Guidelines for applying transitions effectively are provided in the Designer's Pointer on page 31.

*Directions:* Add a slide transition in the file Present as directed.

1. Display your presentation in Slide Sorter view (click the **Slide Sorter view** button or click **View**, **Slide Show**). Note that the Slide Sorter toolbar is automatically displayed.

## Add a Transition Effect for All Slides

2. Click the **Transition** button on the Slide Sorter toolbar or click **Slide Show**, **Slide Transition**. The Transition task pane appears.

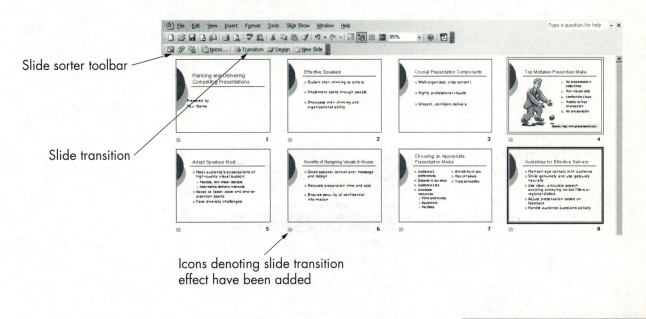

Slide sorter toolbar

Slide transition

Icons denoting slide transition effect have been added

---

### TECHNOLOGY TIP

### Ending the Search for Toolbars

Having trouble finding a toolbar? Just click **View**, **Toolbars** to display a list of toolbars. Check marks appear before toolbars that are currently displayed. Click to add a toolbar to the PowerPoint window. Clearing the check in front of a toolbar will remove it from the PowerPoint window. In the illustration, clicking **View Toolbars**, **Picture** will display the toolbar, and a check mark will be added before "Picture" on the toolbar list.

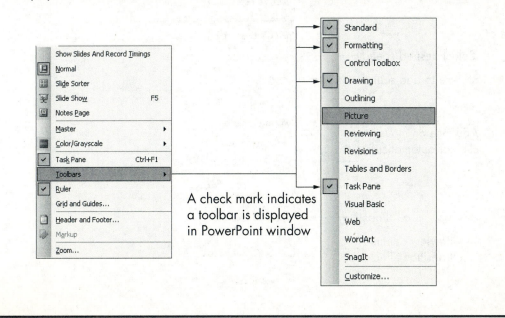

A check mark indicates a toolbar is displayed in PowerPoint window

3. Select the transition effect of your choice from the list.

4. Select the speed of the transition (Slow, Medium, or Fast).

5. Retain the default option to advance the slide on mouse click.

6. Take time to become familiar with each of the transition effects. Then, select the **Push Down** effect at a **Fast** speed setting.

7. Click **Apply to All Slides**. A small transition icon appears below the selected slide to indicate a transition has been set.

To preview the animation effect in the task pane, click **Play**. To view the slide in full screen, click **Slide Show**.

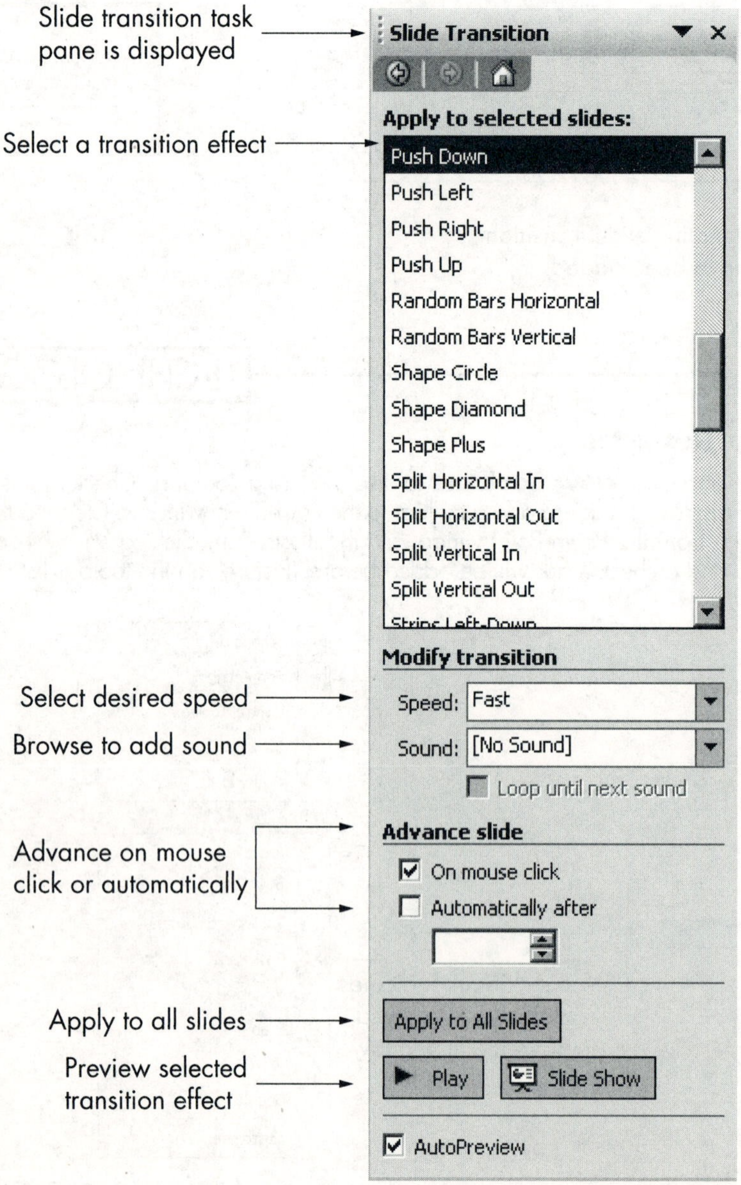

Slide transition task pane is displayed → **Slide Transition**   ▼  ✕

Select a transition effect →

**Apply to selected slides:**

- Push Down
- Push Left
- Push Right
- Push Up
- Random Bars Horizontal
- Random Bars Vertical
- Shape Circle
- Shape Diamond
- Shape Plus
- Split Horizontal In
- Split Horizontal Out
- Split Vertical In
- Split Vertical Out
- Strips Left-Down

**Modify transition**

Select desired speed → Speed: Fast

Browse to add sound → Sound: [No Sound]

☐ Loop until next sound

**Advance slide**

Advance on mouse click or automatically →

☑ On mouse click

☐ Automatically after

Apply to all slides → Apply to All Slides

Preview selected transition effect → ► Play   Slide Show

☑ AutoPreview

```
┌─────────────────────────────────────────────────────────────────────┐
│                                              DESIGNER'S │POINTER│     │
│                                                                       │
│  Applying Appealing Transition Effects                                │
│  Developing a systematic pattern for slide transitions will enhance   │
│  your slide show without creating annoy-ing distractions from your    │
│  message. A good practice is to choose at least two transition        │
│  effects:                                                             │
│                                                                       │
│   •  One subtle effect for content slides. Choose logical display     │
│      of slides such as push down/right, or wipe down/right. For a     │
│      long presentation, you might choose a different transition for    │
│      each section to give the audience a change of pace. A            │
│      transition is not necessary for the first slide if you plan to   │
│      display it prior to a formal introduction.                       │
│                                                                       │
│   •  A more dramatic effect for the divider slides. Draw the          │
│      audience's attention to these slides that are included as        │
│      "signposts" to mark the beginning of each major section of a     │
│      presentation. You will learn more about these coherence devices  │
│      in Project 5.                                                    │
│                                                                       │
│   •  Other transition effects for specimen slides. Some slides may    │
│      require a specific transition. For instance, a dissolve or fade  │
│      smoothly transition may be chosen to direct an audience's        │
│      attention to a dramatic photograph inserted as the background.   │
│      Use constraint in adding too many different tran-sitions for     │
│      these unique elements in your slide show.                        │
└─────────────────────────────────────────────────────────────────────┘
```

## Add a Unique Transition Effect to Selected Slides

8. Click to select Slide 1 (the title slide) in the Slide Sorter view.

9. Click the **No Transition** effect from the Transition dialog box displayed at the right. The icon below Slide 1 in the slide sorter view is removed.

10. Retain the default option to advance the slide on mouse click. This option gives the presenter control over the display of the slide.

You will learn two other advanced transition capabilities in later projects:

• **Advancing slides automatically.** Timed settings advance the slides automatically without a mouse click.

• **Adding sound effects.** Sound will play each time the slide show advances to the next slide.

## ENHANCING WITH CUSTOM ANIMATION

Animation effects allow speakers to add impact to a presentation by directing the audience's attention to important points. Rather than displaying all objects on a slide at once, the speaker chooses a logical order, engaging animation effects and precise timings of these objects. For example, depending on the desired effect, a speaker may choose to display a simple bulleted list all at once or point by point, a letter or word at a time, and with or without a dimming effect on points already discussed.

### Inserting Custom Animation

1. Display the "Effective Speakers" slide in Slide view.

2. Click **Slide Show**, **Custom Animation**. The Custom Animation dialog box is displayed in the task pane. (Alternatively, right-click and click **Custom Animation**.)

## Add an Animation Effect to the Clip Art

3. Select the clip art image.

4. Click **Add Effect**, **Entrance**, **More Effects**. Select **Circle** from the "Basic" category. The animated effect plays automatically for your preview. Click **Play** to view all animation effects applied to a slide; clicking **Slide Show** will allow you to view the animation in full screen. At some point, you may wish to bypass the automatic preview by clearing the **AutoPreview** check box.

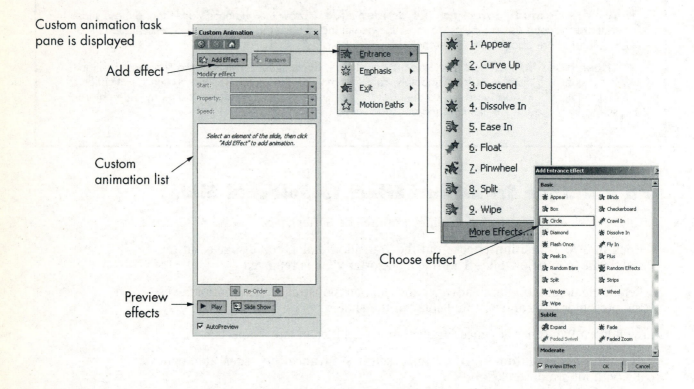

The animated object (the clip art) is added to a list in the Custom Animation task pane. The animation sequences applied to a slide are shown in the list in the order they are added. The numbered icons at the beginning of each sequence indicate the timing of the sequence in relation to other animation events. A non-printing numbered tag that correlates to the effects in the list appears on the slide in Slide view but not in Slide Show view. Each of these icons is annotated in the illustration on page 33.

Explore the four subgroups of animation effects in the "Entrance" category: basic, subtle, moderate, and exciting. Then, return to the Custom Animation menu to explore the animation effects in the remaining three categories: Emphasis, Exit, and Motion Path.

The following options provide control over the precise movement of each animation effect:

• **Start:** Start an animated object with a mouse click or automatically based on timings.

• **Direction:** Select a direction for the selected effect (circle) from the list by clicking the down arrow.

- **Speed:** Select a speed for the effect from the list (Slow, Medium, or Fast) by clicking the down arrow.
- **Remove:** Click **Remove** to eliminate animation; the object is deleted from the animation list and will appear when the slide is displayed.

## Modify an Applied Animation Effect

5. Edit the animation options for the circle animation effect applied to the clip art in Step 4:

   a) Retain the default value that starts the clip art **On Click**.

   b) Set the direction of the box effect to **Out**.

   c) Set speed of the effect to **Medium**.

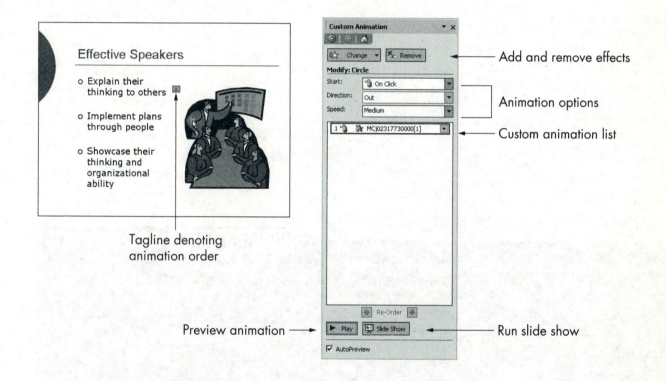

## Add an Animation Effect to the Bulleted List

6. Select the bulleted list.

7. Click **Add Effect, Entrance, More Effects, Wipe**.

8. Change the direction to **From Left** and the speed to **Fast**.

## Change the Animation Order

9. Display the clip art first and the bulleted list second:

   a) Select an animation sequence in the Custom Animation list.

b) Click the up or down arrow to reorder the sequences so that the clip art is displayed first. The taglines on the slide change to denote the revised sequence.

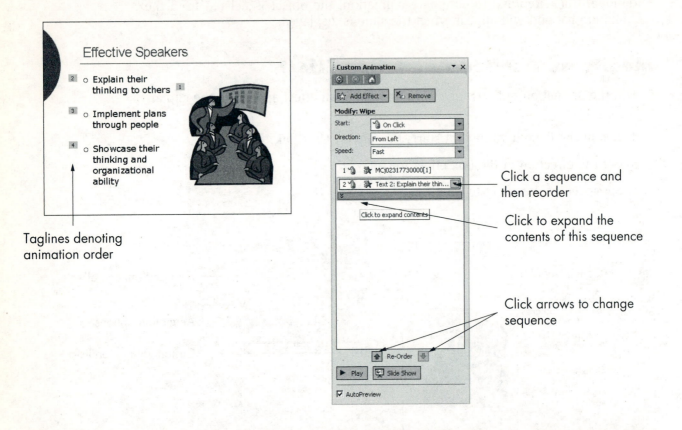

Taglines denoting
animation order

Click a sequence and
then reorder

Click to expand the
contents of this sequence

Click arrows to change
sequence

## PRESENTER'S STRATEGY

### Animating Bulleted Lists with Precision

A systematic pattern for adding animated bulleted lists will provide needed consistency and allow the speaker to direct the audience's attention as needed for comprehension. Follow these practices for animating bulleted lists:

• Apply a subtle animation effect consistently to all bulleted lists in a presentation. Subtle transitions such as wipe, fade, or expand are especially effective because they discreetly reveal information left to right in the direction an audience reads.

• Select holistic or progressive disclosure, depending on the discussion planned for each list.

– **Progressive disclosure (with build).** Items in an animated bulleted list in PowerPoint automatically appear one item at a time until the entire list is built. This build effect, also known as *progressive disclosure of information*, is comparable to moving a blank sheet of paper down an overhead transparency to uncover points as they are discussed. Disclosing text progressively allows the speaker to control the flow of information for targeted impact.

– **Holistic disclosure (without build).** Bulleted lists discussed as a unit should be displayed without a build effect. This effect, also known as *holistic disclosure*, eliminates the distraction caused by a speaker repeatedly clicking the mouse to display the points one immediately after the next with little or no discussion for each point. Examples of slides that should be presented as a unit include an agenda slide previewing the major points in the presentation or a summary slide reviewing a series of slides on a related idea.

## *Introducing Text Without a Build Effect*

1. Click the arrow below the bulleted list in the Custom Animation list to expand the contents, revealing an icon for each bulleted item. Taglines appear before each of the three bulleted items.

2. Edit the Start options to display all items in the bulleted list at once:

   a) Click the down arrow beside the first point and click **Start**.

   b) Choose **On Click** to allow the speaker to click the mouse to display the object.

   c) Repeat Steps a and b for all subsequent points and choose **Start With Previous** in the Start box to display all items in the bulleted list at one time. (Hold down the **Shift** key to select multiple items.)

*Note:* The taglines on the slide show two items in the animation order: The #1 icon denotes the clip art; and #2, the bulleted list.

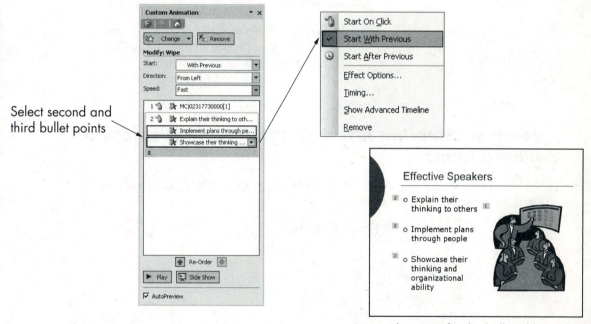

Select second and third bullet points

One tagline (#2) for the bulleted list indicates entire list will appear at once (no build effect)

## *Introducing Text with a Build Effect*

1. Display the "Top Mistakes Presenters Make" slide in Slide view.

2. Click **Slide Show**, **Custom Animation**.

3. Select the clip art and animate to **Fade in** at **Fast** speed.

4. Select the bulleted list and animate to **Wipe from Left** at **Fast** speed.

5. Expand the contents of the animated object. Note that each of the five items is set by default to start with a mouse click; thus, a separate tagline is assigned to each point in the list (#2 through #6).

6. Continue building this slide in the next section.

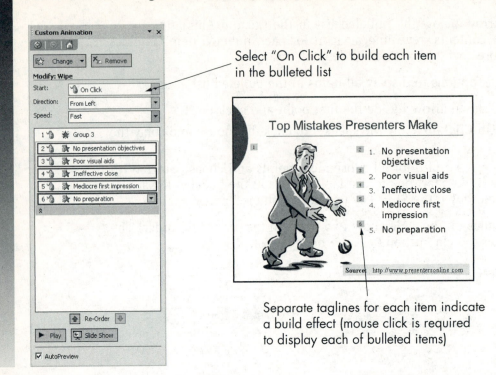

Select "On Click" to build each item in the bulleted list

Separate taglines for each item indicate a build effect (mouse click is required to display each of bulleted items)

## Adding a Dimming Effect to Previously Displayed Bulleted Items

1. Select all five bullet points in the Custom Animation list. (Hold down the **Shift** key to select multiple items.)

2. Click the down arrow and **Effect Options**.

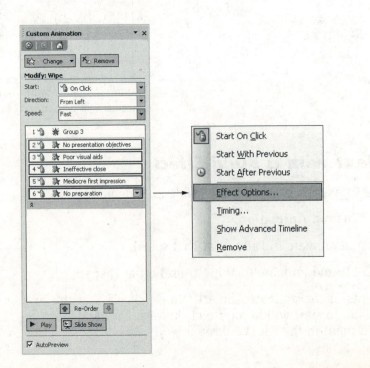

3. Be sure the Effect tab is selected and click the down arrow beside "After animation."

4. Select a color from the palette or click **More Colors** to display additional color choices for a dimming effect. When you advance past a bulleted item, the previous item appears in the color you selected—preferably a slightly lighter color that can still be read easily by the audience. Click **Preview** to critique color choices.

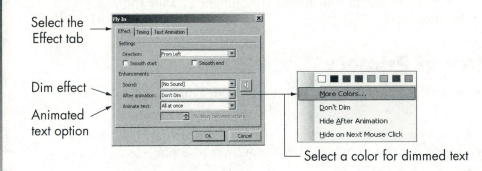

Select the Effect tab

Dim effect

Animated text option

Select a color for dimmed text

5. Click the down arrow beside "Animate text." Note the options for displaying text: all at once, by word, and by letter. After previewing several of these options, retain the default value of introducing the text "all at once."

6. Reorder the animation to display the clip art first and the bulleted list second.

## PRINTING A PRESENTATION

PowerPoint slides can be printed in several formats that are useful as presentation support tools. These options include slides, handouts, notes pages, and outlines. You will learn more about creating highly professional audience handouts and speaker's notes pages in Project 8.

*Directions:* Work through the directions in this section printing only the pages directed by your instructor.

1. Click **File**, **Print**. The Print dialog box appears.

Print range

Number of copies

List of print formats

## Choose the Print Range

2. Note the three print ranges:

*To print all slides:* Select **All**.

*To print a specific slide:* Select **Current Slide**. (This option prints the slide that was selected when the Print command was executed.)

*To print multiple slides:* Select **Slides** and input the number of slides in the dialog box to the right (e.g., 2, 3, 5–12).

## Select the Type of Printout

3. Click the down arrow in the Print What list box to view the available types of output:

- **Slides:** Prints a full-screen view of the slide. Use this option to print slides directly on transparency acetates to be projected on an overhead projector.

- **Handouts:** Prints slides as an audience handout in various formats:

  - **Number of slides per page:** Choose from 2, 3, or 6.
  - **Order slides are printed:** Choose horizontal or vertical. (The thumbnail depicts the slide order.)
  - **Frame slides:** Add an attractive border around each slide.

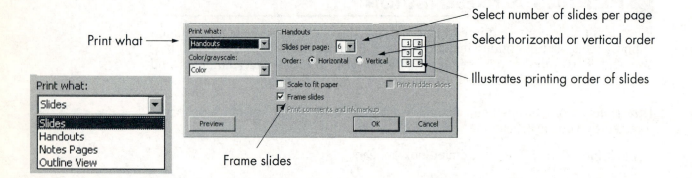

Print what

Print what:
Slides
Slides
Handouts
Notes Pages
Outline View

Select number of slides per page

Select horizontal or vertical order

Illustrates printing order of slides

Frame slides

- **Notes pages:** Prints pages with a miniature slide at the top and any text or graphics input in the notes pane. Refer to the discussion of Slide Show views in Project 1 if necessary.

- **Outline view:** Prints the slide title and text without graphics.

## ▌ DELIVERING A PRESENTATION

Learning to run your slide show professionally is essential to ensuring a successful presentation. You will learn efficient, foolproof ways of moving around in your slide show that will keep the audience's attention focused on the speaker—not the technology. A Presenter's Strategy on page 41 provides additional advice for delivering a seamless presentation.

## *Moving Within a Presentation*

1. Display Slide 1 (title slide) in Slide view.

2. Click the **Slide Show** button. The slide show starts running in full-screen view beginning with Slide 1, the slide that was selected when you began the show.

3. Complete the following instructions to learn to run your presentation professionally. Try the mouse and the keyboard methods to determine the method most convenient for you.

## Advance to the Next Slide

**Mouse:**       Left mouse click

**Keyboard:**   **Enter**, **spacebar**, right arrow key, or **Page Down** key

## Return to the Previous Slide

**Mouse:**       Right mouse click

**Keyboard:**   Left arrow key or **Page Up** key

## Move to a Specific Slide

**Mouse:**       Input the slide number using the numerals on the alphanumeric keypad and press **Enter**.

**Keyboard:**   Right-click and experiment with each of the following movements:

1. Select **Next** to move to the next slide.

2. Select **Previous** to move back one slide.

3. Select **Go to Slide** and select a slide from the list of slide titles.

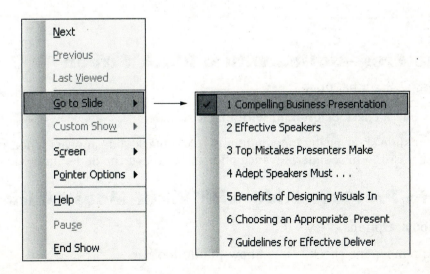

## End a Slide Show

Press the **Esc** key to exit the Slide Show view. Slide 1, the active slide when you clicked the **Slide Show** button, will be displayed in Slide view.

### *Additional Techniques to Ensure Professional Delivery*

1. Display Slide 1 in Slide view and then click the **Slide Show** button to begin running the presentation.

## Black or White Out the Screen

2. Press the **B** key on the keyboard. The screen becomes black.

3. Press the **B** key again to display the slide again.

## White Out the Screen

4. Press the **W** key on the keyboard. The screen becomes white.

5. Press the **W** key again to return to the slide. Alternatively, right-click and select **Screen** and **Black Screen** or **White Screen** as desired.

| Next |
| Previous |
| Last Viewed |
| Go to Slide ▶ |
| Custom Show ▶ |
| Screen ▶ | → | Black Screen |
| Pointer Options ▶ | | White Screen |
| Help | | Show/Hide Ink Markup |
| Pause | | Speaker Notes |
| End Show | | Switch Programs |

## End the Presentation with a Black Screen

6. Click **Tools**, **Options**, **View**.

7. Click to add a check before **End with black slide**.

8. Run your slide show again and you'll note that a black slide appears when you advance past the final slide. Advance once more to exit the Slide Show view.

## Move to Previous Slide with Right Mouse Click

9. Click **Tools**, **Options**, **View**.

10. Click to remove the check before **Show popup toolbar**.

## PRESENTER'S STRATEGY

### Executing a Seamless Delivery

For a polished, professional look, the audience should see the full-screen view and not your untidy work areas (e.g., Normal or Slide Sorter views). To avoid klutzy moves, such as escaping to the work area, that diminish the impact of your delivery, you must rehearse your presentation with your slide show. During these rehearsals, focus on identifying the specific mouse and keyboard controls that work best for you and practice these techniques that make your delivery appear virtually invisible and effortlessly executed.

* Keep the slide show in Slide Show view at all times. Set PowerPoint to end the presentation with a black slide so that you don't have to be concerned about advancing past the last slide and exiting to other, less appealing views.

* Use the left arrow key or page up to move to the previous slide. Program the right-click to move backward without displaying a distracting drop-down menu linking to the slide navigator. This process is time-consuming and directs attention to the technology and away from the speaker.

* Number the slides on your speaker's notes so that you can quickly display a slide needed to answer an audience member's question. There is no need for awkward moves such as exiting to the Slide Sorter view to locate the correct slide or right-clicking to display the slide navigator. Just input the specific slide number and move effortlessly back to a previously displayed slide or advance forward to new slides if you believe the question warrants rearranging the order of your presentation.

* Use the black and white out technique when an audience member asks a question as you are advancing to a new slide. Removing the new information will keep your audience focused on your answer to the question and will allow you to transition into the new topic as you had planned.

11. Display Slide 2 in Slide view. Right-click to return to the previous slide. The slide show moves backward seamlessly without displaying an unattractive menu.

Select View tab ⟶

Hide popup menu ⟶

End with black slide ⟶

## ▪ REINFORCEMENT ACTIVITIES

Add the following slides to the file Present for added reinforcement of the PowerPoint features you learned in this project. Position the slides as shown in the table on page 209.

# Activity 1

1. Display the "Benefits of Designing Visuals In-House" slide in Normal view.

2. Select and insert relevant clip art using Microsoft Clip Organizer or Microsoft Office Online.

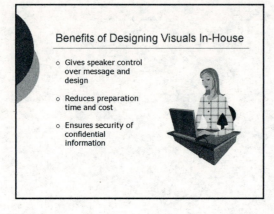

# Activity 2

1. Create the following slide using the Title, Clip Art, and Text layout from the Other Layouts category. Use the Microsoft Clip Organizer or Microsoft Office Online to locate relevant clip art.

2. Add custom animation effects:

   **First:** Title enters with slide (no animation).

   **Second:** Speaker starts with a subtle effect of your choice.

   **Third:** Bulleted list starts with Wipe from Left; build points with no dimming effect.

# Activity 3

1. Display the "Crucial Presentation Components" slide in Normal view.

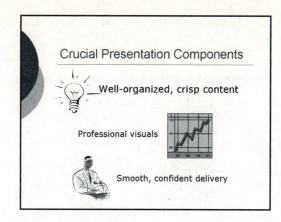

2. Key the title and the first bullet. Click on the bottom center sizing handle and drag to reduce the size of the placeholder to enclose the first bulleted item.

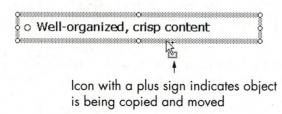

3. Remove the bullet; graphics will be substituted to highlight each point:

   a) Click **Format**, **Bullets and Numbering**.

   b) Select **None**.

4. Create the remaining bulleted entries using the efficient drag-and-drop technique:

   a) Hold down the **Ctrl** key as you drag the text box. An icon with a plus sign appears as you drag the mouse.

   b) Release the mouse to "drop" a second copy on the screen.

   c) Repeat the process to create the remaining bulleted item. Edit the text in each copied text box as shown in the model.

> ○ Well-organized, crisp content

Icon with a plus sign indicates object
is being copied and moved

5. Highlight each point with relevant clip art:

   a) Select three relevant clip art images with a consistent tone using Microsoft Clip Organizer or Microsoft Office Online. Consistent tone is especially important because the images will be displayed on the same slide.

   b) Size and position the images to balance attractively with the text as shown in the model. To size each image exactly the same:

      (1) Select the three images.

      (2) Click **Format**, **Picture** and select the Size tab.

      (3) Input a value for the Height (e.g., "1.5").

(4) With the images still selected, point and drag a corner handle to size as desired.

Size tab is selected ——→

Input exact value for height and/or width

**Format Picture**

| Colors and Lines | Size | Position | Picture | Text Box | Web |

Size and rotate

Height: [1.5"]     Width: [1.45"]

Rotation: [0°]

Scale

Height: [  ]     Width: [  ]

☐ Lock aspect ratio
☐ Relative to original picture size
☐ Best scale for slide show

Resolution: [640 x 480]

Original size

Height:   1.99"     Width:   1.92"     [Reset]

[OK]   [Cancel]   [Preview]

6. Add custom animation effects:

**First:** Title enters with slide (no animation).

**Second:** Light bulb starts with **Center Revolve** effect.

**Third:** First bulleted item starts after previous event (light bulb) with Fade effect.

Apply the same animation effects to the second and third bulleted items and related images.

# Activity 4

1. Create the first slide in the model using the Title and 2-column Text layout from the Text Layouts category. Use the Microsoft Clip Organizer or Microsoft Office Online to locate a relevant clip art image.

2. Add a new placeholder for the recommendation and format attractively with a complementary fill color, line color, and shadow effect.

3. Add custom animation effects:

*Unanimated: Slide title*

**First:** Clip art—subtle effect of your choice.

**Second:** Bulleted list on left—Wipe from Left; build effect with dimming effect.

**Third:** Bulleted list on right—Wipe from Left; build effect with dimming effect.

**Fourth:** Recommendation—dramatic effect. Add a subtle sound effect to bring attention to this summarizing text.

4. Duplicate the slide and edit the content to create the remaining three slides. This technique will ensure consistency in the design of these related slides; clip art selections should convey a consistent tone.

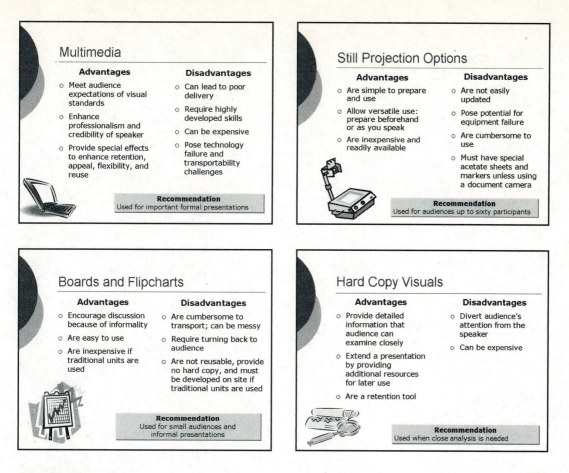

# Activity 5

Add custom animation effects to the remainder of the slides in the file Present as follows:

1. Title Slide—None

2. Adept Speakers Must...

    Bulleted list—Wipe from Left; build effect.

3. Choosing an Appropriate Presentation Media

    **First:** Bulleted list (left)—Wipe from Left.

    **Second:** Bulleted list (right)—Wipe from Left; build with dimming effect.

4. Benefits of Designing Visuals In-House

    **First:** Clip art—dissolve.

    **Second:** Bulleted list—Wipe from Left; build effect.

5. Guidelines for Effective Delivery

    Bulleted list (left)—Wipe from Left; no build effect.

# Slide Order

Sequence slides in the file Present according to the table on page 209. Print the slides and submit as directed by your instructor.

# Enhancing a Presentation with Images and Sound

## LEARNING OBJECTIVES

- Create drawn objects to enhance slides.
- Enhance the appeal of clip art using recolor, group/ungroup, rotation, and cropping tools.
- Use WordArt to add dramatic effects to text.
- Insert photographs as a slide object, slide background, and photo album page.
- Add sound to slide objects and slide transitions.

## USING DRAWING TOOLS TO ENHANCE A PRESENTATION

You will learn to enhance the basic presentation you created in Projects 1 and 2 with enhanced clip art, photographs, drawn objects, WordArt, and sound. Drawn objects, such as rectangles, ovals, and arrows, add a creative flair and provide depth and dimension to a slide. You will explore various ways of enhancing the drawn objects with color, lines, shadows, and other effects.

### Enhancing a Title Slide

*Directions:* Follow the instructions to enhance the original slide as shown.

1. Open the file Present and display Slide 1 (title slide) in Normal view.

Original slide                    Enhanced slide

## Remove the Background Graphic Object

2. Click **Format**, **Background**.

3. Select the **Omit background graphics from master** option.

4. Click **Apply** to remove the object from the title slide only.

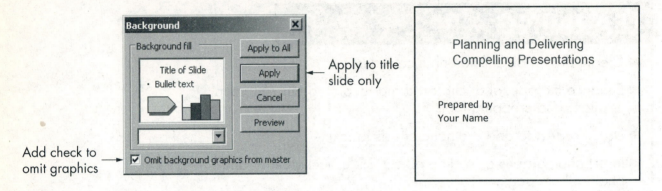

## Enhance the Title for Added Impact

5. Extend the title placeholder to fill the entire width of the slide.

6. Select a creative font face (e.g., Comic Sans) and enlarge the font size to at least 44 points for a dramatic effect.

7. Add a gradient fill. This artistic effect blends two colors, adding dimension to the placeholder and drawing attention to the presentation title.

   a) Click the list arrow to the right of the **Fill Color** button on the Draw toolbar.

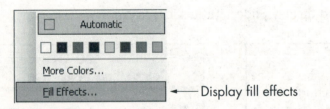

   b) Click **Fill Effects**.

8. Click the Gradient tab and select two colors that complement the template color.

9. Select a shading style that will set the direction of the shading: horizontal, vertical, diagonal up or down, or from corner or center. You can then select a desired variant of the style by clicking the desired thumbnail.

10. Click **Apply**.

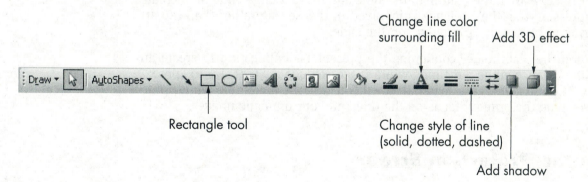

Gradient tab is selected

Select two colors

Select a shading style and variant from the gallery

11. For easy readability, select a font color with high contrast to the fill color. To add depth to the text, click **Shadow** from the Formatting toolbar (or click **Format**, **Font**, and select **Shadow** from the list of effects).

Shadow button

## Add a Border Below the Title

12. Click **AutoShapes**, **Rectangle** (or click the **Rectangle** button on the Draw toolbar) and draw a rectangle that extends the full width of the slide. Position the rectangle below the title placeholder.

Change line color surrounding fill

Add 3D effect

Rectangle tool

Change style of line (solid, dotted, dashed)

Add shadow

13. Add a fill in the rectangle using a complementary color darker than the colors used in the title placeholder.

14. Select the rectangle and click **Shadow** from the Draw Toolbar.

a) Select the shadow effect shown from the gallery of options available (e.g., the shadow appears on the bottom and right of the placeholder in the model).

b) Click **Shadow** again and select **Shadow Settings** to display the Shadow Settings toolbar.

c) Click the right arrow next to **Shadow Color** to select the color of the shadow.

d) Click the down arrow key two times and the right arrow two times to lengthen each side of the shadow slightly.

15. Make other format changes to achieve a desired effect:

a) Add a line to surround the rectangle and choose a complementary color.

b) Explore the appeal of a line style from solid to dotted or dashed.

c) Explore the appropriateness of one of the 3D effects.

## Add Relevant Clip Art

16. Insert a clip art image of a compelling speaker as shown in the model. (Click **Insert**, **Picture**, **Clip Art** or click the **Clip Art** button on the Draw toolbar.)

17. Anchor the clip art at the bottom of the slide and make it large enough to create the impression that the audience is involved in this setting rather than the art appearing to be simply "plastered" on the slide.

18. Reposition the placeholder containing the presenter identification to create an appealing balance in the remaining white space. Reduce the font size to approximately 24 points. Your goal is to balance this text in the remaining white space while keeping the primary focus on the title and your dramatic images.

## Create the Projection Screen

19. Select the **Rectangle** AutoShape on the Draw toolbar and draw the projection screen. Resize and position to create the impression of a projection screen mounted on the wall.

20. Format the rectangle with a black fill and 6-point line.

21. Add a shadow and adjust the shadow color and width for dimension.

22. Add the text box and format the text as shown. Animate the text box to start on mouse click with a Fade Zoom effect at Very Fast speed.

## *Adding an AutoShape to Enhance a Bulleted List Slide*

1. Display the original slide shown in the model in Normal view.

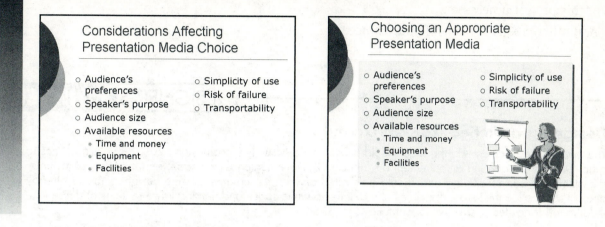

## Create a Projection Screen Behind the Bulleted List

2. Select the **Rectangle** AutoShape on the Draw toolbar and draw the projection screen.

3. Resize and position the rectangle to create the impression of a projection screen behind the two-column list.

## Change the Order of the Objects (Rectangle and Bulleted List)

4. Select the rectangle and click **Draw**, **Order**, **Send to Back** to send the rectangle behind the bulleted list.

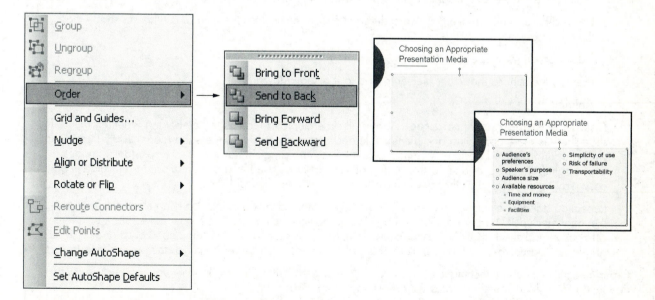

5. Format the rectangle to create the effect of a projection screen:

a) Change the fill color to off-white or gray.

b) Select a complementary line color and line style.

c) Add a shadow and adjust the shadow color and width. Refer to the instructions for enhancing the title slide with a shadowed rectangle at the beginning of this project if necessary.

d) Add other creative effects of your choice.

---

## DESIGNER'S POINTER

### Designing a Unified, Logical Layout

The layout of the elements on the slide should be balanced, visually pleasing, and easy for your audience to read. Decisions regarding arrangement are affected by your audience, message, and the types of multimedia elements you're including and should be limited only by the creativity of the designer. You've already been introduced to the layout principles of maximizing white space and limiting large sections of dense text. Additional principles of effective layout follow:

- **Attempt to give your slide dynamic energy.** For example, adding a shadow or 3D effect pulls an object off the slide, adding dimension and interest. Overlapping objects as illustrated in several of the slides in this project or even positioning an image partially off the slide adds depth and dynamics to an otherwise flat, dull medium. Exercise constraint because overusing visual effects will overwhelm the audience and take attention away from the speaker and the message.

- **Design slides with a clear visual hierarchy that emphasizes the ideas needed to communicate your message effectively.** Understanding the ways in which Western readers distinguish the importance of information provides a crucial foundation for slide layout. Western readers quickly scan from upper left to bottom right to get an overview of a screen image, tend to look at larger items first and smaller items last, are attracted to brighter colors first but look at other colors, interpret items placed above other items as more important than items placed below, look at items that appear heavier first, and are drawn to moving items over static items and sound effects over mute slides. As you create a custom presentation design in Project 4 and complete the other slides in the remaining projects, note the use of these visual techniques to make specific content the primary focal point of your slide.

  - Make it the biggest and brightest or isolate it from other items on the slide.

  - Use a different color, make the item a different shape, or enclose the item in a different shape than the other content on the slide.

  - Add a border or a special effect.

  - Position the item so that other elements lead to it or point toward it.

  - Animate it.

- **Design a unified look and feel.** When all slide elements look as if they belong together, the slide show is more appealing and memorable and communicates your message more clearly than a cluttered, unorganized design. A unified style involves choosing similar colors, shapes, fonts, images, line weights, shadows, and so forth. Placing all clip art to be used in a presentation on one slide is an easy way to eliminate clips that are inconsistent with the overall visual style.

  Repeating standard elements on every slide also gives a unified look and feel. Unifying elements, for example, might include (1) shadows, fills, and borders on objects such as photos, source notes, and quotations; (2) background effects that unify a collection of images on a slide; or (3) the same band of color or a small graphic or logo across the top or bottom of the slide that identifies the presenter or the presentation topic.

Experimenting with visual techniques while allowing your creativity to flow will allow you to structure a unified layout that clearly communicates your most important ideas.

Source: Graham, L. (1999). *Principles of Interactive Design*. Albany, NY: Thomson Delmar.

## Add Relevant Clip Art

6. Insert clip art to create the impression of a speaker delivering a presentation.

7. Change the order of the clip art so that the speaker is standing in front of the projection screen (click **Draw**, **Order** and choose a position as needed).

8. Size and position the clip art to achieve proper balance and perspective.

## ■ WORKING WITH CLIP ART

You can increase the usefulness and appeal of clip art by applying the following techniques: recoloring, grouping/ungrouping, rotating, and cropping.

### *Recoloring Clip Art*

*Directions:* Follow the instructions to recolor the clip art in the title slide.

1. Display the enhanced title slide in Normal view.

2. Select the clip art and click the **Recolor** button on the Picture toolbar. Click **View**, **Toolbars**, **Picture** to display the toolbar if necessary. The color of each segment of the clip art appears in the original column (e.g., the first color in the list is the microphones; next four colors, speaker's clothing; sixth color, lectern; etc.).

3. Select the list arrow in the New column beside the segment you wish to change and select a color. Click **Preview** to see the change.

*Note:* The check mark before the "Original" color for the second color in the list indicates a change has been made already. To return to the original color, click the box and remove the check.

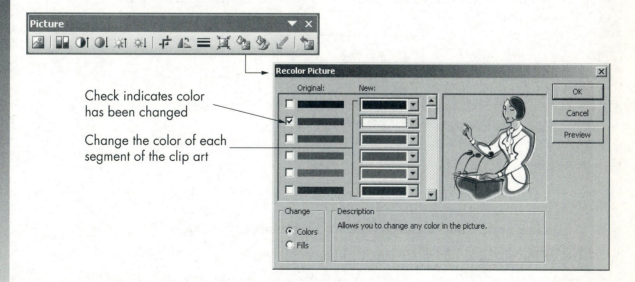

4. Click **OK** when you have made all the necessary changes.

5. Recolor other clip art images in the file Present as needed to make them complementary to the presentation design template.

## *Ungrouping and Grouping Objects*

An ungrouped clip art image can be modified to fit a design. Regrouping the image reduces the number of objects to be animated separately.

***Directions:*** Follow the instructions to enhance the original slide as shown.

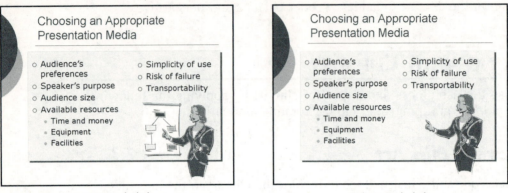

Original slide                                    Enhanced slide

1. Ungroup the clip art:

   a) Click **Draw**, **Ungroup**.

   b) Click **Yes** to convert the picture to a Microsoft Office drawing object.

   c) Repeat the **Draw**, **Ungroup** command until the clip art cannot be ungrouped further. Sizing handles appear for each segment of the ungrouped clip art.

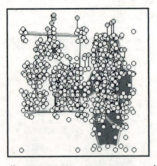

All segments are ungrouped

   d) Click outside the clip art to deselect all sections of the image.

Delete the visual aid from the clip art image:

2. Draw a rectangle with the left mouse click that encloses all segments of the visual and press **Delete**. Repeat this process until all segments of the visual have been deleted.

*Hint:* Holding down the **Shift** key as you click will allow you to select additional segments.

Segments of the visual selected

Regroup the speaker:

3. Use the mouse pointer to draw a rectangle that encloses all segments of the speaker.

4. Click **Draw**, **Group**.

Click group ————→

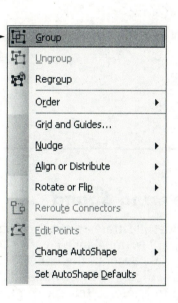

Surround image with rectangle drawn with the left mouse button

Segments of the speaker selected

Segments of the speaker regrouped

5. Resize and position the speaker as needed to achieve the perspective shown in the model.

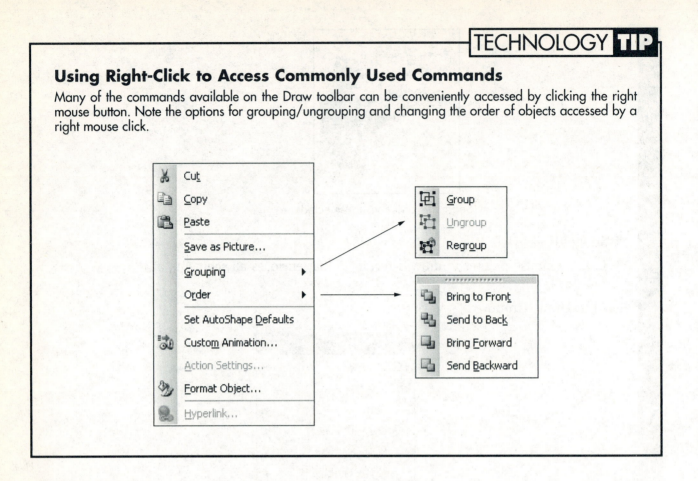

## TECHNOLOGY TIP

### Using Right-Click to Access Commonly Used Commands

Many of the commands available on the Draw toolbar can be conveniently accessed by clicking the right mouse button. Note the options for grouping/ungrouping and changing the order of objects accessed by a right mouse click.

## Adding AutoShapes and Sound

The original slide in the model illustrates several common errors in slide design. First, the small clip art is unbalanced with the text, creating an unappealing, unprofessional look. Second, the bulleted list violates rules of division that require at least two points. Most important, the slide's vague title and overload of text fail to reinforce the speaker's main point: typical business presentations require improvement.

*Directions:* Follow the instructions to enhance the original slide as shown.

Original slide                    Enhanced slide

1. Create a new slide using the Title Only layout from the Other Layouts category.

2. Key the title.

3. Insert the clip art shown by using the keyword "groups" to search Microsoft Clip Organizer or Microsoft Office Online.

## Create a Dialog Box for the Audience's Comment

4. Click **AutoShapes**, **Callouts** on the Draw toolbar. Select one of the four balloons in the top row.

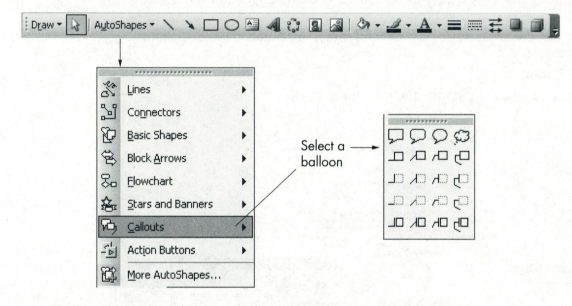

5. Key the following text in the callout box: **Boring and unbearable**.

6. Format the callout box as desired (fill color and effects, line color, line style, shadow, 3D).

7. Format the text as desired (font face, size, and color; bold; shadow).

## Add the Source Note

8. Use the **Text box** button to create a new placeholder for the source note.

9. Key the text: **200 corporate vice presidents surveyed**. Select a readable font size smaller than the title to create a clear hierarchy of importance. That is, the title should appear more important than other text on the slide.

10. Resize the text box to display the text on one line and position the box as shown in the model.

*Hint:* Copying the original source note created for the "Top Mistakes Presenters Make" and then revising would save you time and ensure that the related elements are consistent.

11. Fine-tune the size and position of each object (clip art, callout box, and source note) to produce a realistic effect.

## Add Custom Animation and Sound

12. Click **Slide Show**, **Custom Animation**. Refer to Project 2 to review custom animation if necessary.

13. Edit the Custom Animation dialog box to create the following effects in the order shown:

a) **Unanimated:** Slide title and clip art (start with the slide).

b) **First:** Callout box—Start on mouse click with an engaging effect (e.g., flip, bounce, float).

c) **Second:** Source note—Start with a subtle effect (e.g., expand) on an automatic timing that starts the source note **.2 seconds** after the callout box appears (the previous event):

- Click the down arrow to the right of the source note in the Custom Animation List.
- Click **Timing**.
- Input **.2 seconds** in the spin box for the Delay section.

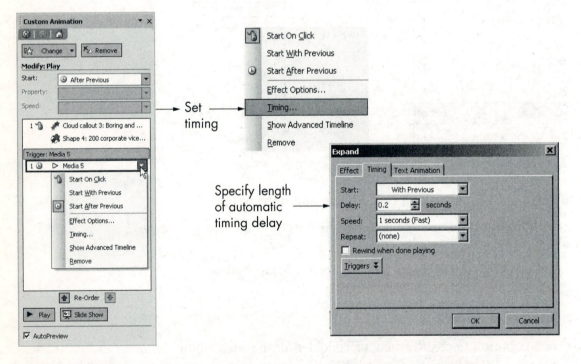

*Note:* You will learn more about advanced animation techniques in Project 6.

## Add a Sound Effect

14. Click the **Clip Art** button from the Draw toolbar (or click **Insert**, **Clip Art**).

15. Click the down arrow beside Selected media file types and uncheck all options except **Sounds**.

16. Search for a sound file of a boring yawn by inputting "yawn" as the keyword for the search.

17. Click to select a sound clip. A sound icon is inserted on the slide, and a prompt to animate the sound appears.

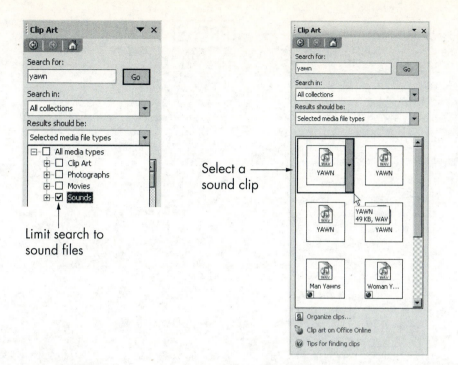

18. Click **Automatically** to play the sound clip without a mouse click. Clicking **When Clicked** allows the speaker to control the play time during the presentation.

To adjust the animation of this media file, right-click on the sound icon and click **Custom Animation**.

## Building Media-Rich Presentations That Comply with Copyright Law

Today's audiences have come to expect media-rich, dynamic presentations. For this reason, electronic presentations must incorporate well-chosen digital elements that connect thematically to the presentation's purpose or brand identity to make an experience real or information more understandable or credible to the audience. Lively, original templates and photos should be chosen over static ones, and boring words and numbers should be replaced with appealing shapes, symbols, images, and edgy layouts that people are more likely to understand and retain. For efficiency and optimal selection, a presenter's toolbox must include a well-stocked professional library of digital media, including templates, backgrounds, photos, sound, and video clips.

Numerous third-party companies, as well as public domain and shareware galleries, provide digital libraries for use in PowerPoint projects. Fortunately, many provide free downloads that help you assess the quality and appropriateness of these collection for your presentation purposes. As you complete this course, you are encouraged to locate useful sites, download several of the free images and templates, and share your evaluation of these sites to your class and instructor.

Regardless of whether you are downloading files from a commercial CD-ROM/DVD, an online subscription, or a free Web site, read the licensing agreement carefully to avoid copyright infringement. Common licensing agreements for commercial digital libraries allow you to use the art on one computer at a time and as part of any document or publication you choose to distribute (same stipulation as with other commercial software). You may not share clip art via a network without a site license.

Your informed use of copyrighted materials will save you embarrassment and your company the cost of an expensive lawsuit and reflect the high ethical standards of a professional presenter.

19. Make the sound icon invisible by moving it off the slide. Alternatively, right-click on the sound icon, click **Edit Sound Object**, and select **Hide sound icon during slide show**. From this menu, you can also edit play options and adjust the volume of the clip.

## ◼ USING PHOTOGRAPHS TO ENHANCE A PRESENTATION

Photographs are useful in helping the audience visualize actual persons, places, or objects. Photographs can be added as a slide object or as the slide background. Special enhancements can be made easily using photo editing software and modifying the slide as a photo album page.

# Inserting a Photograph as a Slide Object with Enhancements

*Directions:* Follow the instructions to complete the slide as shown.

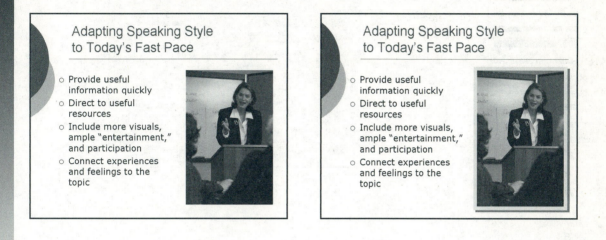

1. Create a new slide using the Title, Text, and Content layout.

2. Key the title and the bulleted list.

## Select a Photo

3. Select a relevant photo using one of the following methods:

   a) Insert a photo from the Microsoft Clip Organizer or Microsoft Office Online.

   b) Scan a photograph or download a file from an Internet site or a digital camera.

## Add a Creative Border for the Photograph

4. Select a relevant photograph, click **Line Style** on the Draw toolbar, and click **More Lines**.

Line style button

5. Be certain the Colors and Lines tab is selected and edit the line to create an appealing border for the photograph:

   a) Select a line color complementary to other colors in the presentation design template.

   b) Increase the line weight to **10 pt** for a more dramatic effect.

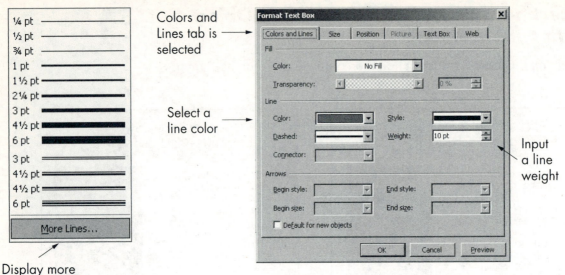

Colors and Lines tab is selected

Select a line color

Input a line weight

Display more line styles

6. Click the **Shadow** button on the Draw toolbar and select a shadow from the gallery. Edit the shadow settings by selecting a shadow color darker than the line color. Extend the shadow to "pop" it off the slide to provide depth and dimension to the slide. Refer to the instructions for editing shadow settings at the beginning of this project if necessary.

7. Animate the slide:

**Unanimated:** Title (comes in with slide).

**First:** Photograph—Start with a mouse click and Dissolve In.

**Second:** Bulleted list—Start with a mouse click and Wipe from Left.

# Inserting a Photograph as the Slide Background and Rotating Text

*Directions:* Follow the instructions to complete the slide as shown.

1. Create a new slide using the Blank layout in the Contents layout category.

2. Omit the background graphics that will distract from the photo background:

a) Click **Format, Background**.

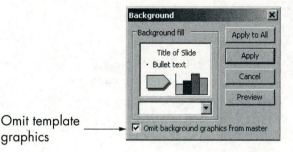

Omit template graphics

b) Click **Omit background graphics from master** and click **Apply** to remove the template object from this slide only.

## Select and Insert the Photograph

3. Insert a photograph from the Microsoft Clip Organizer or Microsoft Office Online (input "speaker" as the keyword) or insert a digital image captured with a digital camera or scanner.

4. Select the photograph. Right-click, select **Save as Picture**. Provide a file name and designate a drive where you wish to save the file. Microsoft automatically saves the photograph as a JPEG graphic image format that can be imported into PowerPoint.

5. Click **Fill Effects, Picture, Select Picture**.

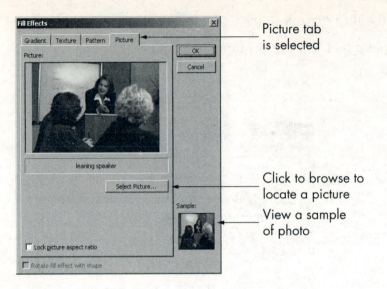

Picture tab
is selected

Click to browse to
locate a picture

View a sample
of photo

6. Browse to locate the photograph file in JPEG format you created in Steps 3–4.

7. Click **Apply**.

## Add and Position a Photo Caption

8. Create a text box that expands across the entire width of the slide and key the text: **Personal Connection a Must**.

9. Format the text as desired (font face, size, and color; bold; shadow).

10. Format the text box as desired (fill color, line color and style, shadow, 3D).

11. Click **Draw**, **Rotate or Flip**, and **Rotate Left 90%**. The text box is rotated to lie vertically at the left of the slide as shown in the model.

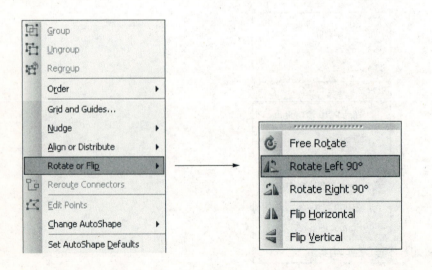

Alternatively, you can click the **Free Rotate** tool (green circle above the top center sizing handle) and drag the text box into the desired position.

Use the free rotate tool to position the text box

## Add a Slide Transition

12. Click **Slide Show**, **Slide Transition**.

13. Select **Dissolve** at **Fast** speed as the slide transition effect.

14. Add a sound effect such as applause or one of your choice to bring attention to this important concept.

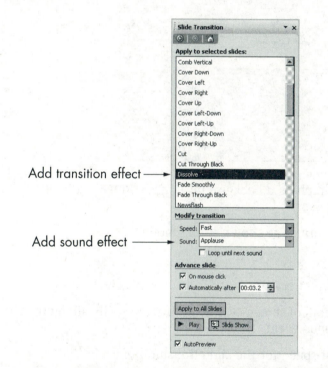

Add transition effect

Add sound effect

## *Editing Photographs in PowerPoint*

Minor adjustments can be made to an image directly in PowerPoint without editing in a separate editing software. Options on the Picture toolbar allow you to change the color to grayscale, black and white, or washout and make it possible to increase or decrease contrast and brightness. To enhance readability of the text in the model, you will "washout" the color in the photograph that is inserted as a dramatic slide background.

*Directions:* Follow the instructions to complete the slide as shown.

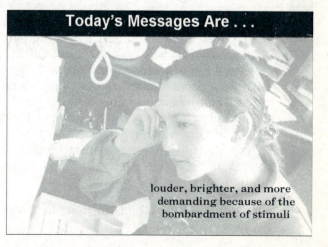

1. Create a new slide using the Blank layout in the Contents layout category.

2. Omit the background graphics that will distract from the photo background.

3. Locate a relevant photo and insert it on the slide.

4. Washout the color to enhance the readability of the text that will appear on top of the photo:

   a) Right-click the photo and click **Format**, **Picture**.

   b) Click the arrow next to the Color box and select **Washout**.

   c) Save the edited photograph and delete the photo on the slide.

Choose washout from the color box

5. Insert the edited photograph as a background image. (Refer to directions for previous slide if necessary.)

6. Add the text boxes and format as shown in the model.

7. Animate:

   **First:** Title—Grow & Turn effect.

   **Second:** Text box at bottom of screen—Grow & Turn automatically with .2 second delay after previous event.

8. Select **Dissolve** and **Fast** speed for the slide transition effect.

## Enhancing Photographs with Photo Editing Software

Photo editing software offers tools for enhancing a photograph scanned or downloaded from the Internet or a digital camera. Microsoft Office Picture Manager 2003, a new component of Office 2003, is primarily a file management tool but does allow for limited image correction, such as adjusting the brightness, contrast, color hue, and saturation; cropping unwanted segments; rotating and flipping; removing red eye; and resizing.

The following project was completed with Microsoft PhotoEditor (available with Office 2002), which has a broader range of editing options than Picture Manager. You may reinstall PhotoEditor or explore the photo editing options in the software available to you (e.g., Microsoft Image Pro and Adobe PhotoShop).

*Directions:* Follow the instructions to create the slide as shown.

Meeting the Demands
of Today's Audiences

1. Create a new slide using any layout and insert a photograph from the Microsoft Clip Organizer.

2. Select the photograph and right-click. Click **Save as Picture**. Provide a file name and designate a drive where you wish to save the file.

3. Delete the slide containing the photograph.

4. Open the photograph file in a photo editing software. Clicking on the file in Explorer will automatically open the file in your default software.

5. Experiment as you explore the menu options. Menus will vary depending on the software used.

**Effects:** The first group of effects enables you to correct minor imperfections in the photograph. The second group of effects is used to add an artistic filter effect. Select a filter and then adjust controls for intensity, direction, and so forth.

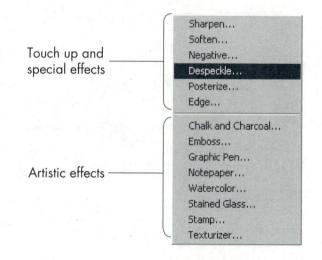

**Image:** Click **AutoBalance** to adjust the brightness and contrast levels of an image automatically or click **Balance** to adjust manually. Use options on the crop menu to create attractive mattes and oval and rectangular images. Rotate images as desired using the options from the **Rotate** menu.

Try these simple adjustments to improve the quality and add an artistic flair to the original photograph shown in the model:

a) Apply the despeckle special effect to reduce a grainy look.

b) Apply the Texturizer, Canvas special effect to add texture and dimension.

c) Save the changes made to the file.

## Creating a Photo Album

The photo album feature allows you to quickly create a handsome photo album of your favorite photos. You can quickly add multiple pictures, choose the layouts and frames, add captions, and then e-mail the file to friends and family or post it on the Web. You also can use this powerful and efficient feature to enhance photographs in a presentation you are delivering.

*Directions:* Follow the instructions to create the slide as shown.

1. Click **Insert**, **Picture**, **New Photo Album**.

2. Click **Picture** and browse to locate the photograph you enhanced in the previous section.

3. Select **1 picture with title** as the picture layout from the drop-down menu.

4. Select **Rounded Rectangle** as the frame shape or an option of your choice from the drop-down menu.

5. Click **Create**.

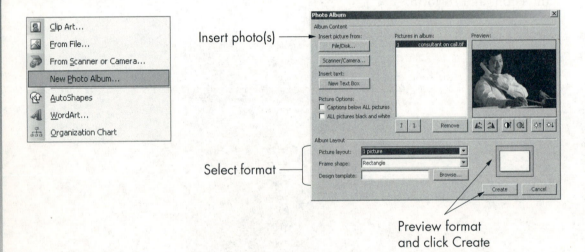

Note that a new PowerPoint presentation was created with a title page and one slide containing the photo in the format you specified.

6. Insert the photo album slide in the file Present:

a) Switch the new presentation (photo album) to Slide Sorter view.

b) Select the slide containing the photo and click **Copy**.

c) Click **Window** and select **Present** from the list of open presentations.

d) Switch the file Present to Slide Sorter view. Click to the left of the slide that will follow the photo album slide.

e) Click **Paste**. The photo slide is reformatted to match the file Present.

f) Close the new presentation (photo album) without saving.

7. Continue building this slide in the next activity.

## Adding WordArt

WordArt displays text creatively using colorful outlines, drop shadows, and a variety of shapes that gives the text a three-dimensional appearance. An eye-catching design using WordArt can help you direct the audience's attention to an important point and enhance the creativity of your presentation. Use WordArt images cautiously. Overuse obviously defeats its purpose for emphasis, and the distortion in the WordArt design can make the text difficult to read.

1. Display the "Consultant on Call" slide in Normal view and click anywhere in the slide.

2. Click the **WordArt** button on the Draw toolbar.

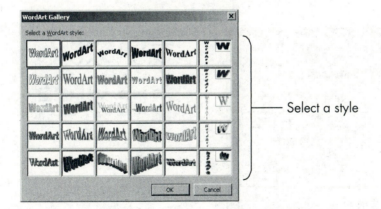

3. Choose a style from the WordArt Gallery.

Select a style

4. Make these changes in the Edit WordArt dialog box:

a) Input the text: **Consultant On Call**.

b) Select a font face and size.

Note that a WordArt toolbar appears on the Draw toolbar after you input text in the WordArt dialog box.

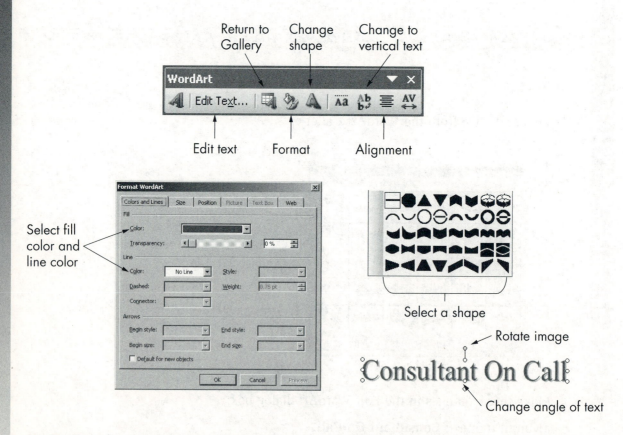

5. Click the **Format WordArt** button and select a fill color and line color complementary to your background.

6. Click the **Change Shape** button and select a shape for the WordArt if you wish to change the default (e.g., triangle down, arch up, can up).

7. Point to the green circle on the WordArt object and drag to rotate as you wish.

8. Design a business card for displaying your contact information:

   a) Create a text box and key your contact information for the sample text.

*Hint:* Keep the size of the card in proportion to a 2 × 3.5 inch business card.

b) Add a parchment texture fill effect (**Draw**, **Fill Color**, **Fill Effects**, **Texture**).

c) Add **6 point triple line** surrounding the card and a subtle shadow to add depth and fullness to the object.

d) Add the image representing your company logo to the top left-hand corner (search for a suitable logo in Microsoft Office Online).

9. Create a text box and insert a company name. Select a creative font as shown. Position attractively at the bottom of the slide.

10. Animate the slide:

**First:** Title—Start with **1 second delay** with an effect of your choice.

**Second:** Photograph—Start with a mouse click with dissolve or a dramatic effect of your choice.

**Third:** Identification—Curve up with 1 second delay after previous event (photo).

## Creating Screen Captures

*Directions:* Follow the instructions to complete the slide shown in the model.

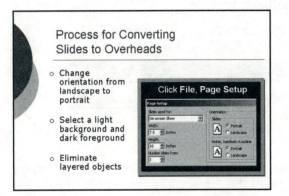

1. Create a new slide using the Title and Text layout.

2. Key the title and bulleted list.

## Capture the Image

3. Display the Page Setup dialog box by clicking **File**, **Page Setup**.

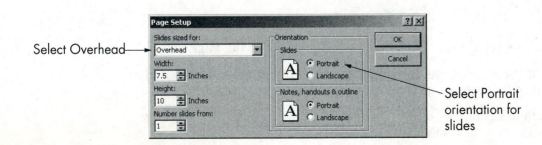

4. Edit the **Page Setup** menu to appear exactly as you wish it captured:

   a) Select **Overhead** in the "Slides sized for" section.

   b) Click **Portrait** in the "Slides orientation" section.

5. Hold down the **Alt** key as you press **PrintScreen** (key located to the right of the **F12** key).

*Note:* The paste icon on the Formatting toolbar becomes active, denoting you have copied an object to the clipboard.

6. Click **Cancel** (you are only capturing the image—*not* executing the command to change the page setup).

## Insert the Captured Image on the Slide

7. Click in the area on the slide where the screen capture will appear.

8. Click **Paste**.

9. Continue building this slide in the next section.

## Cropping Images

1. Select the screen capture. The Picture toolbar should appear when the image is selected. If not, click **View**, **Toolbars**, **Picture**.

2. Click the cropping tool on the Picture toolbar.

Cropping tool

3. Point to the sizing handle in the right center of the selected object. Drag to the left to crop the image to the right of the arrow as shown in the illustration.

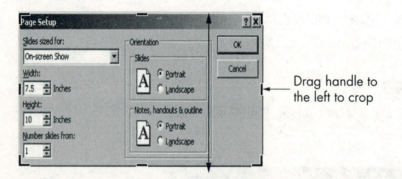

Drag handle to the left to crop

4. Create a text box and key the following text commands: **Click File, Page Setup**.

5. Center the text box directly above the screen capture. Format the font face and font size to balance the text box attractively over the screen capture.

6. Select the **Rectangle** AutoShape on the Draw toolbar to surround the text box and the screen capture with a showcase box.

7. Select the rectangle and send it behind the screen capture and the text box (**Draw**, **Order**, **Send to Back**).

8. Create an appealing format for the showcase box:

   a) Add a fill color of black and a 10-point line. Select an attractive line color, line style, and shadow effect from the Draw toolbar.

   b) Position the showcase box, text box, and screen capture as shown and group these objects to simplify animation.

9. Animate the slides:

   **Unanimated:** Title (come in with the slide).

   **First:** First item of the bulleted list—Wipe from Left.

   **Second:** Grouped image—Center Revolve; start with **1 second delay** after previous event.

   **Third:** Second bulleted item—Wipe from Left.

   **Fourth:** Third bulleted item—Wipe from Left.

## ■ INSERTING SLIDE TRANSITIONS

*Directions:* Follow the instructions to add slide transitions to the slides created in this project.

1. Display the presentation in Slide Sorter view.

2. Select any slides that do not include a slide transition icon below the slide.

3. Click the **Slide Transition** button on the Slide Sorter toolbar.

4. Select **Wipe from Left** at **Fast** speed as the effect.

*Note:* This slide transition effect has been used for all other slides in this presentation except for the slide that contains the photograph as the background, a specimen slide that requires a more dramatic effect.

5. Click **Apply**.

## ■ REINFORCEMENT ACTIVITIES

Add the following slides to the file Present for added reinforcement of the PowerPoint features you learned in this project. Position the slides as shown in the table on pages 209–210.

### Activity 1

1. Complete Project 2, Reinforcement Activity 2, on page 42 if you have not done so already.

2. Recolor the speaker's clothing to complement your presentation design template.

3. Format the bulleted list text box to create the impression of a projection screen for showcasing the speaker's points: add a fill color, a 10-point line slightly darker than the fill color, and a shadow effect.

4. Add the **Wipe from Left** slide transition.

# Activity 2

1. Create the enhanced slide shown in the model using the Title Only layout. Note the improvements over the original slide: a title that clearly describes the slide's purpose, a creative image depicting the reflection on one's audience needed to identify a clear objective, and text reinforcing the exact question to be asked.

| Original slide | Enhanced slide |

2. Locate the speaker on the enhanced slide (search "thinking"). Resize, position, and recolor as shown.

3. Create the audience:

   a) Locate the clip art shown on the original slide (search "presentation").

   b) Ungroup the clip art and delete unneeded segments (words in balloon, computer, and speaker).

   c) Resize and position the remaining images (balloon and audience) as shown in the enhanced model.

   d) Add a shadow effect to the balloon and the audience for added dimension.

   e) Recolor images to complement your template.

   f) Group the balloon and audience.

4. Add the text box and key text: **How do you want the audience to respond to your presentation?** Format the text to bring attention to this key point.

5. Search for a sound file related to thinking (search "hmm") from the Microsoft Clip Organizer or Microsoft Office Online. Animate to play after the speaker is displayed. Hide the sound icon or move it off the slide for invisible delivery.

6. Animate the objects as follows:

   **Unanimated:** Title.

   **First:** Speaker with sound following automatically.

   **Second:** Balloon and audience—Dissolve; after previous with .2 second delay.

   **Third:** Text box—Stretch.

7. Add the **Wipe from Left** slide transition.

# Activity 3

1. Create the slide shown in the model using the Title, Text, and Clip Art layout.

2. Omit the bullet and format the text for emphasis and appeal (**Format**, **Bullets and Numbering**, **None**). Locate a photograph from the Microsoft Clip Organizer or Microsoft Office Online and format attractively.

3. Copy the source note text box used in the presentation Present. Edit the source of this quotation: **Source: H. Dennis Beaver, "Visual aids: How much is too much?"** *ABA Banking Journal.*

4. Animate the objects as desired and reorder in the custom animation list: (1) title, (2) photograph, (3) quote, and (4) note source starting on an automatic timing immediately after the quote.

5. Add the **Wipe from Left** slide transition.

# Activity 4

Locate a quotation related to planning and delivering compelling presentations and design your own slide similar to the model in Activity 3. Position the slide with related content in the file Present.

# Activity 5

1. Create the slide shown in the model.

2. Locate three photos and save them as JPEG files. Format the photos as rounded rectangles using the photo album feature.

3. Use WordArt to create the text: **Relies on Speaking Skills**.

4. Animate the objects:

   **First:** Photos—Fly in from Left (presenter), from top Right (telephone), and from Bottom (group talking).

   **Second:** Word Art—Grow & Turn.

## Activity 6

1. Create the slide shown in the model.

2. Omit the graphics from the background to allow more space for the screen capture.

3. Create a screen capture of a useful Web site for presenters (e.g., **http://www.presentations.com** or **http://www.powerpointers.com**). Crop the image to omit the browser toolbars.

4. Add an attractive text box for displaying the Internet address.

5. Animate the objects as desired and reorder in the custom animation list: (1) title, (2) screen capture, and (3) Web address starting automatically .2 seconds after photograph.

6. Add the **Wipe from Left** slide transition.

**Additional Resources**

Insert a screen capture of a Web site of your choice.

Insert the Internet address.

## Slide Order

Sequence slides in the file Present according to the table on pages 209–210. Print and submit as directed by your instructor.

# Creating a Custom Presentation Design

- Edit the master slide to modify standard design elements consistently and efficiently.

- Modify the color scheme of a standard presentation design to fit a topic and the needs of a specific audience.

- Create a custom template for a company that reflects its corporate identity and displays a high standard of quality and originality.

## CUSTOMIZING POWERPOINT

A designer can easily adjust standard design elements within a presentation to meet specific presentation needs. Custom designs are created using a slide master to ensure the consistency required in a professional design and to maximize the designer's efficiency in preparing the slides. Changes you will make in this project include (1) editing the slide master, (2) modifying the color scheme of a standard presentation design, (3) creating a custom presentation design for a specific topic and a company, and (4) reformatting slides to be produced as overhead transparencies.

### Editing the Slide Master

A slide master controls the standard elements displayed in the title slide, all other slide layouts, and handouts. Any change input on the slide master automatically reformats each slide in the presentation, eliminating the time-consuming process of revising each slide individually and checking and double-checking for consistency. The following activity will illustrate the efficiency of using the slide master to make universal changes to the file Present.

To maximize your efficiency, always edit the slide master as you experiment with the design of your slide show. That means avoiding the temptation to make "quick" changes directly on presentation slides rather than on the slide master. Why? Suppose you edit the slide master to apply a different font face and color for the title slide. These updates in the slide master will *not* override manual edits made to individual slides! Updates appear only on new slides you add to the presentation and slides you've not manually edited.

*Directions:* Follow these instructions to modify the slide master for the file Present. You will change the font face, size, and color; edit the bullet for the first and second bullet levels; and enhance the title placeholder.

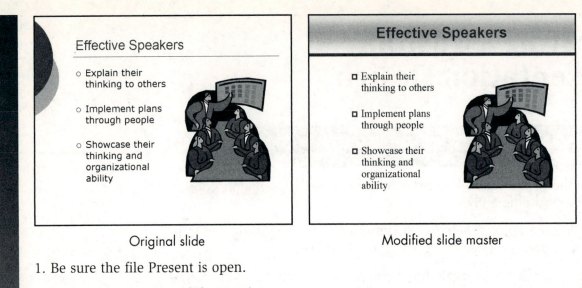

Original slide                    Modified slide master

1. Be sure the file Present is open.

2. Click **View**, **Master**, **Slide Master**.

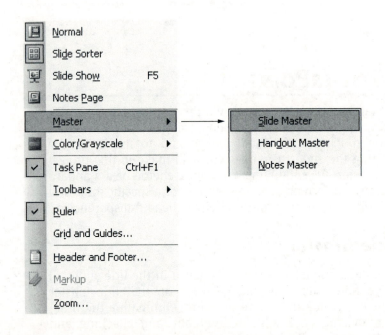

3. Click the **Insert New Slide Master** button.

Click to insert new slide

## Revise the Title Placeholder

4. Click in the Title placeholder and make the following changes:

   a) Select a sturdy font that can be read easily from a distance (e.g., Arial). Add bold and a shadow effect. Refer to the Designer's Pointer related to font selection and size on page 79.

## DESIGNER'S POINTER

### Choosing Lively, Readable Fonts

Follow these general guidelines for making font choices that (1) an audience can easily read on a projected visual, (2) are fresh and interesting, and (3) clearly define the importance of the various sections of text (e.g., slide title, text, source notes):

1. Limit the number of fonts within a single presentation to at least two but no more than three to prevent a cluttered and confusing look.

2. Choose interesting fonts that convey the mood of a presentation and are a fresh change from the most commonly used (e.g., Times New Roman and Helvetica). For example, for a less formal presentation, consider informal fonts such as Comic Sans MS and Tahoma.

3. Choose sturdy font faces that can easily be read from a distance, perhaps in a darkened room. Avoid delicate fonts with narrow strokes that wash out, especially when displayed in color. Likewise, avoid italic, decorative fonts, and condensed fonts because the letters are close together and can be difficult to read. Examples of poor choices include *Times New Roman, Italic;* ALGERIAN (decorative); and Abadi MT Condensed. Good choices are illustrated in the following table.

4. Use fonts that are large enough for the audience to read. General guidelines for slides projected in a typical presentation room (approximately 30 participants) appear in the following table, but font sizes must be adjusted for larger rooms. Larger fonts are also needed when transmitting via videoconference; the fuzziness resulting from compressed video makes text smaller than 44 points difficult to read. The Technology Tip on page 81 provides a point reference to help you understand point size.

5. Create a hierarchy of importance among the standard elements (slide title, bulleted lists, and source notes) by varying the font size and the font face.

   a) Use different font sizes for the slide title, bulleted list, and other text on the slide to enable the audience to recognize differences in the importance of these items. The slide title should be keyed in the largest font to draw the audience's attention to the title, followed by the bulleted list, and then other text on the slide (e.g., source notes, text within AutoShapes).

   b) Use a sturdy sans serif font for the slide title and a serif font for bulleted text to further distinguish the slide title from other text. When presenting by videoconference, use all sans serif fonts because these plain, simple fonts are easier to read with the fuzziness of compressed video.

### Recommendations for Font Faces and Sizes

| Slide Element | Recommended Font Type | Recommended Font Size | Examples |
|---|---|---|---|
| Slide title | **Sans serif** A font without cross-strokes known as serifs. (*Sans* means "without.") Has simple, blocky look that is appropriate for displaying text, as in the slide title or headlines of a newspaper or magazine. | 24 to 36 points | Arial<br>Century Gothic<br>**Arial Black**<br>Verdana |
| Bulleted list | **Serif** A font with short cross-strokes that project from the top and bottom of the main stroke of a letter—the type that typically is read as the main print in textbooks and newspapers. | 18 to 24 points | CG Times<br>Times New Roman |
| Other text | **Serif** | No smaller than 14 points | See serif examples. |

b) Change the text alignment of your presentation design's current setting. Click the desired alignment from the **Alignment** buttons on the Formatting toolbar (or click **Format**, **Alignment** and choose the desired format: left, center, or right align).

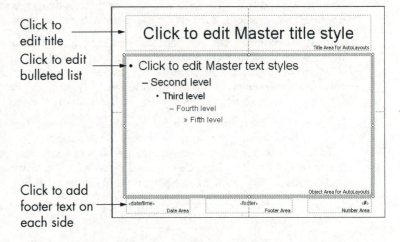

Select text alignment: left, center, or right

c) Enhance the placeholder to draw the audience's attention to the title first. Follow these suggestions or develop ideas of your own:

Click to edit title

Click to edit bulleted list

• Omit the graphic objects on the slide master if you believe they will conflict with the new design. Note that the graphic circles and horizontal line below the title placeholder were deleted from the slide master.

• Change the fill color of the placeholder to a shade slightly lighter than the slide background or add a special fill effect (gradient, patterned, or texture).

Click to add footer text on each side

• Add a narrow border in a subtle color and/or add a shadowing effect.

• Resize the placeholder to extend the full width of the slide.

## Modify a Bullet

5. Click **Click to edit Master text styles** in the bulleted list placeholder.

6. Change the font face and font size for the first level to a selection of your choice.

7. Click **Format**, **Bullet**.

8. Be sure the Bulleted tab is selected. The Numbered tab allows you to select a numbering style, which is used to indicate a required sequence (1, 2, 3...).

Select for bullets or numbers

Modify size

Modify color

Select character or picture

9. Click **Customize** to select a new bullet.

   a) Explore the various categories and available bullets for each category by clicking the drop-down list.

   b) Select the **Wingdings 2** category and click the bullet shown or any category and bullet of your choice.

Display different categories of bullets

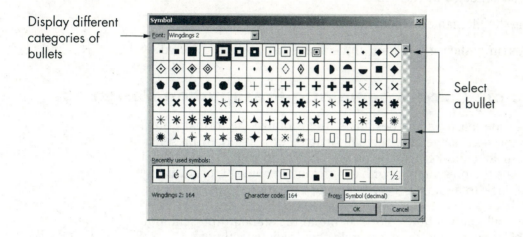

Select a bullet

10. Click **OK** to return to the Bullets and Numbering dialog box and change the appearance of the bullet.

    a) Increase the bullet size by double-clicking in the Size text box and inputting a number larger than 100 percent (e.g., "120").

    b) Select a new bullet color by clicking the Color list arrow and selecting a color complementary to the presentation design.

11. Click **OK** to return to the slide master.

12. Click **Second Level** and modify the appearance of the second-level bulleted items following the same process (Steps 8–11).

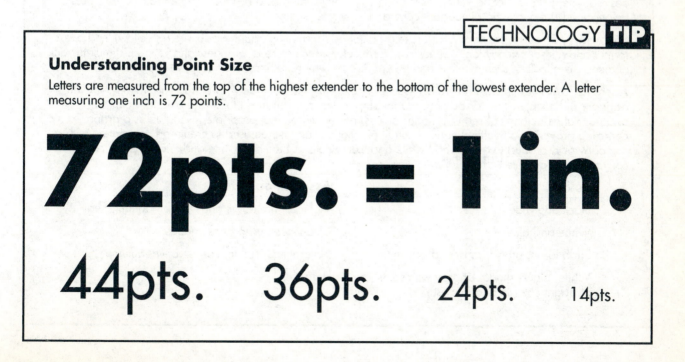

## TECHNOLOGY TIP

### Understanding Point Size

Letters are measured from the top of the highest extender to the bottom of the lowest extender. A letter measuring one inch is 72 points.

# 72pts. = 1 in.

44pts.    36pts.    24pts.    14pts.

## Preview Changes to the Slide Master and Print Selected Slides

13. Click **Close Master View** to exit the slide master and return to Normal or Slide Sorter view (the view you were using when you accessed the slide master).

14. Advance through the presentation and note the modifications made to the slide master that are now reflected in each slide.

15. Save the file using the file name **Present-new**.

16. Print Slides 1–3 as an audience handout, three slides per page, if directed by your instructor.

### Modifying the Color Scheme of a Presentation Design

Changes in the slide master allow designers to customize the format of text and template objects. Changes to the color scheme of a standard presentation design can help a speaker use the power of color to convey a particular mood, to associate the presentation with a company or concept, or to simply give an original look to a familiar PowerPoint presentation design.

*Directions:* You will apply a new color scheme to the standard presentation design you applied to the file Present-new in the previous activity.

1. Be sure the Present-new file is open.

2. Read the Designer's Pointer below related to guidelines for effective color selection.

## DESIGNER'S POINTER

### Selecting an Effective Color Scheme

Color is the most exciting part of the presentation design. The colors you choose and the way you combine them determine the overall effectiveness of your presentation and add a personal touch to your work. Your strategic choice of color will aid you in (1) conveying the formality of the presentation; (2) creating a desired tone; (3) associating your presentation with your company, a product, or the topic of your presentation; and (4) emphasizing important components of your slide.

**Formality/Effect:** Conservative colors (e.g., blue) add formality; brighter colors (e.g., yellow) lend a less formal and perhaps trendy look. Generally, warm colors, such as reds, oranges, and yellows, stimulate your audience; cool colors, such as blues and greens, create a more relaxed and receptive environment.

**Association:** An audience naturally associates colors with certain ideas: green for go, money, growth, or financial health; yellow for caution; red for stop, danger, or financial loss; and blue for calm. Because of a natural association of red with financial loss, red would be inappropriate in a table or a graph depicting growth or a healthy financial condition. Colors can also be used to create an association with a company or a product (e.g., red and white and Coca-Cola or blue and white and Pepsi). Other colors to convey widely accepted effects follow:

| Color | Association/Effect |
| --- | --- |
| Black and red | Violence, fire, love, anger, debt, danger, heat |
| White and blue | Cleanliness; crisp pure images |
| Earth tones, brown, tans, and off-whites | Naturalness, stable, conservative, autumn |
| White, black, shades of gray with splashes of bright color to add interest | High-tech |

*Continued*

| Purple, black, gold, rich red Black/gold/white combination | Elegance, luxury, power, royalty |
| --- | --- |
| Green | Money, growth, nature, freshness, environmentally friendly, spring |
| Yellow | Cheerful, energy, creativity, autumn |
| Orange | Joy, creativity, encouragement, success, autumn |
| Blue | Sky, sea, water, peace, knowledge, stability, trust, loyalty, wisdom, integrity |

**Differentiation:** Color helps the audience distinguish between different design elements such as the slide title appearing in a color brighter than the bulleted list. Color can also be used to (1) highlight specific text or emphasize key elements in a graph, (2) connect a set of numbers in a table that are to be considered as a group, (3) color code related components in a diagram or organization chart, and (4) print pages on paper of different colors to help the audience find a particular sheet in a handout.

To avoid an overwhelming, distracting design, limit colors to no more than three colors on a slide and follow these steps for selecting an effective color scheme for your presentation visuals:

1. **Determine the medium you will use for displaying the visual.** The color scheme needed for optimal readability varies depending on your use of an electronic presentation, overhead transparencies, or a Web page.

| Output Medium | Background/Foreground |
| --- | --- |
| Overhead transparencies shown in a well-lit room | Light background Dark text |
| Electronic presentation and 35-mm slides presented in a darkened room | Medium to dark background Light text |
| Electronic presentation in a well-lit room | Light background Dark text |
| Web page | Light background Dark text |

2. **Choose the background color first because this area displays the largest amount of color.** Consider the preliminary issues of formality, effect, association, and differentiation discussed previously.

3. **Choose foreground colors—one for the slide title and a second for the text.** Both colors should contrast highly with the background color selected so that the text can be read easily. Black text against a white background, the color scheme used traditionally in overhead transparencies, has the greatest contrast. A blue background with yellow text contrasts well, but a yellow background with white text would be difficult to read because of low contrast.

   After you have chosen the background and foreground colors, evaluate the readability of the font(s) you have chosen. Colored text tends to wash out when projected; therefore, be certain that the fonts are sturdy enough and large enough to be read easily using the color scheme you selected.

4. **Choose the accent colors that complement the color scheme.** Accent colors are used in small doses to draw attention to key elements: bullet markers, bars and slices in charts, background fills of boxes, geometric shapes, selected text, or drawings that are color coded for emphasis.

Project your presentation ahead of time in the room where you are to make your presentation so that you can adjust the color scheme. This process is essential because colors display differently on a computer monitor than they do on projection devices. You can also check the readability of the text and double-check for typographical errors at the same time.

## Apply a Standard Presentation Design

3. Click **Format**, **Slide Design** (or click **Design** on the Formatting toolbar).

4. Click **Color Schemes** and preview samples of the available standard color schemes for the presentation design template applied to the file Present-new. The colors used for each standard design element (background, text colors, fills, shadows, etc.) are illustrated in the thumbnail of each color scheme.

5. Click a color scheme and click **Apply to All Slides** to convert all slides in the file to the new standard color scheme.

6. Advance through the slide show evaluating the appeal of the new color scheme. Select other standard color schemes until you are satisfied with one.

Click to display
gallery of color
schemes

Click to edit a
standard color
scheme

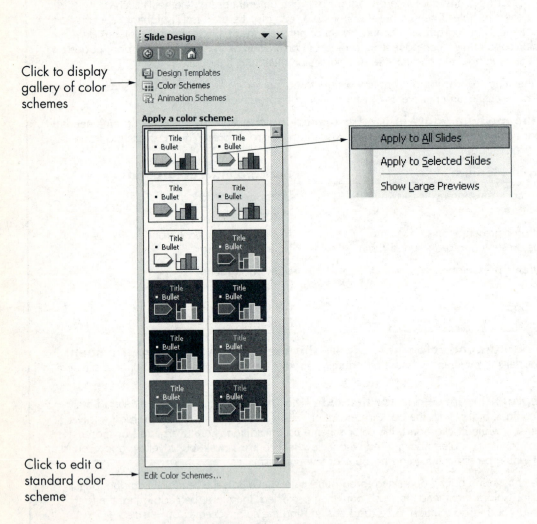

## Modify a Standard Presentation Design

7. Display the gallery of standard presentation designs as you did in Steps 3–4.

8. Click **Edit Color Schemes** (option below the gallery of designs). Refer to the preceding illustration.

9. Select the Custom tab and note the color of each element in the color scheme as shown in the list and the thumbnail.

10. Click the color thumbnail for the Background option and click **Change Color**.

11. Select the Standard tab and select a color for the slide background from the standard color wheel that is displayed.

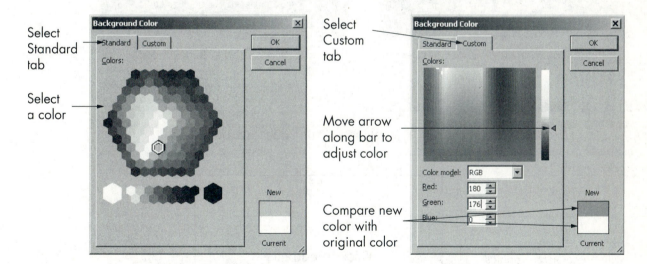

12. Click **OK** and advance through the slide show to evaluate the appeal of the new background color now applied to the slides. Select other standard color schemes until you are satisfied with a specific color.

13. Return to the Edit Color Scheme dialog box and select the Custom tab to mix a color if the exact color you want is not shown on the standard color wheel. Refer to Steps 3–4 if necessary.

14. Click up and down on the color bar to darken and lighten the color, comparing the new color to the original color as you experiment with various choices.

15. Click **OK** and evaluate the appeal of the new background color applied to the slides. Return to the Custom tab and modify the color until you are satisfied with it.

16. Change the color of other design elements in the color scheme as required. To allow for easy readability, be certain the contrast between the new background color and the text colors is high.

17. Print Slides 1–3 as an audience handout, three slides per page, if directed by your instructor.

# DESIGNING A CUSTOM PRESENTATION DESIGN

Use of stock presentation designs that provide no association with a company and/or the topic may give the impression that a speaker is unprepared, pays little attention to details, and perhaps lead to the logical conclusion that the company this speaker represents is incompetent as well.

## *Reinforcing a Presentation Topic*

Presenters who want to set themselves apart devote the time and energy needed to develop powerful, creative designs that reinforce the topic being discussed. Creative templates that reinforce presentations by using vivid word imagery, such as those developed around creative analogies, are easily developed. In the following activity, you will see how lively, upbeat fonts and colors and related template images reinforce the speaker's message, extolling the benefits of facilitating employees' efforts to maintain a healthful lifestyle.

*Directions:* Follow the instructions to create a custom template that a team of consultants might develop for a presentation recommending that a client company establish a corporate wellness program.

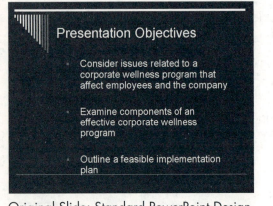

Original Slide: Standard PowerPoint Design

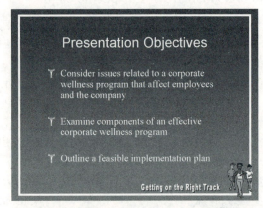

Enhanced Slide: Custom Template Reflecting Presentation Topic

## Develop the Custom Design

1. Open a new presentation by clicking **File**, **New**. A Title slide using the default presentation design (blank) is displayed.

Open blank presentation with no color or graphics →

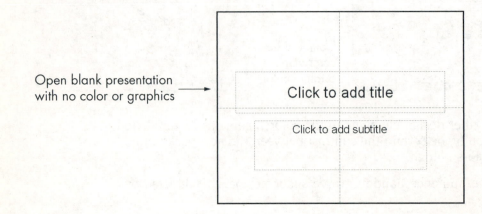

## Select the Color Scheme

2. Read the Designer's Pointer on pages 82–83 to review the systematic process for developing an effective color scheme.

3. Select the color scheme for each standard design element in the presentation using the following recommendations or your own preferences:

   - **Background:** Gradient blue using a horizontal variant with dark medium blue at the top and a slightly lighter shade at the bottom.
   - **Title text:** Yellow.
   - **Text for level 1 of bulleted list:** White.
   - **Fills:** Medium green.

## Edit the Master Slide

4. Review the design principles for selecting fonts presented in the Designer's Pointer on page 79 if necessary.

5. Select fonts to convey an upbeat mood consistent with the theme that healthy employees are happy, productive, and satisfied with the company.

   - **Slide title:** Select an informal sans serif font such as Berlin Sans FB Demi.
   - **Text for bulleted list:** Select an informal serif font such as Lucida Bright.

6. Select a bullet associated with the wellness theme, such as the figure lifting the barbell (select Webdings font, symbol #134, after selecting **Format**, **Bullet**).

7. Format the motto **Getting on the Right Track** using a WordArt style that is easy to read and selecting fill and line colors with high contrast to the slide background (e.g., yellow, gray).

*Note:* This short phrase, anchored in the bottom right corner of the slide, will keep the audience focused on the purpose of the presentation throughout the delivery.

8. Add a clip art image to the right of the motto that conveys the intended message of happy, healthy employees (e.g., diverse group of people working out or participating in other types of wellness programs).

9. Add a narrow border around the slide to add unity to the motto and clip art; this gives the sense of a "track" for these employees and the company.

   a) Use the **Rectangle** AutoShape on the Draw toolbar to draw the border.

   b) Change the fill color to **No Fill**, the line color to white, and the line width to 6 points (click the **Line Style** button on the Draw toolbar).

## Create Slides

1. Design a title page for the slide assuming you are the consultant making the presentation.

2. Build the slide shown in the model that details the presentation objectives and thus serves as an agenda to preview the major points in the presentation. Key the following bulleted text on this slide:

   - **Consider issues related to a corporate wellness program that affect employees and the company**

- Examine components of an effective corporate wellness program
- Outline a feasible implementation plan

## Save and Print the Slide Show

3. Save the file as **Wellnesstemplate**.

4. Print the slide show as an audience handout if directed by your instructor.

## Reflecting a Company's Image

A speaker representing a company in competitive business presentations must develop a strong custom presentation design (template) that clearly reflects the company's professional image and unique corporate identity and the topic being discussed.

*Directions:* Follow instructions to create a custom template for a company of your choice or one designated by your instructor.

## Research the Company and Prepare a Sketch

1. Obtain copies of the company's printed materials (e.g., letterhead, brochures, annual report) and visit the company's Web site. Identify graphical elements, approved company colors, and logos the company is already using to create the company's identity.

2. Review the Designer's Pointers in this project to be sure you understand design principles related to font and color selection.

3. Sketch a draft of your design.

4. Reproduce or download from the company's Web site high-quality images to use in the design. Keep in mind that poor reproductions will reflect negatively on the company. Be sure to clear any copyright restrictions.

## Create and Print the Slides

5. Create the title page and one bulleted list providing text of your choice (e.g., the company's major products, locations, or significant achievements). Refer to the Designer's Pointer on pages 89–90 related to developing effective content for slides.

6. Save the file using your company name as the file name.

7. Print the slide show as an audience handout if directed by your instructor.

## Reformatting Slides for Overheads

You can easily create professional overhead transparencies with PowerPoint. If you know in advance your output medium is overheads, create the overhead using the default presentation design (blank). If you learn that you must deliver the presentation using overhead transparencies after your slide show is developed, you will need to modify your slides. Specifically, you will fit your visuals to the setup of the overhead projector, minimize excessive amounts of color print, and reduce the number of slides because of the additional time needed to display overheads versus projecting slides.

**DESIGNER'S POINTER**

## Composing Slide Content: Key to Successful Delivery

Although it has become the standard presentation design tool, PowerPoint has received harsh criticism from graphic-design guru Edward Tufte and others. Much of this criticism relates to inappropriate emphasis on format rather than audience-focused content; the proliferation of bulleted lists as a substitute for logical, coherent discussion of pertinent information; and boring delivery styles. Without relevant content and skillful delivery, the presenter can easily be upstaged by the show. The impact of the PowerPoint presentation depends on the presenter's ability to use the tool to support a meaningful, well-organized message. Compelling slide content that keeps the speaker as the central focus of the presentation is essential to a successful delivery.

Well-organized, crisp slide content enhances the audience's ability to grasp the meaning and find immediate value in the information. Follow these simple rules for writing concise, meaningful content for your PowerPoint slides. Study the sample slides that illustrate effective and ineffective principles.

- **Limit the number of slides used in a single presentation.** Too many visuals can overwhelm, bore, and tire the audience, so give the audience a welcome break to simply listen. Prepare visuals needed to direct the audience's attention to major points and to clarify or illustrate complex information.

  When possible, place ideas to be compared on the same slide to guard against overload but more importantly to allow the audience to view all relevant data for easy synthesis and interpretation. In this example, placing the advantages, disadvantages, and recommendations for each visual type on a single slide allows for quick, coherent delivery of a vast amount of information. Imagine the frustration of today's fast-paced audiences if the designer had created three separate slides for each visual type—12 slides to develop one main point.

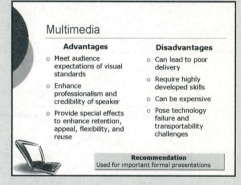

- **Include only one major idea on each visual, with a descriptive title highlighting the idea.** The title should reflect the exact content of the slide in a way that will engage the audience's attention.

- **Write concise, to-the-point statements that you want the audience to remember.** Avoid the tendency of many speakers to clean up their notes and put everything they intend to say on the slide. The clarity of precise language will enable an audience to focus briefly on key points while keeping primary attention on the speaker's explanations. Good slides will facilitate an extemporaneous delivery rather than a speaker's monotonous reading of scripted slides. Short text lines also are easier for the eye to follow and open up the slide with appealing white space. The revised slide on page 90 eliminates scripted text that could lead to poor delivery—the first major point and the final two subpoints.

- **Use powerful visual communication to quickly and effectively convey information.** Images and shapes are more visually appealing and memorable than words, and they enable audiences to grasp information more easily. What's more, today's audiences expect media-rich, dynamic visuals, not a speaker's dense notes simply cleaned up, put onscreen, and used as a crutch during a boring and unbearable delivery. In the "Average Presentation Rated" slide you created in Project 3, the speaker rejects the standard design of bulleted lists and random clip art and instead creates a strong conceptual image of an ineffective presentation, complete with boring speaker and inattentive audience to reinforce the dire need for improved business presentations. Note the power of other conceptual slides you've created thus far in this text.

*Continued*

- **Develop powerful bulleted lists.** Follow these simple guidelines:

  a) Begin by making the items in the bulleted list parallel in structure. If one item is presented in a different way grammatically, it appears out of place and weakens the emphasis given to each item in the list. The inconsistency also may distract the audience's attention from the message.

  b) Be certain that the items in a bulleted list appear together for a similar purpose. Does each item in a list serve the same purpose? Does each major point relate to the key concept revealed in the slide title? Does each subpoint relate to its major point, and so on?

  c) Limit the number of points in a bulleted list to increase the audience's retention and facilitate a smooth flow of ideas. In your draft, look for overlap and repetition that will allow you to collapse the content into a short list that an audience can remember more easily.

- **Reflect legal and ethical responsibility in the design of presentation visuals.** Presentation visuals should be uncluttered and easily understood and should depict information honestly. Be certain that you have cleared the copyrights on all multimedia and content on your slide.

- **Proofread the presentation visuals carefully.** Misspellings in handouts or displays are embarrassing and diminish your credibility.

Concise, Targeted Bulleted List: Poor (*left*) and Good (*right*) Examples

### Benefits

Υ Happy, healthy workers yield high returns for the company
Υ Lower health care costs
 — Employee sickness and injuries
Υ Increase in employee productivity and efficiency
Υ Reduction in employee absenteeism
Υ Recruitment and retention are increased
 — Employees feel management values them and their well-being; happy employees are less likely to leave
 — Can recruit more successfully when company has an innovative, "people first" image

**Getting on the Right Track**

### Corporate Wellness Program Yields High Returns

Υ Lowers health care costs resulting from employee sickness and injuries

Υ Increases employee productivity and efficiency

Υ Reduces employee turnover and absenteeism

Υ Improves recruitment and retention as the company is recognized to be innovative and supportive of employees

**Getting on the Right Track**

- Uses a descriptive title that captures the single idea—the key idea of high returns that prepare the audience for the list of benefits that follow.

- Retains only bulleted items that are benefits of implementing a corporate wellness program. Excludes the first point, a transition statement that the speaker should say, not read from the slide.

- Collapses the content into four precise, coherent statements. (1) Combining absenteeism and medical costs and the subpoint eliminates choppiness and an outlining error: A point cannot be divided unless it divides into at least two parts. (2) The final point in the revised slide is a tight, targeted summary of the final point and its subpoints.

- Uses parallel structure for remaining bulleted items (all past tense verbs) that allows for a smooth flow of information.

*Directions:* Follow the instructions to format the company template you just created for overheads.

1. Be sure the Wellnesstemplate file is open.

2. Resave the file using the file name Wellness-overhead.

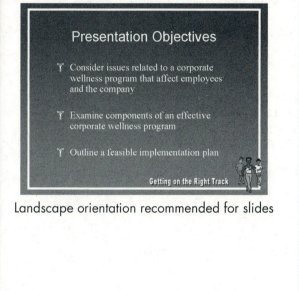

Landscape orientation recommended for slides

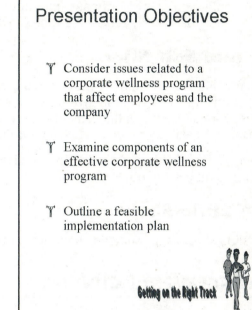

Portrait orientation recommended for transparencies

## Change the Slide Orientation to Portrait

3. Review the Designer's Pointer on page 93 to learn more about slide orientation.

4. Click **File**, **Page Setup**.

5. Change the "Slides sized for" to **Overhead** (default setting is on-screen show).

6. Change the orientation for the slides to Portrait (default setting is landscape). Retain the default to print notes, handouts, and outline in portrait orientation for easy reading of these documents, which are typically printed on paper.

| | Page Setup | ? ☓ |
|---|---|---|
| Select overhead → | **Slides sized for:** Overhead ▾ | OK   Cancel |
| Note changes in slide dimensions | **Width:** 7.5 ⬍ Inches   **Height:** 10 ⬍ Inches   **Number slides from:** 1 ⬍ | **Orientation** — **Slides** A ◉ Portrait ○ Landscape ← Select portrait orientation for overheads |
| | | **Notes, handouts & outline** A ◉ Portrait ○ Landscape ← Retain portrait orientation for slides printed on paper |

## Modify the Color Scheme and the Format

7. Change the background to white. (Click **Format**, **Background**.)

8. Edit the slide master to include font colors for the slide title and the bulleted list that have high contrast with the white background.

9. Modify the objects on the slide master to remove large areas of color and large logos that would require an inordinate amount of color. Your goal is to include splashes of color that clearly reflect the tone of the presentation.

## Critique and Edit Slides

10. Redesign any slides with animated layers (e.g., overlapping objects that hide after animation). Create a separate overhead for each layer or develop a simple bulleted list with appealing enhancements that require small amounts of color. You will learn to create these layered effects in Project 6.

11. Check each slide for changes needed in the size and the position of objects because of the reduced width.

## Print the Slide Show

12. Print the slide show as an audience handout if directed by your instructor.

## ■ REINFORCEMENT ACTIVITIES

Add the following slides for added reinforcement of the PowerPoint features you learned in this project.

## Activity 1

Use an online database to locate the following article that compares effective speaking to the successful ski jump:

Wilson, A. B. (1996, June/July). Ache for the impact: Four steps to powerful oratory. *Executive Speeches*, 6–7.

Design a custom template to reinforce the ski analogy that adheres to the presentation design guidelines presented in this project. Create a title slide and at least one slide that illustrates a key point made in the speech and that displays the standard slide elements. Be prepared to share with your instructor and the class the rationale for your design choices. Print the slides as an audience handout.

## Activity 2

Use an online database to locate an actual speech made by a company executive. Specify "speech" as the publication type or search only in periodicals that publish speeches, such as *Executive Speeches* or *Vital Speeches of the Day*. Design a custom template that reflects the company's corporate identity and the speaker's topic based on your knowledge of the company and information gleaned from your review of the company's home page. Create a title slide and at least one slide that illustrates a key point made in the speech and displays the standard slide elements. Be prepared to share with your instructor and the class the rationale for your design choices. Print the slides as an audience handout.

## Formatting Slides and Handouts to Fit Presentation Needs

You must choose a page layout orientation appropriate for the presentation visual you are creating:

- Choose landscape orientation for computer presentations and 35-mm slides. This horizontal placement provides a wide view that (1) creates a pleasing, soothing feeling similar to looking over the horizon; (2) provides longer lines for text and images; and (3) ensures that no content is included so low that the slide cannot be seen properly.

- Choose portrait orientation for overhead transparencies. This vertical placement positions the text to be read across the shortest side of the page, which makes additional lines available for text. The sides of a horizontally arranged slide would not be visible if projected on an overhead projector.

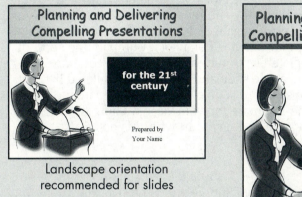

Landscape orientation
recommended for slides

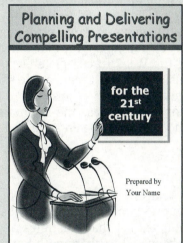

Portrait orientation
recommended for overheads

Slides, note pages, and outlines printed using portrait orientation are more convenient for readers because we are accustomed to reading pages in a vertical format (longest side at the left rather than at the top).

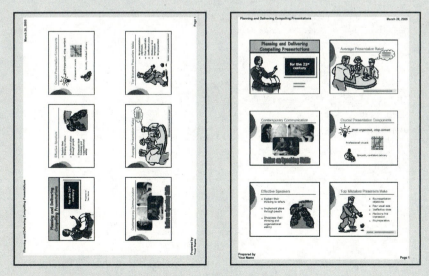

Handouts printed in landscape orientation *(left)* are less convenient to read than portrait orientation *(right)* because they must be turned sideways to be read.

# Activity 3

Design a custom template to reinforce the topic of a presentation you are currently developing following the presentation design guidelines presented in this project. Create a title slide and at least one bulleted list that illustrates a point in the speech and displays the standard slide elements. Be prepared to share with your instructor and the class the rationale for your design choices. Print the slides as an audience handout.

# Activity 4

In small groups, brainstorm to identify a creative analogy for presenting the main points of a presentation on a topic of your choice or one assigned by your instructor. For example, sports images and terminology could be used in a speech on team presentations (e.g., the winning game plan, organizing a committed team, practicing important plays, exhibiting appropriate sideline behavior). Compare the sport of surfing to "surfing the Web" to complete electronic job searches or compare handling stress to diffusing a bomb. Create a title slide and at least one bulleted list that illustrates a key point and displays the standard slide elements. Be prepared to share with your instructor and the class the rationale for your design choices. Print the slides as an audience handout. Be creative and have fun with this activity.

# Activity 5

Develop a custom template for your college or university to be used in a recruitment or orientation presentation to new or prospective students. Create a title slide and at least one bulleted list that illustrates a key point and displays the standard slide elements. Be prepared to share with your instructor and the class the rationale for your design choices. Print the slides as an audience handout.

# Editing for Coherence and Accuracy and Rehearsing for Effective Delivery

## DESIGNING COHERENCE DEVICES

Showcasing the organizational structure of a presentation will assist you in delivering a presentation that an audience perceives to be coherent—a logical, smooth progression of ideas. In this project you will create (1) an agenda slide to preview major divisions of a presentation, (2) divider slides to mark the beginning of the major points in a presentation, and (3) a summary slide to preview several content slides related to one major idea. Refer to the Designer's Pointer on page 96 for additional information about the value of planning coherence devices.

### Creating an Agenda Slide

A simple bulleted list can provide a concise preview of the main points in your presentation and the order in which you plan to cover them. Other, more creative techniques will capture the audience's attention and set the stage for a dynamic presentation. You will see both approaches as you complete the activities in this project.

*Directions:* Follow the directions to create the agenda slide as shown.

Simple agenda slide          Elaborate agenda slide

1. Be sure the file Present is open.

2. Create a new slide using the Title layout from Text Layouts category.

3. Insert a photograph as the slide background as shown in the model.

4. Key the bulleted list and add a transparent fill color that will enhance the readability of the text while allowing the background image to be seen. You'll need to experiment with the settings based on the contrast required to set the text apart from the background (click **Fill Color** and add values

## DESIGNER'S POINTER

### Supplementing Spoken Transitions

Content that follows a clear, logical organizational pattern is fundamental to an effective presentation. A writer includes headings to serve as signposts to mark the major and minor divisions of a report. Likewise, a speaker uses verbal cues to transition an audience through a presentation smoothly. These cues include a preview of the main points to be covered before moving into the body of the presentation and use of transition words such as *first, next,* and *finally.*

You will also want to supplement spoken transitions with slides that move the audience logically and smoothly through the presentation. An agenda slide can convey presentation goals, divider slides serve as road signs to mark major sections, and other slides can draw attention to question-and-answer periods.

Divider slides that transition the audience logically and smoothly from one point to the next in a presentation should be designed to dramatically and distinctly differ from content slides. A few basic design suggestions follow:

- Include a descriptive title that engages the audience's attention and perhaps an image that reinforces the major idea on each divider slide.

- Select a slightly different color scheme and perhaps a different fill effect (e.g., pattern, texture) that is complementary to the presentation template but that the audience will clearly identify as the signpost marking a new section.

- Consider selecting a subtle, relevant sound effect to bring added emphasis to this pivotal point in your presentation. A subtle sound will not be distracting because the presentation will have only a few divider slides.

If time is limited, simply design the divider slides using the Title layout. The simple repositioning of the slide title will signal this slide as a signpost indicating a new major point.

in the transparencies spin buttons). Select a high-contrast font to stand out from the transparent fill.

Edit fill effects →

Set transparency range →

5. Add custom animation consistent with other bulleted lists in the presentation: **Wipe from Left** on **Fast** speed; do not build.

6. Add a slide transition effect that is slightly more dramatic than the **Wipe from Left** used in other slides and add a subtle sound effect if desired (e.g., chime, jingle).

## Creating Divider Slides

A divider slide is positioned at the beginning of each major point of a presentation to remind the audience where the speaker is in the organizational structure and to target attention to this new discussion. Study the Designer's Pointer on page 96 before creating divider slides for the file Present.

## Create a Master Divider Slide

*Directions:* Follow the instructions to create the master divider slide design for the file Present as shown.

1. Create a new slide using the Title Only layout.

2. Remove the graphic image from the slide background (click **Format**, **Background** and remove the check mark).

3. Add a texture effect to the slide background that resembles a wall in a presentation room (e.g., canvas). (Click **Format**, **Background**, **Fill Effects**, **Texture**.)

4. Create a text box and format the title: **Challenges Facing Today's Speakers**.

5. Select a relevant image of your choice.

6. Resize and position the text and image as shown in the model.

7. Use the **Rectangle** AutoShape on the Draw toolbar to create the impression of a table extending the full width of the slide.

   a) Add a background texture that resembles a table (e.g., walnut, oak, medium wood).

   b) Add a shadow to add dimension to the AutoShape.

8. Add custom animation as desired to bring added attention to this divider slide, signaling the beginning of the first major point in the presentation.

9. Select a distinctive slide transition that will be used to transition to all divider slides in the file Present. Add a subtle sound effect that will direct the audience's attention to this change of topic (e.g., chime, jingle).

## Copy the Master Slide to Create Each Divider Slide

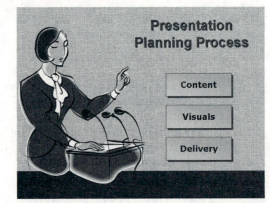

*Directions:* Follow the instructions to use the master slide to create an additional divider slide for the file Present.

1. Copy the master divider slide "Challenges Facing Today's Speakers" that you created in the previous section. If necessary, refer to Project 1 for instructions for copying slides.

2. Edit the title: **Presentation Planning Process**.

3. Highlight the subpoints using AutoShapes rather than a bland bulleted list.

   a) Use the **Rectangle** AutoShape to create the first major point of this subdivision: **Content**.

   b) Add a gradient fill that blends a primary color in your presentation template and the earth tones introduced in the wood table and the canvas wall.

   c) Add a shadow to add dimension to the AutoShape.

   d) Create the remaining points by copying and editing the model you've just designed.

4. Animate the three rectangles: **Curve up together on mouse click**.

### Creating a Summary Slide

A summary slide, like an agenda slide, aids an audience in understanding the organizational structure and flow of a presentation. A summary slide previews the content of a series of slides related to a supporting idea for a major point in the presentation. PowerPoint's summary slide feature makes creating this device of coherence very simple. The software automatically compiles a simple bulleted list containing the slide titles of any slides you select.

*Directions:* Follow the instructions to build the summary slide for four slides in the file Present. This slide will preview slides, providing more detailed information about each of the four types of visuals.

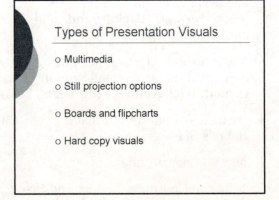

## Create the Slides to Be Included on the Summary Slide

1. Complete Project 2, Reinforcement Activity 4, on page 44 if you have not done so already. Alternatively, you may create these four slides and key the slide titles only:

    **Slide 1:** Multimedia.

    **Slide 2:** Still Projection Options.

    **Slide 3:** Boards and Flipcharts.

    **Slide 4:** Hard Copy Visuals.

## Select the Slides to Be Included on the Summary Slide

2. Go to Slide Sorter view and select the four slides to be included on the summary slide (hold down the **Shift** key as you click to select multiple slides). The slides are (1) "Multimedia," (2) "Still Projection Options," (3) "Boards and Flipcharts," and (4) "Hard Copy Visuals."

3. Click the **Summary Slide** button from the Slide Sorter toolbar. A new slide containing the slide title "Summary Slide" and a bulleted list of the titles of the four selected slides appears in front of the selected slides.

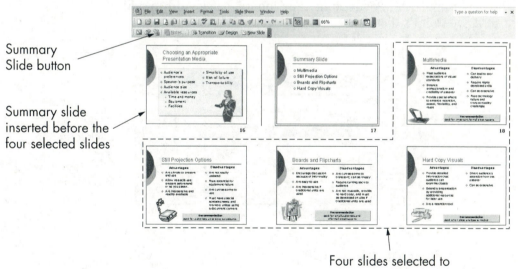

Summary Slide button

Summary slide inserted before the four selected slides

Four slides selected to create summary slide

4. Display the summary slide in Normal view and edit the slide:

    a) Input the new title: **Types of Presentation Visuals**.

    b) Change the capitalization style in the bulleted list so that only the first word in each bulleted item is capitalized.

    c) Increase the spacing between the lines to balance the text on the page (click **Format**, **Line Spacing**, select **2** for double spacing).

## Add a Slide Transition

5. Click the **Slide Transition** button on the Slide Sorter toolbar.

6. Select **Wipe from Left** as the slide transition for consistency with other slides in the presentation.

# ■ PROOFREADING A SLIDE SHOW

A speaker will lose credibility instantly if slides contain spelling and grammatical errors. A systematic plan for proofreading includes using PowerPoint's speller to locate spelling errors and the style checker to ensure consistency in several styles:

## *Using the Speller*

Follow the instructions to check the spelling in the file Present.

1. Click **Tools, Spelling**.

2. Select the appropriate correction from the Spelling dialog box that appears when a spelling error is detected.

   a) Click **Change** to accept a recommended spelling or select the correct spelling from the list provided and then click **Change**.

   b) Click **Ignore All** to ignore all instances of a word if the spelling is correct but does not appear in PowerPoint's dictionary. Click **Add** to add the word to PowerPoint's dictionary.

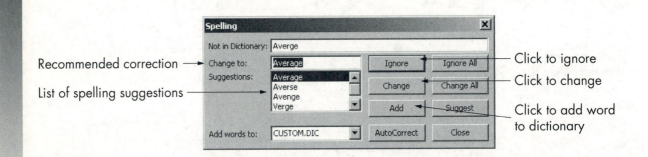

3. Save the presentation to update the file with any corrections made while running the speller.

## *Using the Style Checker*

In addition to checking spelling, the style checker checks for visual clarity, capitalization, and end punctuation.

1. Enable Style Check:

   a) Click **Tools, Options** and select the Spelling and Style tab.

   b) Click the **Check Style** check box.

Select Spelling and Style tab

Check to enable style check

Change options

Specify rules under the Case and End Punctuation and Visual Clarity tabs

2. Click **Help**, **Show the Office Assistant** to enable the Office Assistant (the paper clip assistant).

3. Click the light bulb that appears beside a style error and select the appropriate option for correcting the problem.

In the illustration, PowerPoint recognizes an inconsistency in the capitalization of a bulleted list and displays several options. The designer would click **Change the text to sentence case** to correct the capitalization style for each bulleted list and may also choose to change the style checker options to AutoCorrect this error in all other presentations.

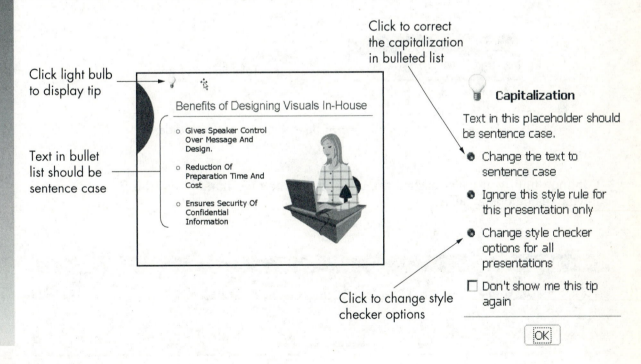

Click to correct the capitalization in bulleted list

Click light bulb to display tip

Text in bullet list should be sentence case

Click to change style checker options

## ▮ REHEARSING A PRESENTATION

Running the Rehearse Timing feature while making a dry run of your presentation gives you a record of the actual time of the presentation and the time spent on each slide. Use this information to enhance your presentation in a variety of ways.

For example, you can locate errors in logical development and flow and content, develop a smooth transition from one point to the next, and enhance your delivery skills. Additional suggestions are provided in the related Presenter's Strategy on page 104.

*Directions:* Follow the instructions to use the rehearsal timings to practice your delivery using the file Present.

1. Go to Slide Sorter view and click the **Rehearse Timings** button on the Slide Sorter toolbar. The slide show automatically goes into the Slide Show view.

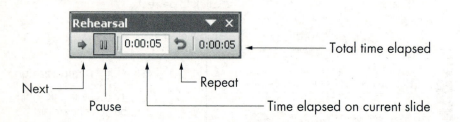

Rehearse Timings button

2. Advance through the presentation as if you were delivering the actual presentation. Use the buttons in the Rehearsal dialog box superimposed on the slide to refine your delivery:

   a) Click **Next** to move to the next slide.

   b) Click **Pause** to stop the clock as you review your notes, rethink your discussion, and so on.

   c) Click **Repeat** to reset the clock so that you can deliver the slide again.

Rehearsal

0:00:05          0:00:05 ← Total time elapsed

Next

Pause

Repeat

Time elapsed on current slide

3. Continue until you have reached the last slide in the presentation and the following dialog box appears:

**Microsoft Office PowerPoint**

The total time for the slide show was 0:00:22. Do you want to keep the new slide timings to use when you view the slide show?

Yes          No

Click **Yes** to record the new slide timings. The slides are displayed in Slide Sorter view, with the timings for individual slides displayed below each slide as shown in the following illustration. You can easily review the timings to identify areas of improvement.

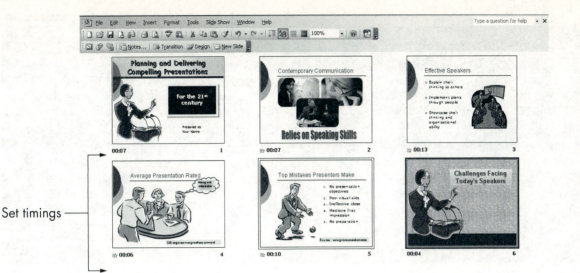

Set timings

## *Running a Slide Show with Timings*

Once you have recorded timings during rehearsals (as shown in the previous illustration), you must decide each time you run the presentation whether to run it manually or with the set timings.

***Directions:*** Follow the instructions to run a presentation manually and with set timings.

1. Click **Slide Show**, **Set Up Show**.

2. Note the two selections in the Set Up Show dialog box:

   a) Click **Manually** to advance the slide on a mouse click.

   b) Click **Using timings**, **if present** to allow the slides to advance automatically using the set timings.

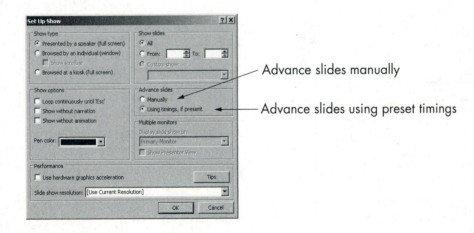

Advance slides manually

Advance slides using preset timings

3. Run the file Present using the set timings. Run the show a second time using the manual setting.

PRESENTER'S **STRATEGY**

### Rehearsing to Fit a Time Slot

After you've completed a dry run of your presentation using the rehearsal timings, analyze the "total time spent" values and edit your presentation to fit your time slot. For example, a slide with a timing longer than 1 minute may contain too much information and should be divided into one or more slides. On the other hand, the lengthy timing could simply pinpoint difficult content that requires additional thought and deliberate practice to present concisely and coherently.

Run your presentation with set timings as you rehearse to help you maintain the pace needed to fit a predetermined time slot. However, run the presentation manually during your actual presentation because preset timings prevent you from adapting the presentation to the audience's needs and entertaining questions, managing interruptions, and so forth. Preset timings are critical when designing presentations to be run automatically at exhibit areas or that will be sent to potential customers/clients with voice commentary replacing a live presenter.

## ■ REINFORCEMENT ACTIVITIES

Add the following slides to the file Present for added reinforcement of the PowerPoint features you learned in this project. Position the slides as shown at the end of the project.

## Activity 1

The original agenda slide (*left*) uses a simple bulleted list to draw a clear roadmap of the three sections of a presentation that focuses on the three-part process for developing compelling presentations. A more creative approach involves using word pictures and images to make the main points memorable, as shown in the improved version (*right*). The improved agenda slide can be modified slightly to create complementary divider slides to mark the major three sections of the presentation.

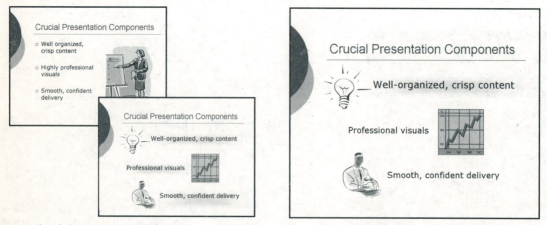

Agenda slide—original *(left)*; improved *(right)*          Divider slide—point 1

1. Open the file Present and display the slide "Crucial Presentation Components" in Normal view.

## Create the Master Divider Slide

2. Copy the agenda slide to create a master divider slide.

3. Draw the audience's attention to the first main point by adding a gradient fill in the text box. The design will subtly emphasize the relevant point without adding clutter that competes with the three important images and text.

   a) Apply a gradient fill color to the text box. Select a shading style **From center** and the Variant style with darkest color in the center.

   b) Change the transparency of the fill effect from 15 to 40 percent.

4. Add a slide transition with a subtle sound effect (e.g., key jingle).

5. Add custom animation to create the desired effect.

## Add the Divider Slides

6. Create a copy of the master divider slide.

7. Copy the formatting style of the first text box using the Format Painter:

   a) Select the text box for the first major point.

   b) Click **Format Painter** from the Formatting toolbar:

Format Painter button

8. Click the second text box. The gradient fill is automatically applied.

9. Repeat the process to create the remaining divider slide.

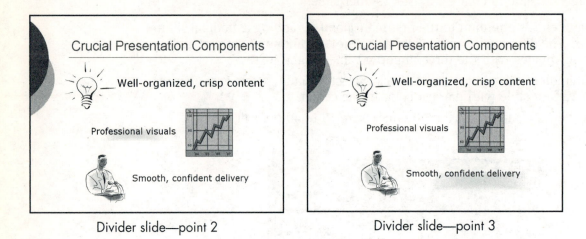

Divider slide—point 2                    Divider slide—point 3

# Activity 2

The original agenda slide uses a simple bulleted list and a single image as a clear road map for a presentation focusing on the three aspects related to employment interviews. Designing powerful visuals to develop an analogy between interviewing and a Hollywood movie creates a memorable slide show that should hold the audience on the edge of their seats.

Original slide                    Enhanced slide

1. Open the new presentation using a presentation template related to concept of business success or the topic of job interviewing.

2. Create a new slide using the Title Only layout from the Text Layouts category.

3. Click **AutoShapes**, **More AutoShapes** and insert the film strip. Resize to fit the width of the slide as shown in the model.

4. Insert relevant clip art for each of the three "acts" of this feature presentation: the employment interview.

5. Add an upbeat sound effect to play as the film is displayed. Search Microsoft Office Online or **http://freeplaymusic.com** (e.g., select a .10 second .MP3 clip from the motivational category). Move the sound icon off the slide to minimize distraction.

6. Add custom animation:

   **First:** Film—Fade on mouse click after title.

   **Second:** Film—Flash bulb (from Emphasis category) after previous event to bring added attention to the film.

   **Third:** Sound file with previous event.

7. Apply a slide transition such as **Fade Through Black** to give a Hollywood effect.

## Create Divider Slides

8. Copy the agenda slide and edit the title for each of the three "acts" of this presentation.

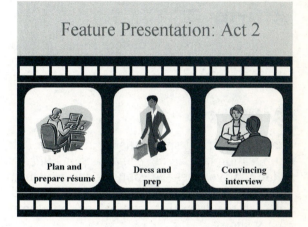

9. Retain the current animation. Alternatively, ungroup the film and group into segments so that an emphasis effect such as **Flash Bulb** can be added only to the clip art and text box in the act being introduced (e.g., "Plan and prepare résumé" for Act I).

10. Apply the same slide transition used for the agenda slide (Activity 1).

11. Save the presentation as **Interview**.

## Create an Attention-Getter Slide

12. Open the presentation Interview and create a new slide using the Title Only layout from the Text Layouts category.

13. Create this conceptual slide that creates blooper shots of an actual interview. Use the **Rectangle**, **Rounded Rectangle**, and **Balloon** AutoShapes for designing the set. Place the applicant's response in a text box in front of the rectangle. In Project 6, you will learn to use an advanced animation feature to replace the first blooper response with the next, and so on.

14. Add a sound reflecting the interviewer's reaction (e.g., moan, gong). Move the sound icon off the slide to minimize distraction.

15. Add custom animation:

    **First:** Blooper in text box—Fade on mouse click after title.

    **Second:** Balloon with interviewer's reaction—Faded Zoom.

    **Third:** Sound file with previous event.

16. Apply a slide transition such as **Fade Through Black** to give a Hollywood effect.

### Create a Presentation Summary Slide

17. Create a copy of the bloopers slide you must create for the Interview file.

18. Edit the title, add a photo of an interview and clip art of a film slate, and add WordArt for the text: **A Wrap!**

19. Add custom animation:

    **First:** Title—Fade on mouse click after title.

    **Second:** Text Box—Center Revolve.

# Activity 3

Create an agenda and divider slides using the main points of a presentation you are currently developing or the corporate wellness speech for which you created the custom design template in Project 4. Save using a file name of your choice.

# Activity 4

Locate a printed speech using an online database or the Internet (e.g., search by publication for *Executive Speeches* or *Vital Speeches of the Day*). Develop an agenda slide that you believe captures the road map the speaker has established for the development of the presentation; divider slides that creatively mark the beginning of each major section; compelling, attention-getting slides; and presentation summary slides.

# Slide Order

Sequence slides in the files Present and Interview according to the table on pages 210–212. Print and submit as directed by your instructor.

# Adding Creative Animation Techniques

- Use automatic timings to enhance a slide show and to allow the presenter to deliver a seamless, professional slide show.

- Create dazzling effects with Hide on Next Mouse Click and Hide After Animation techniques.

## CREATIVE ANIMATION TECHNIQUES

Animation directs the audience's eyes to a specific object, as demonstrated in the simple animation used in Project 2 (e.g., building a bulleted list and controlling the precise timing of when objects enter the slide). Learning the three advanced animation techniques presented in this project will empower you to create effects that will reinforce important points in ways that your audience will find compelling. These techniques include (1) using automated timings, (2) using Hide on Next Mouse Click animation, and (3) using Hide After Animation.

### Using Automated Timings

*Directions:* Follow the instructions to enhance the original slide as shown.

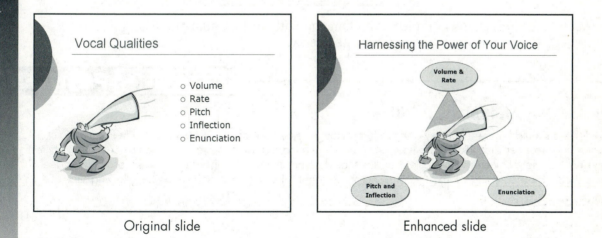

Original slide                    Enhanced slide

1. Create a new slide using the Title Only layout from the Text Layouts category.

2. Insert a relevant image to reinforce the concept of sounds made by the human voice.

3. Click **AutoShapes**, **More AutoShapes** and select the triad.

4. Recolor each oval using a color scheme that is complementary to your presentation design. Add a shadow to add dimension to the diagram.

5. Ungroup the AutoShape (click **Draw, Grouping, Ungroup**). Refer to Project 3 to review the steps for grouping and ungrouping clip art if necessary.

6. Select the top oval and key the text: **Volume & Rate**.

7. Select an appealing font large enough for the audience to read. Add bold-face and shadow as needed for readability and appeal.

8. Repeat Steps 6–7 to create the text for the remaining ovals.

9. Animate the diagram:

   **First:** Isosceles Triangle: Dissolve → Start on Click → Fast speed.

   **Second:** Clip art: Dissolve → Start with Previous → Fast speed.

   **Third:** Top oval: Fly in from Top → Start on Click → Medium speed.

   Bottom left oval: Fly in from Bottom Left → Start After Previous with .2 second delay → Medium speed.

   Bottom right oval: Fly in from Bottom Right → Start After Previous with .2 second delay → Medium speed.

*Note:* Refer to sections in Project 2 (enhancing with custom animation) and Project 3 (setting automatic timing) as necessary.

---

## DESIGNER'S POINTER

### Balancing Multiple-Line Titles

Slide titles should be brief, but they must be long enough to be informative, as you learned in Project 4. Balancing a longer slide title on two lines is a more appealing format than stretching the title on one line across most of the width of the slide. Multiple-line titles should be arranged in the inverted pyramid format; that is, each line should be succeeding shorter than the line preceding it. Note the arrangement of the following slide title:

**Unbalanced:**                    Ten Common Mistakes Made by Presenters


                                   Ten Common Mistakes Made
                                        by Presenters


**Inverted Pyramid Format:**              Ten Common Mistakes
                                        Made by Presenters

## Using the Hide on Next Mouse Click Animation Technique

The Hide on Next Mouse Click animation technique allows you to create multiple layers on a single slide. Specific layers are displayed with precise timing. In the following project, a speaker displays on an AutoShape resembling a projection screen three separate layers of text and images. Each layer depicts a common problem with visuals. Enabling the audience to visualize the problems rather than read a bland bulleted list of problems increases the power of the communication.

*Directions:* Follow the instructions to enhance the original slide as shown.

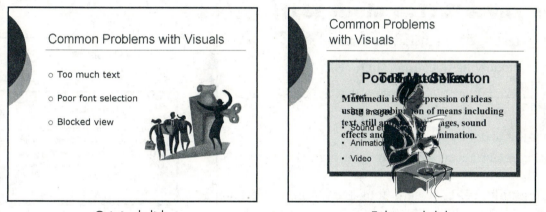

Original slide                                   Enhanced slide

1. Preview the four layers of images before you begin building the slide. A showcase box displays three separate visual effects built on one slide using the Hide After Mouse Click animation effect. When the speaker advances through the slide show, the previous text disappears and the next layer is displayed in the showcase box.

| | | | |
|---|---|---|---|
| Layer 1 | Layer 2 | Layer 3 | Layer 4 |
| Showcase box | Too Much Text | Poor Font Selection | Blocked View |

2. Create a new slide using the Title Only layout from the Text layouts category.

3. Key the title: **Common Problems with Visuals**.

4. Set the zoom at 25% to provide a large desktop area to the right of the slide. (Use the **Zoom** button on the standard toolbar or click **View**, **Zoom**.)

## Create Layer 1 (Showcase Box)

5. Use the **Rectangle** AutoShape on the Draw toolbar to create a projection screen that serves as a backdrop or showcase box for a series of three images that illustrate common problems with visuals.

6. Select a fill color; line color, width, and style; and shadow effect to give the projection screen a realistic appearance. Refer to the instructions for creating a showcase box in Project 3 if necessary.

7. Animate the showcase box: Fade → Start on Click → Medium speed.

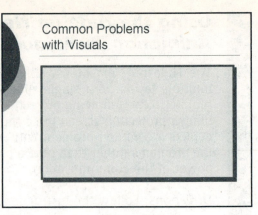

Layer 1

## Create Layer 2 (Too Much Text)

8. Create a text box to fit inside the rectangle.

9. Input the following title: **Too Much Text**.

10. Press **Enter** and key the paragraph that appears on the Layer 2 slide.

11. Format the text:

    a) **Title:** Select a sans serif font face (e.g., Univers or Arial) with font size of 40 points.

    b) **Paragraph:** Select a serif font (e.g., Times New Roman) with a font size of 34 points.

12. Resize and reposition the text box so that the text appears to be projected on the projection screen.

13. Animate Layer 2 (Too Much Text) as follows:

    a) Wipe from Left → Start on Click → Medium speed.

    b) Modify the effects options to hide Layer 2 (Too Much Text) when the slide advances to the next layer:

    • Click the down arrow beside the object in the Custom Animation list.

    • Click **Effect Options**.

    • Click the down arrow beside After Animation and select **Hide on Next Mouse Click**.

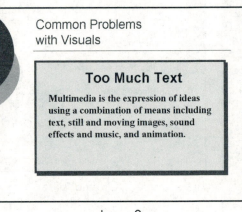

Layer 2

Select Hide on Next Mouse Click

## Create Layer 3 (Poor Font Selection)

14. Copy Layer 2 (Too Much Text) to save time and ensure consistency in the design of each layer:

    a) Select the text box you created for the first layer.

    b) Hold down the **Ctrl** key as you click on and then drag the object over into the gray area outside the slide.

15. Edit the copy of Layer 2 that is positioned on the slide. Refer to the following illustration for assistance.

    a) Input the new title: **Poor Font Selection**.

    b) Delete the unneeded text.

    c) Click the **Bullets** button on the Formatting toolbar and key the text:

       • **Text**

       • **Still images**

       • **Sound effects and music**

       • **Animation**

       • **Video**

    d) Select a narrow, hard-to-read font face with a font size no larger than 18 points for the bulleted list.

    e) Refer to the Technology Tip on page 114 for aligning the text in the bulleted list.

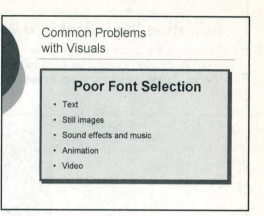

Layer 3

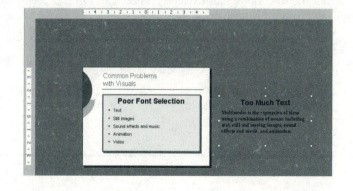

16. Animate Layer 3. Because you edited a copy of Layer 2, no further changes are needed. Confirm the animation settings if you wish: Wipe from Left → Start on Click → Medium speed → Hide on Next Mouse Click *(removes Layer 3, allowing the next layer to be displayed)*.

## Create Layer 4 (Blocked View)

17. Copy Layer 3 and edit the copy positioned on the slide. Refer to the illustration of the desktop above for assistance.

    a) Input the new title: **Blocked View**.

    b) Delete the paragraph.

Layer 4

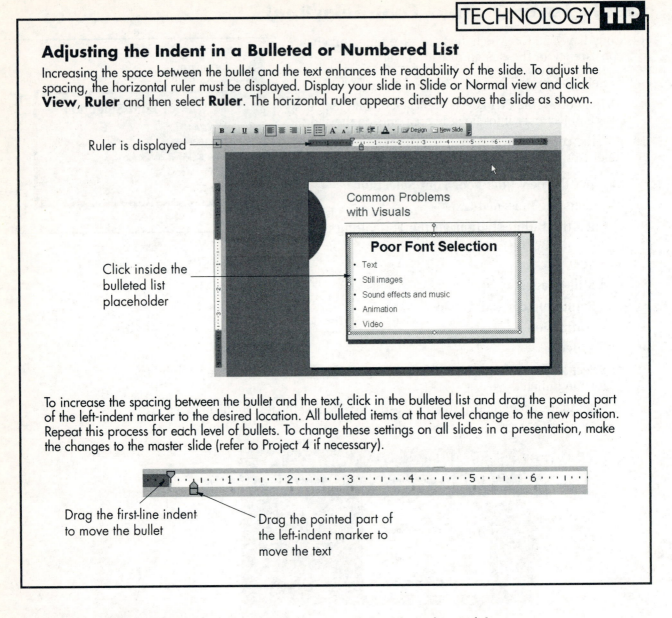

### Adjusting the Indent in a Bulleted or Numbered List

Increasing the space between the bullet and the text enhances the readability of the slide. To adjust the spacing, the horizontal ruler must be displayed. Display your slide in Slide or Normal view and click **View**, **Ruler** and then select **Ruler**. The horizontal ruler appears directly above the slide as shown.

Ruler is displayed →

Click inside the bulleted list placeholder →

To increase the spacing between the bullet and the text, click in the bulleted list and drag the pointed part of the left-indent marker to the desired location. All bulleted items at that level change to the new position. Repeat this process for each level of bullets. To change these settings on all slides in a presentation, make the changes to the master slide (refer to Project 4 if necessary).

Drag the first-line indent to move the bullet

Drag the pointed part of the left-indent marker to move the text

---

c) Insert a clip art image of a speaker facing forward directly in front of the projection screen.

d) Group the title and the clip art so that they can be animated to appear together. Alternatively, animate the speaker to start with the previous event (the title of the layer: Blocked View).

18. Animate Layer 4 by editing the animation settings copied from Layer 2: Center Revolve → Start on Click → Medium speed → Don't Dim.

*Note:* Changing the Hide on Next Mouse Click effect to Don't Dim can be omitted because the next mouse click will advance to the next slide.

## Position Layers on the Slide

19. Drag Layer 4 (Blocked View) off the slide and into the work area.

20. Position Layer 2 (Too Much Text) in front of the showcase box, making sure it is balanced attractively in the showcase box.

21. Position Layer 3 (Poor Font Selection) directly on top of Layer 2 (Too Much Text).

22. Position Layer 4 (Blocked View) directly on top of Layer 3 (Poor Font Selection).

## Preview Animation

It's now time to run the slide show and check the results of all these effects:

- **Slide Title:** Appear with the slide.

- **Showcase Box:** Fade.

- **Layer 2 (Too Much Text):** Wipe from Left → Hide on Next Mouse Click.

- **Layer 3 (Poor Font Selection):** Wipe from Left → Hide on Next Mouse Click.

- **Layer 4 (Blocked View):** Center Revolve → Don't Dim. (Next mouse click advances to the next slide.)

## Using the Hide After Animation Technique

*Directions:* Follow the instructions to enhance the original slide as shown.

1. Create a new slide using the Title Only layout from the Text layouts category.

2. Change the background color to black to resemble a movie reel (click **Format**, **Background**).

3. Key the title and insert a clip art image of an effective speaker. Size and position as shown in the model.

4. Search "marquee" in Microsoft Clip Organizer or Microsoft Office Online to locate the clip art image. Key the text and format as shown in the model.

## Create a Master Star

5. Click **AutoShapes**, **Stars and Banners**.

6. Select the **5-point Star** and draw the star.

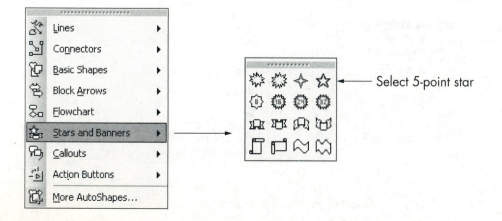

Select 5-point star

7. Create a realistic twinkling effect:

   a) Add a gradient fill effect by blending either blue, white, or yellow. Select a shading style and a variant of your choice. Placing the lighter color in the center will give the star a 3D effect, as though the star is pushing out from center.

   b) Add a shadow effect of your choice and a shadow color slightly darker than the fill effect.

   c) Drag on the star's rotate handle in the direction you want to rotate the star.

AutoShape without
enhancements

Enhanced star

8. Animate the master star: Expand → Start with Previous → Fast speed.

## Copy the Master Star to Create Additional Stars

9. Select the star and hold down the **Ctrl** key as you drag the object. An icon with a plus sign appears as you drag the slide, indicating an object is being moved and copied.

10. Drop the star anywhere on the screen; you will reposition the stars later.

11. Repeat the process until you have created several stars.

12. Vary the size of the stars and reposition them to create an appealing design. (Refer to the model to view a possible placement of stars.)

## Animate Selected Stars to Hide

13. Identify two or three stars that you would like to appear and then hide after they are displayed.

14. Modify the custom animation for each of these stars:

   a) Click the down arrow beside the object in the Custom Animation list.

   b) Click **Effect Options**.

   c) Click the down arrow beside After animation and select **Hide After Animation**.

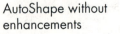

Select Hide After Animation

## Edit the Animation Order and Slide Transition

15. Click **Slide Show**, **Custom Animation** and verify the animation order and effect of each object:

- **First:** Speaker: Start on Click → Dissolve.
- **Second:** Marquee: After previous → Split Vertical Out.
- **Third:** Series of stars that expand and start with the previous event. Selected stars hide after animation. Reorder the stars in the animation list to display the stars in a sequence you consider appealing.

16. Add a dynamic slide transition (Fade through Black or Newsflash) with sound effect (e.g., applause) to bring added attention to the important point presented on this specimen slide.

## Other Animation Enhancements

For added dazzle, experiment with these additional animation techniques if time permits:

1. Add an exit custom animation effect for objects you wish to disappear. The Hide After Animation technique simply hides the object after the entrance animation effect has played.

   a) Select the object and add the entrance animation effect as directed in Step 15.

   b) Select the object and add an exit animation effect: **Custom Animation**, **Add Effect**, **Exit**, **Dissolve Out** (or an effect of your choice).

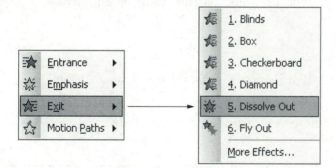

2. Create a motion path (i.e., an invisible track you lay on the slide for an object to move on). You can move text from one place on your slide to another, create a hand-drawn entrance or exit for an image, or lay a path that an arrow could follow at crucial points in your narrative to show a process. The motion path depicted by the dotted line in the model moves the star in a circular motion around the speaker. To set a motion path:

Star moves on circular motion path around the speaker

a) Click **Custom Animation**, **Add Effect**, **Motion Paths**; choose a path from the list of preset or custom paths.

b) Change the path by selecting and dragging on the path. You'll need to experiment to get the effect exactly as you want it. Refer to the Microsoft Office Help to learn more about this advanced animation effect.

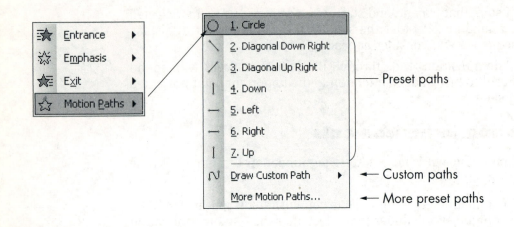

## ■ REINFORCEMENT ACTIVITIES

Add the following slides to the file Present for added reinforcement of the PowerPoint features you learned in this project. Position the slides as shown at the end of the project.

### Activity 1

Follow the instructions to build a slide that depicts a different image as each bulleted item is displayed.

1. Preview the four layers of images before you begin building the slide.

2. Create a new slide using the Title, Text, and Clip Art layout from the Other Layouts category.

3. Key the bulleted list and add custom animation: Wipe from Left → Start on Click → Fast speed → Build and dim effect.

4. Select a relevant image to reinforce the concept described in the first bulleted item.

5. Add custom animation: Ease In → With Previous Event → Medium speed → Hide on Next Mouse Click.

6. Reorder the image to follow the first bulleted item. Drag the clip art off the slide into the work area as you create the next layer.

7. Repeat the process to insert and animate the remaining three images.

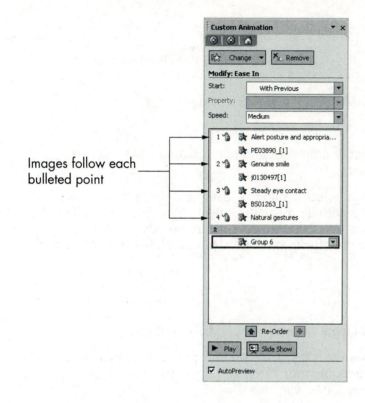

Images follow each bulleted point

8. Position the first image (posture) on the slide as shown in the model, making sure it is balanced attractively with the text. Layer the other three images in the order they are to be discussed.

9. Preview the animation and check for accuracy in the effects and timing and for optimal placement of the graphics.

## Activity 2

Build the slide shown in the model.

1. Choose one of the explosion shapes from AutoShapes or choose a shape of your own.

2. Animate the following objects as indicated. Extend the automatic timing to allow the audience .2 seconds to view an item before the next one is displayed.

   • **First:** AutoShape: Diamond → Start on Click → Fast speed.

   • **Second:** Text box (went up in smoke): From Top-left → Start on Click → Medium speed.

   • **Third:** Text box (bent out of shape): From Top-right → Start After Previous → Medium speed.

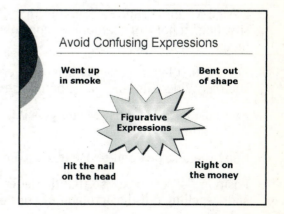

- **Fourth:** Text box (hit the nail on the head): From Bottom-left → Start After Previous → Medium speed.
- **Fifth:** Text box (right on the money): From Bottom-right → Start After Previous → Medium speed.

# Activity 3

Edit a copy of the slide created in Activity 2 to build three additional slides that illustrate other types of confusing expressions:

- **Acronyms:** FYI, ASAP, FASB, HMO, or others of your choice.

- **Slang:** Cool, buck, flop, dis, or others of your choice.

- **Sports analogies:** Caught off guard, drop back and punt, batting a thousand, way off target, or others of your choice.

*Note:* The Hide After Animation effect could be used on these four slides. However, because the timings are automatic, a "disappear" exit animation effect for the AutoShape and the four text boxes would be required to hide these objects. In this case, displaying the effects on four separate slides is a simpler design technique.

# Activity 4

1. Create a slide using the Blank layout from the Contents Layout category.

2. Select three to five photos related to a topic of your choice (e.g., attractions in a city of your choice, favorite spots on your campus, highlights of an activity of one of your student groups, your latest vacation).

3. Build a creative slide using the Hide After Animation effect to showcase these photographs. You may wish to use the photo album feature for importing the photographs and developing interesting frame shapes efficiently (refer to Project 3 if necessary). Add a related slide title and photo captions and relevant sound if you wish.

4. Save in a separate file.

# Activity 5

1. Create a slide using the Blank layout from the Contents Layout category.

2. Design a simple slide background that depicts an image of your college/university (e.g., photo of memorable spot on campus with low contrast, wallpaper image of your logo).

3. Key the first letter of your college/university's acronym using a bold, sturdy font such as Wide Latin in a large point size (at least 60 points).

4. Add custom animation: Magnify → After Previous → Fast speed → Hide After Animation.

5. Copy the text box and revise it to create the remaining letters of the acronym.

6. Position the text boxes so that the letters appear in various locations across the slide, spelling out the acronym of your college/university several times.

7. Add a second slide containing a series of photos related to the college/university (optional). Follow the instructions provided in Activity 4.

8. Add your college/university fight song or other music to play with the slide.

9. Save in a separate file.

## Activity 6

Revise the slide from the file Present shown below to include the circular motion path around the speaker. Refer to the discussion on page 117 if necessary.

## Slide Order

Sequence slides in the file Present according to the table on pages 212–213. Print and submit as directed by your instructor.

# Creating Compelling Tables and Charts

## LEARNING OBJECTIVES

- Design a compelling table, bar chart, and pie chart.
- Add creative enhancements to charts for added clarity and appeal.

## ■ CREATING TABLES

Displaying text in a columnar format helps a speaker clarify large quantities of data. PowerPoint simplifies the process of creating highly professional tables.

*Directions:* Follow the instructions to enhance the original slide as shown.

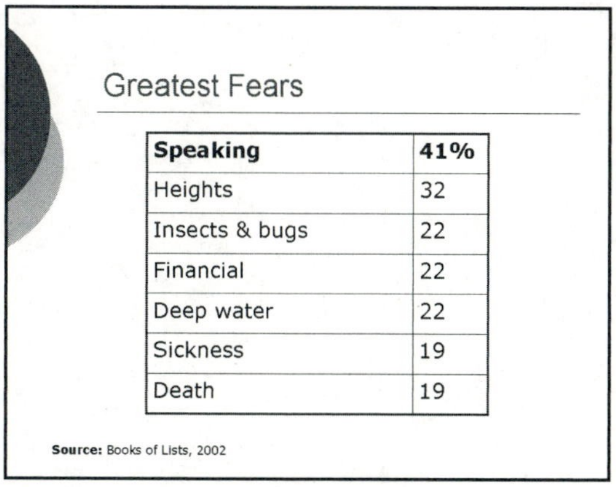

Original slide

Enhanced slide

1. Create a new slide using the Title and 2 Content layout from the Content Layouts category.

2. Key the title in the Title placeholder. Note that the revised title clearly conveys the key thought presented in the data—public speaking anxiety is normal.

3. Click the **Clip Art** icon in the Left Content placeholder.

4. Select relevant clip art from Microsoft Clip Organizer or Microsoft Office Online, using "fear" as the search term. Resize and position the clip art as shown in the model.

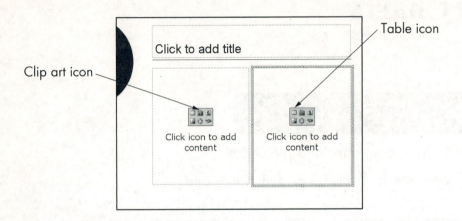

## Create the Table

5. Click the **Table** icon in the Right Content placeholder.

6. Enter **2** for number of columns and **7** for number of rows.

7. Key the data shown in the model in the cells of the table. Use the arrow keys to move from cell to cell.

| | |
|---|---|
| Speaking | 41% |
| Heights | 32 |
| Insects & bugs | 22 |
| Financial | 22 |
| Deep water | 22 |
| Sickness | 22 |
| Death | 19 |

**Insert Table**

Number of columns:
2
Number of rows:
7
OK     Cancel

## Format the Data

8. Highlight the second column and click **Right Align** from the Formatting toolbar.

9. Highlight the first row (Speaking) and format for emphasis: Change the font size to approximately 18 points and add boldface. Decrease the font size at least 2 points for the remaining items in the list.

10. Click **Format**, **Table** and select the Text Box tab. Select **Middle** to center the text within the rows.

Select Text Box tab

Choose alignment

**Format Table**

Borders | Fill | Text Box

Text alignment: Middle

Internal margin
Left: 0.1"     Top: 0.05"
Right: 0.1"    Bottom: 0.05"

☐ Rotate text within cell by 90 degrees

OK     Cancel     Preview

## Resize the Table and Add a Source Note

11. Point to the right border until a two-headed arrow appears. Click and then drag the mouse to the left to reduce the width of the right column and increase the width of the left column of the table. Reduce the height of the table until the table is positioned as shown in the model.

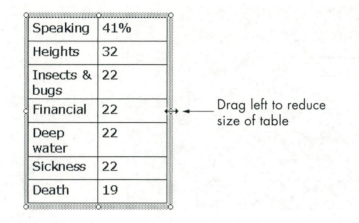

| Speaking | 41% |
| Heights | 32 |
| Insects & bugs | 22 |
| Financial | 22 |
| Deep water | 22 |
| Sickness | 22 |
| Death | 19 |

← Drag left to reduce size of table

## Format the Table

12. Highlight the first row (Speaking) and click **Format**, **Table** (or right-click and click **Border and Fills**).

13. Select the Fill tab, click **Fill Effects**, and select a gradient fill blending two colors complementary to the design template. Select the **From Center** shading style and the variant that places the lighter color in the center. Putting the lighter color in the center will give the table a 3D look, as if it's raised in the center.

14. Highlight the remaining rows and apply the same gradient fill you applied to the first row, except lighten the colors to create a receding effect on these rows.

Select Fill tab

Select Fill Effects

**Format Table** dialog box with tabs Borders, Fill, Text Box; options Fill color, Automatic, More Colors..., Fill Effects..., Background; buttons OK, Cancel, Preview.

Select Gradient tab

Select two colors

Choose a shading style and variant

**Fill Effects** dialog box with tabs Gradient, Texture, Pattern, Picture; Colors: One color, Two colors, Preset; Color 1, Color 2; Transparency From, To; Shading styles: Horizontal, Vertical, Diagonal up, Diagonal down, From corner, From center; Variants; Sample; Rotate fill effect with shape.

15. Highlight the entire table and click **Format**, **Table** (or right-click and click **Border and Fills**).

16. Select the Borders tab and use the buttons or select the diagram to eliminate all borders in the table (outside and inside).

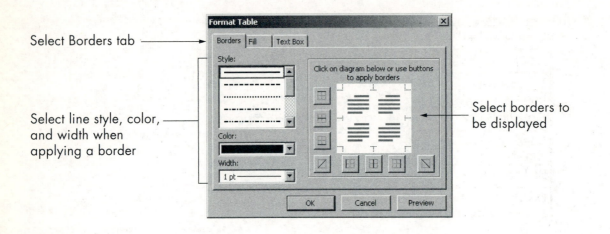

Select Borders tab

Select line style, color, and width when applying a border

Select borders to be displayed

*Note:* You may wish to use the **Rectangle** AutoShape to create a showcase box slightly larger than the table. Create an appealing format that adds dimension to the table. Add a complementary fill and line color and experiment with a creative line style of various widths and with shadows.

## Animate the Slide

17. Click **Slide Show**, **Custom Animation**.

18. Animate the slide as follows:
    - **First:** Clip art: Crawl from Left → Start on Click → Medium speed.
    - **Second:** Table: Split, Vertical Out → Start on Click → Fast speed.
    - **Third:** Source note: Dissolve → Start After Previous with .2 second delay → Fast speed.

## ▮ CREATING CHARTS

Well-designed, appealing charts help the speaker convey quantitative information without overwhelming the audience. You will learn to enhance PowerPoint's basic default charts to create a bar chart and a pie chart that reflect good rules for formation of graphic aids. You will also learn to change the chart type to be certain you have depicted the data in a logical manner for the decision maker. Guidelines for selecting a graphic type that depict data most effectively are included in the Designer's Pointer on page 127.

## DESIGNER'S POINTER

### Applying Graphic Design Principles

Charts, like other presentation graphics, should be designed to clarify, reinforce, or emphasize a particular idea and should contribute to the overall understanding of the idea being discussed. They should be uncluttered and easily understood and depict information honestly. However, because important decisions are often made on the basis of charts, presenters must take special care in designing simple, yet appealing charts that clearly convey meaningful information.

Selecting the graphic type that will depict data in the most effective manner is one of the most important decisions you must make in designing a meaningful chart. After identifying the primary idea you want the audience to understand, you are then able to choose a graphic type that will depict the data in a meaningful way. Use the following guidelines to help you choose an appropriate graphic type:

| Graphic Type | Objective |
|---|---|
| Table | Shows exact figures |
| Bar chart (column or horizontal) | Compares one quantity with another quantity |
| Line chart | Illustrates changes in quantities over time |
| Pie chart | Shows how the parts of a whole are distributed |

Once you've input the data in PowerPoint's datasheet, you can view your data in several chart types until you identify the type that communicates your primary idea most effectively. To view the data in a different chart type, click **Chart**, **Chart Type** and select a different chart type and subtype.

A competent designer cannot assume that a software application will produce these results automatically. Although the latest generation of presentation software programs guide users away from the worst errors of taste and judgment, they often do not reflect good rules for formation of accurate and appealing graphics. A few changes in PowerPoint's default settings will arrange a chart according to appropriate design rules that enhance appeal and clarity. In this project, you will begin pie charts at the 12 o'clock position, beginning with the largest slice and descending in clockwise order; you will position labels and percentages inside or beside pie slices for optimal readability; and so forth. Note other enhancements in appeal and clarity resulting from changes in default settings as you complete this project.

## Creating a Column Chart

A bar chart is effective for comparing quantities at a specific time, whereas a line chart is effective for comparing quantities over time and illustrating trends. The bar chart is referred to as a column or vertical chart when the bars are presented vertically, as shown in the following slide, and as a horizontal bar chart when the bars are presented horizontally. The chart must be labeled clearly so that the audience understands key points; however, the audience's intended use of the data determines the extent of labeling (e.g., inclusion or omission of specific values and gridlines). To avoid visual distortion, the quantitative axis should begin at zero. Avoid 3D effects in projected visuals to improve readability.

*Directions:* Follow the instructions to enhance the original slide by editing PowerPoint's default values.

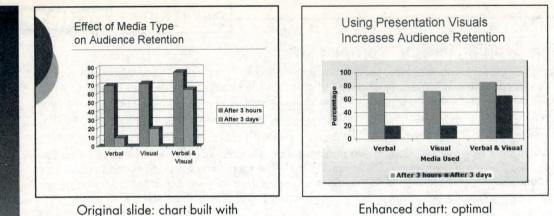

Original slide: chart built with
software default values

Enhanced chart: optimal
appeal and readability

1. Create a new slide using the Title and Chart layout from the Other Layouts category.

2. Key the title in the Title placeholder. Note that the revised title reveals the interpretation of the data and allows the audience to grasp immediately the meaningfulness of the information as it relates to speaker's point—the perceived worth of presentation visuals.

3. Consider whether the background object should be deleted to allow more space for the chart and eliminate unnecessary clutter. (To remove the graphics, click **Format**, **Background** and click to place a check in front of **Omit background graphics from master**.)

## Select a Chart Type

4. Double-click the Chart placeholder.

5. Click **Chart**, **Chart Type**.

6. Be sure the Standard Types tab is selected and note the various types of charts that can be built.

7. Click **Column** and select the first option—the clustered chart. Note the various types of column charts displayed in the gallery.

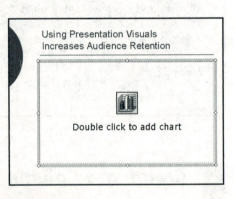

Select Standard
Types tab

Select chart
subtype

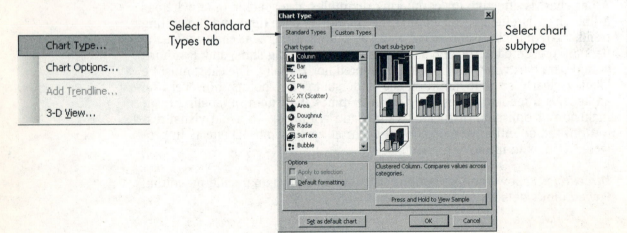
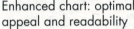

**TECHNOLOGY TIP**

## Steering Clear of Common Charting Snafus

A first look at the numerous options in the charting mode can be overwhelming, but practice will provide the confidence needed to create appealing and meaningful charts. Here are a few tricks to help you avoid some of the initial frustrations of working in Chart Mode:

First, if you accidentally click off the chart and return to the slide, just double-click the chart to return to Chart Mode. To verify that you are working in Chart Mode, look for **Chart** as an option on the Menu toolbar and a diagonal border surrounding the chart.

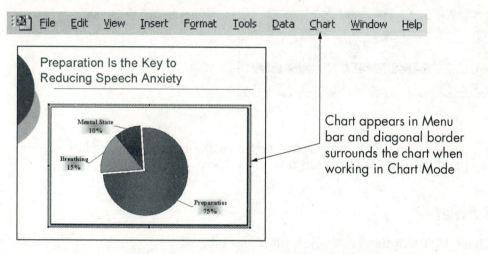

Chart appears in Menu bar and diagonal border surrounds the chart when working in Chart Mode

Next, if your chart has extra space to the right of the third column and a blank entry in the legend key as shown in the illustration, you likely deleted the data in Column D and Row 3 but not the column and row. Follow these commands:

1. Select the unneeded column(s) (Column D) and click **Edit**, **Delete**, **Entire Column** (or right-click and click **Delete**).

2. Select the unneeded row(s) (Row 3) and click **Edit**, **Delete**, **Entire Row** (or right-click and click **Delete**).

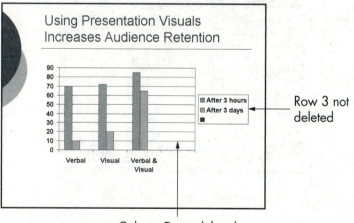

Row 3 not deleted

Column D not deleted

Last, right-clicking the mouse displays a list of context-sensitive prompts that quickly assist you in revising the format of a specific section of the chart. Right-click freely and have fun exploring the numerous ways you can enhance the appeal and meaningfulness of charts you create with Microsoft Office Chart Mode.

## Edit the Sample Datasheet to Build the Column Chart

8. Click in the first cell of the sample datasheet and input the data. Use the arrow keys to move to the next cell.

9. Input all remaining data and delete any sample data that remain (Column D and Row 3). Refer to the Technology Tip on page 129 if the structure of your column chart still includes the extra row and column.

| | | A | B | C | D | E |
|---|---|---|---|---|---|---|
| | | Verbal | Visual | Verbal & Visual | | |
| 1 | After 3 hours | 70 | 72 | 85 | | |
| 2 | After 3 days | 20 | 20 | 65 | | |
| 3 | | | | | | |
| 4 | | | | | | |

Click to exit datasheet

10. Exit the datasheet to allow more space for formatting the column chart. To redisplay the datasheet for later revisions, click **View**, **Datasheet**.

## Input Labels

11. Click **Chart**, **Chart Options** and select the Titles tab.

12. Input the x-axis label: **Media Used**.

13. Input the z-axis (or y-axis) label: **Percentage**.

*Note*: Omit a chart title because the title will appear as the title of the slide for added impact.

Select Titles tab

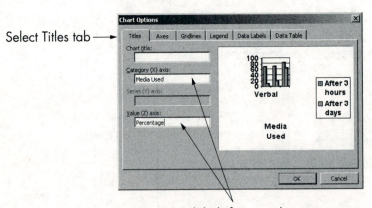

Input labels for x- and y-axes

## Format the Legend

14. Click **Chart**, **Chart Options** and select the Legend tab.

15. Click **Bottom**. Positioning the legend below the chart allows space for increasing the size of the chart for easy readability on a projected visual.

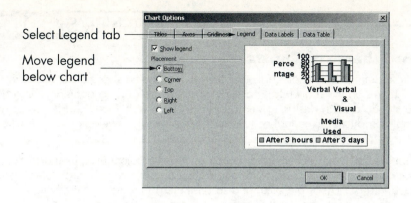

Select Legend tab

Move legend
below chart

## Size the Chart

16. Hold down the **Shift** key and click on a corner handle to drag the chart. Enlarge the chart to occupy the space below the slide title, allowing adequate, even margins on all four sides. Use the model as a guide.

## Enhance the Chart Format

You will now make four changes to enhance the appearance of the default column chart: (1) add a fill behind the chart area to add dimension to the slide, (2) increase the size of the labels for easier readability of text on a projected visual, (3) change the alignment of the y-axis label, and (4) edit the bar colors. As you edit the chart, take note of other ways you can modify a column chart to increase visual appeal.

## Get Acquainted with the Chart Edit Technique

17. Be sure you are in the Chart Mode, which allows you to modify a chart. Refer to the Technology Tip on page 129 if necessary.

18. Experiment with the use of the right mouse click to identify areas to be formatted.

   a) Move the mouse near the part of the chart you wish to format until a prompt identifying the selected section of the chart appears (e.g., Format _____ Area). For example, pointing slightly below the top border of the chart selects the chart area (i.e., the entire chart, including the bars, labels, legend, etc.) and the Format Chart Area prompt appears.

   b) Right-click, click **Format _____**, and input any changes in the dialog box that appears.

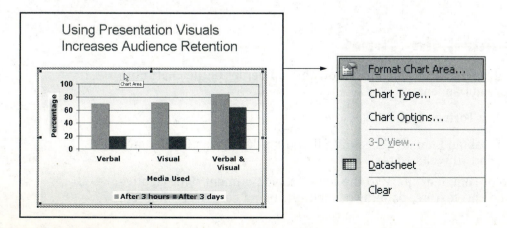

**DESIGNER'S POINTER**

## Modifying the Color Scheme of Charts

If your presentation will include a number of charts, take the time to modify the slide color scheme to reflect the fill colors of the elements on the chart (e.g., bars, pie slices, levels of an organization chart). Devoting time to planning a standard chart design will ensure a consistent look for all charts in a presentation and will save you valuable production time that can be spent more wisely developing and practicing the presentation.

The last four scheme colors in the Edit Color Scheme dialog box control the colors used in charts. For example, the Fills color is the color that will appear inside any AutoShape drawn on a slide in this presentation as well as the first value in a bar chart, pie slice, and so on. Refer to Project 4, Modifying the Color Scheme of a Presentation Design, to review the procedure for editing a color scheme.

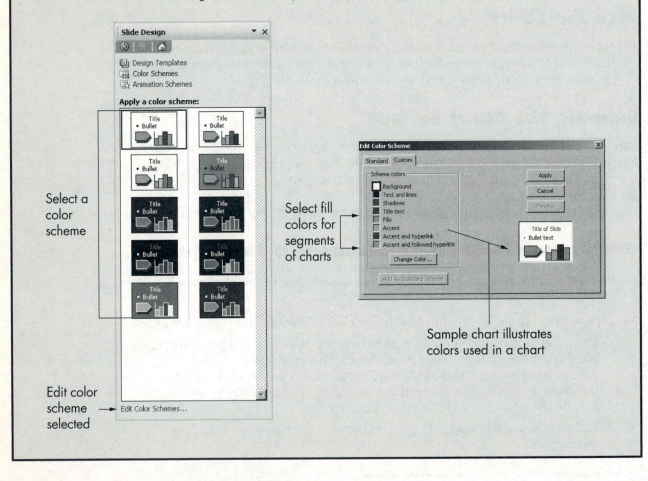

## Add a Fill Behind the Chart

19. Select the chart area by pointing slightly below the top border of the chart until the Chart Area prompt appears.

20. Right-click and click **Format Chart Area**.

21. Select the Patterns tab and create appealing fill and border effects for the area surrounding the chart (the chart area).

   a) Select a fill color complementary to the template. Experiment with creative fill effects (gradient, texture, pattern, or picture), being certain to choose a format that allows the audience to read the chart easily. Refer to Project 3 if necessary.

b) Select a line style, color, and weight complementary to the fill color.

Select Patterns tab ⟶

Select line style, color, and weight

Select a fill color complementary to the template

Consider a creative fill effect (gradient, texture, pattern, or picture)

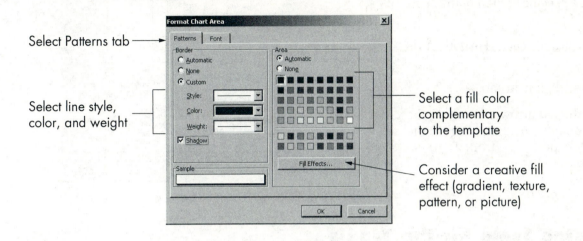

## Adjust the Font Size and Color of the Text

22. Select the Font tab to specify the font face and font size of the labels (x- and y-axes) and the legend.

a) Select an interesting, yet readable font (e.g., Arial) and select **Bold** as the font style and **20** points for font size to ensure readability.

b) Select a font color that has high contrast with the fill effect and that complements the design template.

Select Font tab

Change font style and size

Change font color

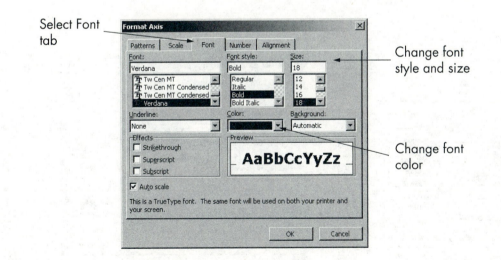

*Note:* Editing the chart area allows you to edit the font attributes of all three labels with one command. To modify one of these labels (the x- or y-axis or the legend), select the label you wish to edit, right-click and select **Format**. Then, click the Font tab, and input your changes.

## Change the Alignment of the Y-axis Label

23. Select the Value Axis Title area by clicking near the label "Percentage." If necessary, refer to Steps 17–18 for selecting a specific section of the chart for editing.

24. Right-click and click **Format Axis Title**.

25. Select the Alignment tab.

26. Point to the red arrow controlling the orientation of the text and drag to the 12 o'clock position (from 0 to 90 degrees).

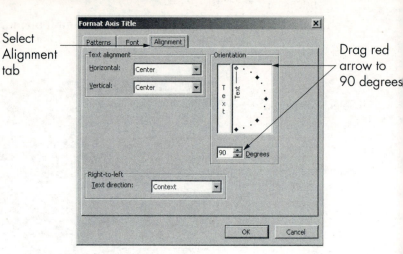

Select Alignment tab

Drag red arrow to 90 degrees

## Change the Scale for the Y-axis

To improve the readability and appeal of the y-axis scale, increase the size of the scale interval and change the maximum value to reflect the percentages depicted in the chart.

27. Select the Value Axis by pointing near the y-axis values.

28. Right-click and click **Format Value Axis**.

29. Input the following changes to the scale:
   - Maximum value: 100.
   - Minimum value: 0.
   - Major unit: 20.

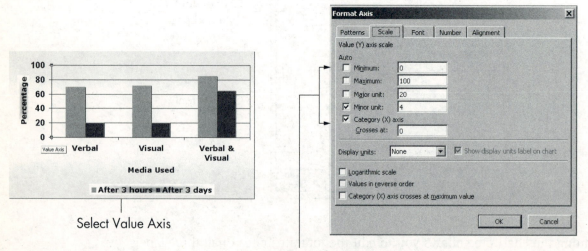

Select Value Axis

Specify the minimum and maximum values and the major unit

## Change the Bar Colors

Recolor the bars, striving for high contrast with the fill effect behind the column chart (the chart area) and an appealing color scheme consistent with other filled objects in the file Present.

30. Select the first series (After 3 hours) by pointing to and clicking one of these bars. Selection handles will appear on the "After 3 hours" bars at each point along the x-axis.

31. Right-click and click **Format Data Series**.

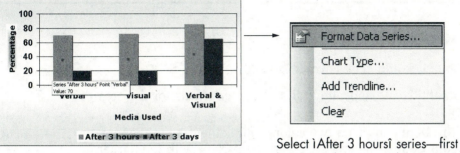

Select ìAfter 3 hoursî series—first bar at each point on the x-axis

32. Select the Patterns tab and select a fill color for the bars. Choose a color complementary to the design template that has high contrast with the fill behind the column chart (the chart area). Experiment with creative fill effects (gradient, texture, pattern, or picture). Try a horizontal or vertical two-color gradient with the lighter color in the middle to give the bars a 3D look (they will look as if they are raised in the middle).

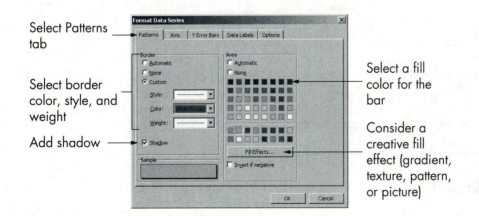

33. Repeat the process to recolor the "After 3 days" data series. The contrast between the colors you select for the two data series should be high so that the audience can easily distinguish between the two values. The Designer's Pointer on page 136 highlights another important consideration for color components in a chart.

34. Get acquainted with other ways you can modify the format of the data series by clicking the other tabs: axis, y-error bars, data labels, and options.

### Ensuring Accessibility to the Color Impaired

Almost 10 percent of the population is color impaired, meaning that some colors are inaccessible to them, appearing instead as a confusing blend of grays. Distinguishing reds and greens appears to be a consistent problem, with dim lighting only worsening the color distortion.

To provide equal access to your slide content, avoid designs that require your audience to distinguish between red and green. For example, avoid using red and green as the colors of adjacent bars or pie slices and don't use red and green to differentiate between important points (e.g., red text on a green background or green text on a red background).

## Enhance the Labels

35. Select the legend. Right-click and click **Format Legend**.

36. Select the Patterns tab and create appealing fill and border effects for the area surrounding the legend.

   a) Click **Fill Effects**, **Gradient** and blend two colors complementary to the template. Select the **From Center** shading style and the variant with the darker of the two colors in the center.

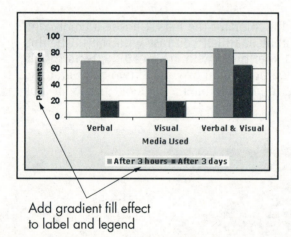

Add gradient fill effect
to label and legend

   b) Omit the border surrounding the legend to eliminate unnecessary clutter.

37. Create the same gradient fill on the y-axis label.

## Animate the Chart

38. Click **Slide Show**, **Custom Animation**.

39. Select **Wipe from Bottom** in the Entry Animation box. This upward effect reinforces the concept that the use of multimedia (verbal and visual) increases retention both short and long term.

40. Click the down arrow to the right of the chart object in the Custom Animation list.

41. Click **Effect Options** and select the Chart Animation tab.

42. Select **By series**. Click **Play** and note the "After 3 hours" bars are displayed first, followed by the "After 3 days" bars.

43. Add a sound effect if you wish.

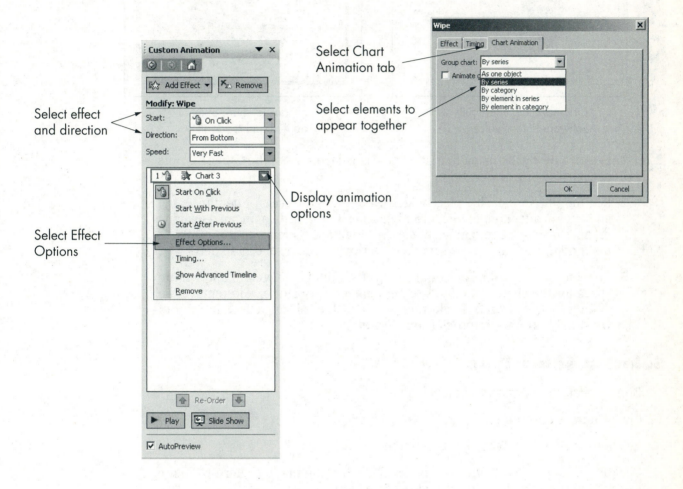

## Creating a Pie Chart

A pie chart is effective for showing how the parts of a whole are distributed. The whole is represented as a pie, with the parts becoming slices of the pie. Limit a pie chart to no more than six slices to avoid problems with complex, dense labeling. The largest slice or the slice to be emphasized should be placed at the 12 o'clock position and can be exploded for added emphasis. Preferably, place the label and value inside or just outside each slice to ease the audience's burden of interpreting the graph. A legend is a less effective method for identifying slices because the audience's attention is split between the pie and the legend.

*Directions:* Follow the instructions to enhance the original slide by editing PowerPoint's default values.

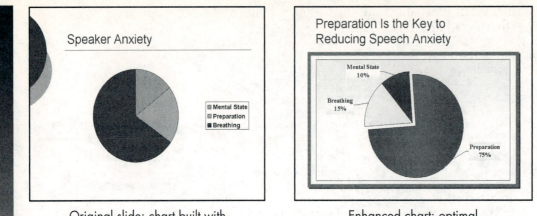

Original slide: chart built with
software default values

Enhanced chart: optimal
appeal and readability

1. Create a new slide using the Title and Chart layout from the Other Layouts category.

2. Key the title in the Title placeholder. Note that the revised title directs the audience's attention to the meaningfulness of the data in an engaging manner. The title communicates clearly how the data relate to the speaker's main point—research-based strategies for overcoming speech anxiety.

3. Consider whether the background object should be deleted to allow more space for the chart and eliminate any unnecessary clutter. (To remove the graphics, click **Format**, **Background** and click to place a check in front of **Omit background graphics from master**.)

## Select a Chart Type

4. Double-click the Chart placeholder.

5. Click **Chart**, **Chart Type**.

6. Be sure the Standard Types tab is selected.

7. Click **Pie** from the Chart Type dialog box and select the first pie chart. Note the various types of pie charts displayed in the gallery.

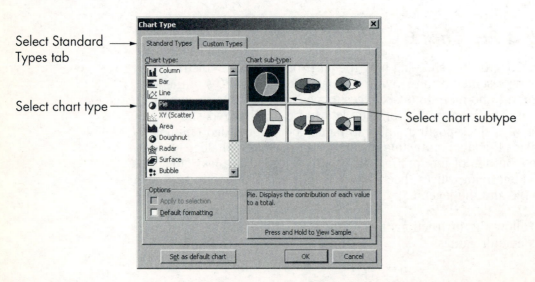

Select Standard Types tab

Select chart type

Select chart subtype

## Edit the Sample Datasheet

8. Click in the first cell and input the data. Use the arrow keys to move to the next cell.

| | | A | B | C | D |
|---|---|---|---|---|---|
| | | Mental State | Preparation | Breathing | |
| 1 | | 10 | 75 | 15 | |
| 2 | | | | | |
| 3 | | | | | |
| 4 | | | | | |

Lehman Project 7 - Datasheet — Click to exit the datasheet

9. Input the remaining data and exit the datasheet. To redisplay the datasheet for later revisions, click **View**, **Datasheet**.

10. Delete any unneeded rows and columns. Refer to the Technology Tip on page 129 if necessary.

## Input the Chart Title

11. Do not include a title in the chart because the title will appear in the Title place-holder. If you wish to include the title in a chart, click **Chart**, **Chart Options**, select the Titles tab, and input the title.

## Format the Labels Beside the Pie Slice for Improved Readability

12. Click **Chart**, **Chart Options** and select the Data Labels tab.

13. Click **Category name** to display the labels with the pie slide (e.g., Preparation).

14. Click **Percentage** to display the value and a percent sign beside the pie slice (e.g., 75%).

15. Be sure the **Legend key** option is not checked. A legend, containing color-coded squares for each value, is not needed when the value will appear outside the appropriate pie slice.

16. Be sure a check appears before the **Show leader lines** option. Lines that direct the audience's eyes from the pie slice to the related value will appear when you later drag the label away from the pie.

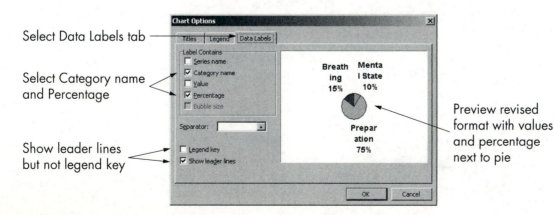

Select Data Labels tab

Select Category name and Percentage

Show leader lines but not legend key

Preview revised format with values and percentage next to pie

## Omit Legend

The legend is displayed by default in the Chart layout, but it is unnecessary when the value is displayed with the pie slice.

17. Click **Chart**, **Chart Options** and select the Legend tab.

18. Click to remove the check in front of the **Show Legend** box.

## Animate the Chart

19. Click **Slide Show**, **Custom Animation**.

20. Add a **Wipe from Top** animation effect or an effect of your choice.

21. Click the down arrow to the right of the chart object in the Custom Animation list.

22. Click **Effect Options** and select the Chart Animation tab.

23. Select **By category**.

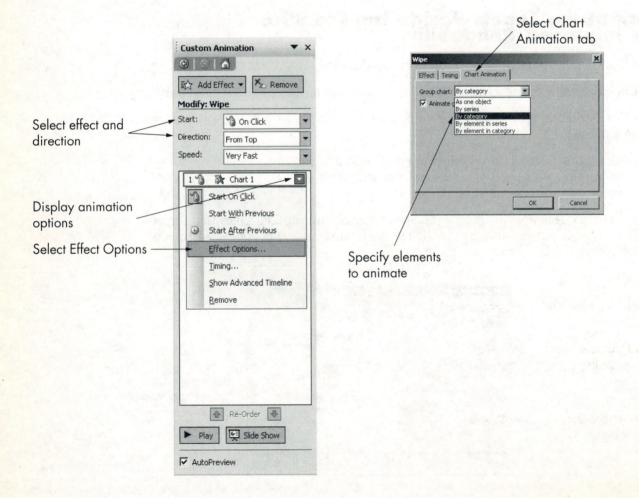

## Enhance the Chart Format

You will make the following changes to enhance the appearance of the default pie chart: (1) increase the size of the chart for improved readability on a projected visual, (2) change the angle of the pie slices to adhere to guidelines for constructing pie charts, (3) change the slice colors for optimal contrast, and (4) explode the largest slice for added emphasis. As you proceed through the menus, take the time to acquaint yourself with other ways pie charts can be modified for added visual appeal.

## Get Acquainted with the Chart Edit Technique

24. Be sure you are in the Chart Mode and not in your slide. Refer to the Technology Tip on page 129 if necessary.

25. Experiment with the use of the right mouse click to identify areas to be formatted.

   a) Move the mouse pointer near the part of the chart you wish to format until a prompt appears identifying the selected section of the chart (e.g., Format _____ Area). For example, pointing slightly below the top border of the chart selects the chart area (the entire chart, including the slices, labels, legend, etc.) and the Format Chart Area prompt appears.

   b) Right-click, click **Format** _____, and input any changes in the dialog box that appears.

## Size the Chart

26. Point near the pie to select the Plot Area. Right-click and click **Format Plot Area**.

27. Hold down the **Shift** key and click on a corner handle; drag the handle to enlarge the chart to occupy the space below the slide title.

28. Point to the border between the sizing handles, click, and drag to balance the pie on the slide.

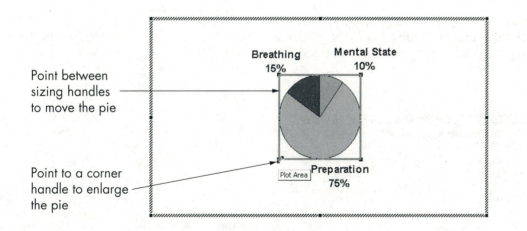

## Delete the Plot Marker

The rectangular border surrounding the Plot Area allows you to easily identify this section of the chart for enlarging the pie size and making other modifications. This useful design tool must be deleted once the pie chart has been built.

29. Select the Plot Area and right-click and click **Format Plot Area**.

30. Click **None** to specify no border around the plot area.

Omit border ⟶

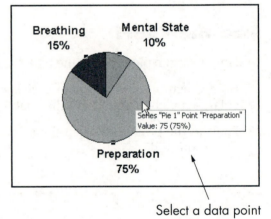

## Change the Angle of the Slices

PowerPoint's default setting must be adjusted to position the largest slice or the slice to be emphasized at the 12 o'clock position, a commonly used guideline for constructing pie charts.

31. Point near one of the pie slices to select a Data Point area. Right-click and click **Format Data Point**.

*Note:* The angle can be changed if all data points are selected.

32. Select the Options tab.

33. Change the angle of the slice by clicking the spin arrow until the largest slice rotates to the 12 o'clock position. Key an exact value if necessary to align perfectly in position.

Select a data point

Select Options tab ⟶

Click to change angle of slice ⟶

Largest slice is at the 12 o'clock position

## Increase the Font Size of Data Labels

34. Select the Data Labels area. Right-click and click **Format Data Labels**.

35. Select the Font tab and change the font size to **20** points to increase the readability of the labels.

## Position the Data Labels and Add Leader Lines

36. Point to one of the data labels and click until the sizing handles appear.

37. Drag the label away from the pie slice to display the leader lines. Position the label for balance and appeal.

38. Reposition the other labels following the same process. Use the model as a guide.

## Add a Fill Behind the Chart

39. Select the chart area. Right-click and click **Format Chart Area**.

40. Select the Patterns tab.

41. Apply the same fill and border effects that you applied to the column chart to ensure consistency throughout the Present file. Reference the instructions for adding a fill effect to the column chart if necessary.

## Change the Slice Colors

You will recolor the pie slices, striving for high contrast with the fill effect behind the pie chart (the chart area) and an appealing color scheme consistent with the column chart in the file Present.

42. Select the largest slice (Preparation). Right-click and click **Format Data Series** (**Preparation**).

43. Select the Patterns tab and select a color used in the column chart that will bring maximum attention to this most important slice in the pie.

Select Patterns tab ──→

Select border style, color, and width

Select fill style, color, and width, as well as effects

## Explode a Slice for Emphasis

44. Select the largest slice (Preparation).

45. While holding down the mouse key, drag to move the slice away from the pie slightly—just enough to provide added emphasis to this important relationship. Use the model as a guide.

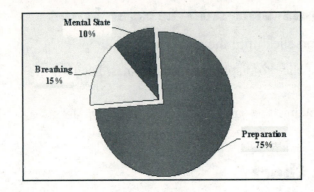

## Enhance the Labels

46. Select the data series. Right-click and click **Format Data Labels**.

47. Select the Patterns tab and apply the same gradient fill that you applied to the legend and y-axis label of the column chart. Omit the border surrounding the labels to eliminate unnecessary clutter.

## ■ ADDING CREATIVE ENHANCEMENTS

Today's audiences (decision makers) look to effective speakers who can assist them in extracting needed information and meaning from the immense quantity of information available as a result of today's information explosion. The fundamental techniques you've already learned—selecting an appropriate chart for the data, using an engaging title that tells the audience exactly what should be learned from the chart, and using a simple design that clarifies key data—are critical to controlling and managing information for your audiences. Depending on your audience's use of the information, you can further simplify the design to emphasize the key idea and to eliminate "chartjunk," decorative distractions that bury relevant data. Business presenters are also incorporating techniques that result in powerful, creative graphics that live up to a new standard of information graphics design set by news programs, *USA Today, Newsweek,* and other professional publications.

### DESIGNER'S POINTER

### More Creative Design Ideas...

Try integrating clip art images outside of charts or overlapping charts to aid the audience in visualizing your key point. Recall the use of the clip art of the nervous speaker beside the table of top fears to highlight the anxiety associated with public speaking. Two side-by-side pie charts showing changes in the age demographics of the workforce could be enhanced by adding simple clip art images of workers of different ages (e.g., younger worker overlapping the pie chart in the earlier time span and an older worker overlapping the pie chart for the present or projected time span). Pictures added as a fill effect inside bars and slices can add appeal as long as the photo selected is not overly distorted. Note other creative enhancements applied to graphics in printed or electronic sources.

## *Eliminating Chartjunk*

*Directions:* Follow the instructions to build the slide as shown.

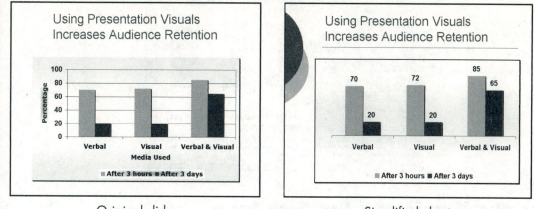

Original slide                    Simplified chart

1. Make a copy of the column chart ("Using Presentation Visuals Increases Audience Retention") that you built earlier in this project. Refer to Project 1 for copying instructions if necessary.

2. Revise the slide title to reflect that percentages are being depicted; this addition is essential because the axes labels are not displayed in the simplified chart.

## Remove Labels

3. Double-click on the chart to edit the chart in Chart Mode.

4. Click **Chart**, **Chart Options** and select the Titles tab.

5. Delete the titles you input previously for the x-axis (Media Used) and the y-axis (Percentage).

## Add Values and Remove Gridlines

6. Click **Chart**, **Chart Options** and select the Data Labels tab.

7. Click **Value** to add the exact value above each bar.

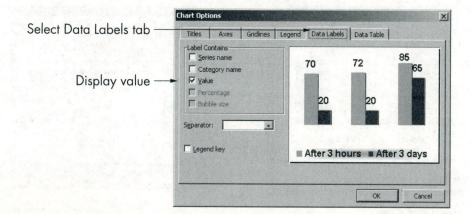

8. Click **Chart**, **Chart Options** and select the Gridlines tab.

9. Deselect the major and minor gridlines for the x- and y-axes.

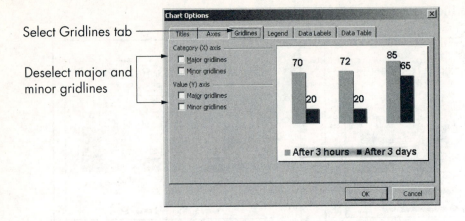

## Remove the Y-axis and the Plot Area

10. Click **Chart**, **Chart Options** and select the Axes tab.

11. Deselect the y-axis by removing the check for **Value (y) axis**.

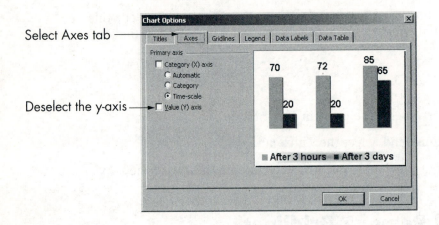

12. Select the Plot Area. Right-click and click **Format Plot Area**.

13. Click **None** as the border.

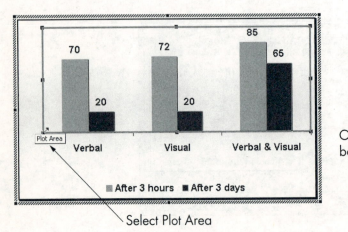

## Adding Eye-catching Fill Effects

*Directions:* Follow the instructions to build the slide as shown.

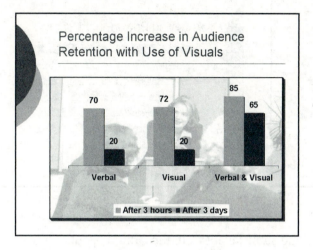

1. Make a copy of the column chart ("Percentage Increase in Audience Retention with Use of Visuals") that you built earlier in this project.

2. Select a digital photograph obtained from Microsoft Clip Organizer, a scanner, or digital camera.

3. Open the photograph file in a photo editing software (e.g., Microsoft Photo Editor or Microsoft Office Picture Manager). Create a transparent effect that will allow easy readability of the chart that will be superimposed over the photograph (e.g., decrease the contrast and increase the brightness, soften the edges, or apply the washout effect). Refer to Project 3 if necessary. Save the changes.

4. Add the photograph in the chart area.

   a) Select the chart area. Right-click and click **Format Chart Area**.

   b) Select the Patterns tab and click **Fill Effects**, **Picture**.

   c) Browse to insert your photograph.

# ■ INSERTING SLIDE TRANSITIONS

Add the **Wipe from Left** slide transition to the slides created in this project. Refer to Project 2 if necessary.

# ■ REINFORCEMENT ACTIVITIES

Add the following slides for added reinforcement of the PowerPoint features you learned in this project. Position the slides as shown in the table on pages 213–214.

# Activity 1

Build the slide containing two layers shown in the model.

Layer 1

Layer 2

1. Create a new slide using the Title and Table layout from the Other Layouts category.

2. Key and format the table and source note as shown. To separate the rows, point to a row border, select, and drag in any direction when the four-head arrow appears. Adjust until the spacing is equal between all rows.

*Hint:* Editing a copy of the slide "Public Speaking Tops List of People's Great Fears" would save you time.

3. Select a relevant image to reinforce the concept that misuse of PowerPoint is annoying (search "annoying" in Microsoft Clip Organizer).

4. Add an annoying sound effect. Hide or position the sound icon off the screen to play automatically after the clip art.

5. Animate the slide:

   **First:** Clip art: Pinwheel (or other dramatic effect) → Start on Click → Fast speed → Hide on Next Mouse Click.

   **Second:** Sound effect → After Previous.

   **Third:** Table: Split, Vertical Out → Start on Click → Fast speed.

   **Fourth:** Source note: Dissolve → Start After Previous with .2 second delay → Fast speed.

# Activity 2

Prepare a line chart showing earnings per share for the past 5 years for a company of your choice. Obtain the data from either a printed or online copy of the company's annual report. Provide an engaging title that interprets the data depicted in the chart and add animation to emphasize the most important data.

# Activity 3

Select a chart from a corporate annual report or other leading publication and evaluate its effectiveness in clarifying or reinforcing major points (e.g., appropriate chart type; accurate labeling; engaging title that reveals key; simple, uncluttered design;

honest representation of the data). Build the chart incorporating your suggestions for improvement. Animate to emphasize the most important data. Be prepared to discuss your improvements with your instructor or the class.

## Activity 4

Build a chart that presents compelling data to support a key point in a presentation you are currently developing. Alternatively, depict key data related to a timely issue (e.g., legal and ethical implications of technology; e-commerce; work/family balance; computer usage policies, including Internet filtering; disaster recovery planning; bullying in the workplace). Select a chart type that will convey the data in the most effective manner. Refer to the Designer's Pointer related to chart types on page 127 if necessary. Strive for a simple, uncluttered design that presents the data clearly and honestly. Provide an engaging title that interprets the data depicted in the chart and add animation to emphasize the most important data.

## Slide Order

Sequence slides in the file Present according to the table on pages 213–214. Print and submit as directed by your instructor.

# Developing Useful Speaker's Notes and Professional Audience Handouts

## LEARNING OBJECTIVES

- Create speaker's notes designed to aid a speaker during delivery.

- Enhance the professional appearance of handouts printed using the PowerPoint print option by adding identification information in the header and footer positions.

- Create professional audience handouts that extend the presentation and enhance the credibility of the speaker using the Master Handout and export to Microsoft Word features.

## ■ CONSTRUCTING USEFUL SPEAKER'S NOTES PAGES

PowerPoint can be used to construct useful notes pages that aid the speaker in delivering a smooth, professional presentation. Two techniques are available for creating notes pages in PowerPoint: (1) adding speaker notes while running the presentation for practice purposes and (2) inserting notes directly in the Notes pane of the Normal view.

### Adding Speaker's Notes While Rehearsing

*Directions:* Follow the instructions to create speaker's notes for one slide in the file Present. Print and submit a copy to your instructor if directed.

1. Begin running the file Present in Slide Show view as if you were rehearsing your presentation.

2. Right-click when you have advanced to the "Effective Speakers" slide, where you will stop rehearsing to input your notes—smooth transitions, trigger statements, and so on.

3. Click **Speaker's Notes** from the menu.

4. Key the text shown in the illustration in the Speaker Notes dialog box.

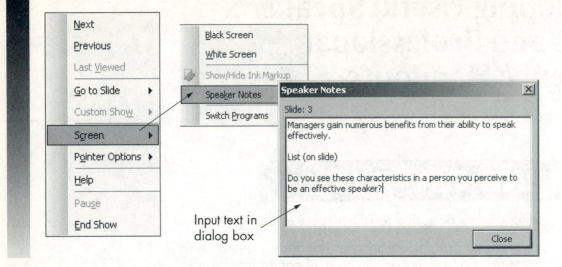

Input text in dialog box

## Edit Notes in the Notes Pane

5. Press the **Esc** key and display Slide 2 in the Normal view. The text you keyed while running the presentation in the Slide Show view appears in the Notes pane as shown in the following illustration.

6. Select all the text in the placeholder by holding **Ctrl** and pressing **A** (**Ctrl+A**).

7. Increase the font size to at least 14 points so that the notes can be read easily in a darkened room (adjust the size of the print to a speaker's needs for a specific presentation).

---

## PRESENTER'S STRATEGY

### Developing Useful Notes Pages

Surprisingly, speakers frequently rely on notes less than they should. Under speaking pressure, speakers panic at the sight of dense, poorly prepared notes and thus attempt to deliver the presentation without notes, or they read a complete script. Preparing useful speaker's notes will reduce speaker anxiety and enhance a speaker's ability to deliver the presentation extemporaneously. Follow these guidelines for developing the content and format of useful speaker's notes to support your next presentation:

### Content

Use trigger statements that prompt you to remember the next point and highlight the logical flow of the slide. Include additional detail for content that demands precision and accuracy, for example, the introduction and conclusion, statistics, quotations, or a joke or humorous story with a punch line.

### Format

Develop an uncluttered, easy-to-read design for the notes page following these suggestions:

• Allow plenty of white space and a uniform structure (e.g., bulleted list, outline, headings).

• Print in a large, easy-to-read font.

• Print on full-size pages that can be turned without distraction and number all pages so that they can be reordered quickly if they are dropped or mishandled.

• Keep notes neat, with no last-minute confusing revisions, such as arrows denoting major reordering of ideas that likely wouldn't be understood under the pressure of speaking.

8. Revise the notes if necessary. Add emphasis where needed (e.g., boldface, bulleted lists).

9. Continue to the next section.

Drag borders between panes for more space in Notes pane

Click in Notes pane to edit notes

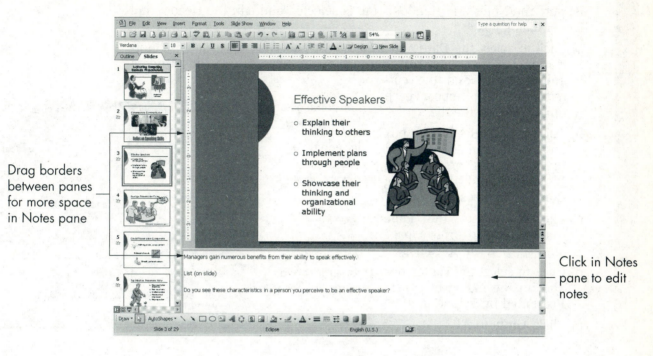

## Adding Speaker's Notes in the Notes Pane

*Directions:* Create speaker's notes for one slide in the file Present following the guidelines for writing and formatting useful speaker's notes provided in the Presenter's Strategy on page 152. Print a copy to submit to your instructor if directed.

1. Display a slide of your choice in Normal view and set the zoom at 66% so that the text can be read easily.

2. Key the text—a few trigger statements to prompt your thoughts and remind you of the logical flow of the discussion for this slide.

3. Select all the text in the placeholder by holding **Ctrl** and pressing **A** (**Ctrl+A**).

4. Increase the font size to at least 14 points so that the notes can be read easily in a darkened room (adjust the size to fit a speaker's needs for a specific presentation).

5. Add emphasis where needed (e.g., boldface, bulleted lists).

6. Continue to the next section.

## Adding a Header and a Footer to the Notes Pages

Add informative headers and footers to notes pages to identify them clearly for later use. Adding page numbers is especially helpful for keeping pages ordered correctly.

*Directions:* Add a header and a footer to the notes pages of the file Present. Print a copy to present to your instructor as directed.

1. Click **View**, **Header and Footer**.

2. Be sure the Notes and Handouts tab is selected and edit the Header and Footer dialog box:

   a) Click to select the **Date and time** box if you wish to print this information on each slide. Key the date in the dialog box. Click **Update automatically** and the current date will appear each time you open the file.

   b) Click to select the **Header** box and, in the dialog box, input the title of the presentation: **Planning and Delivering Compelling Presentations**.

   c) Click to select the **Page number** box to print a page number on each notes page.

   d) Click to select the **Footer** box and, in the dialog box, key: **Presented by** *Your Name*.

   e) Click **Apply to All**.

Select Notes and Handouts tab

Include date and update automatically

Add header and footer text and page number

## Print the Notes Page for Selected Slides

3. Click **File**, **Print** and edit the Print dialog box:

   a) Select **Slides** in the Print range box, then input the number of the slide you wish to print.

   b) Select **Notes Pages** in the Print what box.

   c) Click **OK**.

Select slides to be printed

Specify Notes Pages format

# ■ CREATING PROFESSIONAL AUDIENCE HANDOUTS

Audience handouts must reflect the same degree of professionalism as the slide show and the speaker's delivery. Create professional handouts that increase a speaker's credibility by editing the Handout Master and exporting presentation slides to Microsoft Word for more elaborate formatting.

## PRESENTER'S STRATEGY

### Extending a Presentation with Audience Handouts

The appropriate time for distributing handouts depends on the presentation's purpose. If you want the audience to take notes, you will need to distribute a handout early, but recognize that the audience's attention will be split between reading the handout and listening to you. Although taking notes helps retain the audience's attention, providing too much detail actually discourages note taking. Thus, be selective in the slides included in the handout and the amount of detail included on the slide. Distributing handouts at the end of the presentation or providing access to electronic handouts (e-handouts) is useful for providing supplementary information that will extend the usefulness of the presentation.

Regardless of the distribution time, an appealing, highly professional handout provides an opportunity to increase your credibility and to provide phone numbers, Web addresses, and other contact information. This information serves as a powerful advertisement for a presenter and his or her company.

If you are generating the handout from a PowerPoint slide show, simply edit the Master Handout to include an appealing header and footer as shown in the illustration. Then, choose the print format that meets your presentation need (two, three, or six slides to a page).

Handout generated in PowerPoint with appealing identification and slides printed six to page.

Handout generated in PowerPoint printed three to a page. Limited slide content encourages note taking.

## *Editing the Handout Master*

*Directions:* Follow the instructions to change the format of the handout master for the file Present. Print a copy to present to your instructor if directed.

1. Click **View**, **Master**, **Handout Master**. You will add identification information to the four placeholders on the handout master (shown in the following illustrations).

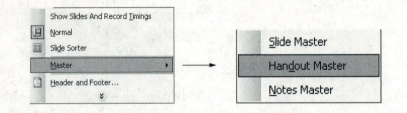

2. Edit the Header placeholder:

   a) Click in the Header placeholder and input the title of the presentation: **Planning and Delivering Compelling Presentations**.

   b) Select a font face of your choice and set the font size to 9 points and boldface.

   c) Resize the placeholder so that the text appears on one line.

3. Edit the Date placeholder:

   a) Click in the date area.

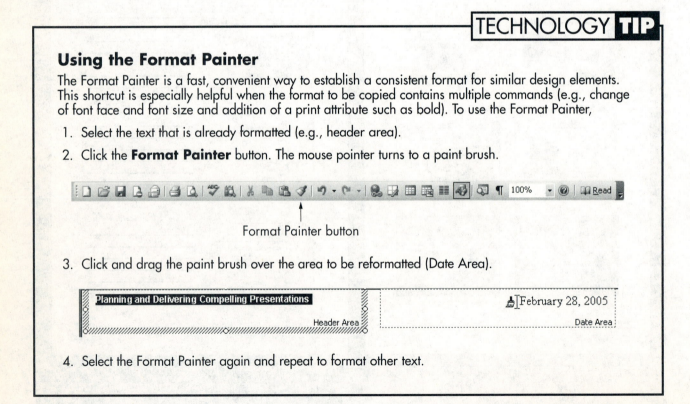

## TECHNOLOGY TIP

### Using the Format Painter

The Format Painter is a fast, convenient way to establish a consistent format for similar design elements. This shortcut is especially helpful when the format to be copied contains multiple commands (e.g., change of font face and font size and addition of a print attribute such as bold). To use the Format Painter,

1. Select the text that is already formatted (e.g., header area).

2. Click the **Format Painter** button. The mouse pointer turns to a paint brush.

Format Painter button

3. Click and drag the paint brush over the area to be reformatted (Date Area).

Planning and Delivering Compelling Presentations                    February 28, 2005

Header Area                                                         Date Area

4. Select the Format Painter again and repeat to format other text.

b) Highlight the text that appears in the placeholder (Date/Time) and key the date. Format it to match the text in the other placeholders using the shortcut illustrated in the Technology Tip on page 156.

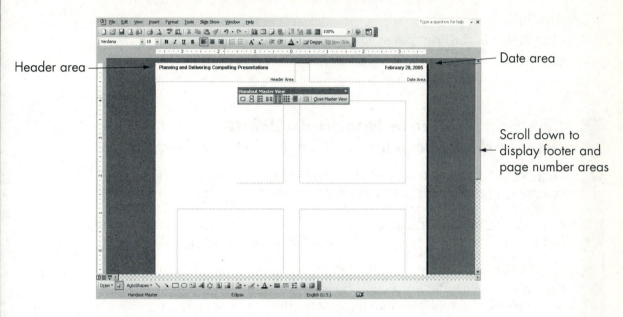

Header area

Date area

Scroll down to display footer and page number areas

4. Edit the Footer placeholder:

a) Click in the Footer placeholder and input **Prepared by** *Your Name*.

b) Press **Enter** and key the title of the course you are taking that requires you to complete this presentation.

c) Format the text to match the text in the other placeholders using the shortcut illustrated in the Technology Tip on page 156.

5. Edit the Page Number placeholder:

a) Click in the Page Number placeholder.

b) Input the word **Page** before the text that appears in the placeholder (#). Format the word *Page* and # to match the text in the other placeholders using the shortcut illustrated in the Technology Tip on page 156.

Scroll up to display header and date areas

Footer area

Page number area

6. Click **Close Master View** to return to either the Normal or Slide Sorter view.

## Print Handouts for Slides 1–3

7. Click **File**, **Print**.

8. Edit the Print dialog box:

   a) Select **Slides** in the Print range box and input **1-3**.

   b) Select **Handouts** in the Print what box and select **3 per page**.

9. Click **OK**.

## Creating Audience Handouts Using the Send-to-Microsoft Office Word Feature

Editing the Handout Master enhances the appeal of slides created using the PowerPoint print option. Exporting slides to Microsoft Office Word provides additional template layouts as well as the power of Microsoft Office Word to create a custom format that works best for your presentation. Refer to the Designer's Pointer on page 160 for additional advice on preparing these custom handouts.

*Directions:* Follow the instructions to export the presentation file Present to Microsoft Office Word and then input notes in the available space.

1. Click the **Color/Grayscale** button on the Standard toolbar and select the **Pure Black and White** button to convert the slides to black and white. Omit this step if you intend to print using a color printer.

Color/Grayscale

Color

Grayscale

Select Pure Black and White → Pure Black and White

2. Click **File**, **Send to**, **Microsoft Office Word**.

| | | |
|---|---|---|
| New... | Ctrl+N | |
| Open... | Ctrl+O | |
| Close | | |
| Save | Ctrl+S | |
| Save As... | | |
| Save as Web Page... | | |
| File Search... | | |
| Permission | ▶ | |
| Package for CD... | | |
| Web Page Preview | | |
| Page Setup... | | |
| Print Preview | | |
| Print... | Ctrl+P | |
| Send To | ▶ | |
| Properties | | |

Mail Recipient (for Review)...
Mail Recipient (as Attachment)...
Exchange Folder...
Online Meeting Participant
Recipient using Internet Fax Service...
Microsoft Office Word...

3. Take a moment to study the five available layouts: Notes next to slides, Blank lines next to slides, Notes below slides, Blank lines below slides, and Outline only. Each of these formats can be accomplished through the PowerPoint print option, except for adding "Notes next to slides" and printing "Blank lines below slides."

4. Select **Notes next to slides**. The Notes pane will appear in a notes column to the right of the slide thumbnail.

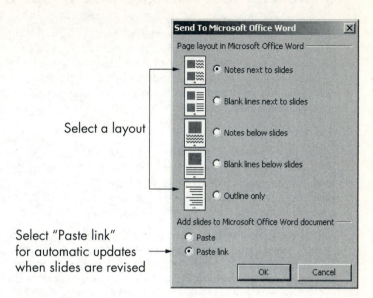

Select a layout

Select "Paste link" for automatic updates when slides are revised

*Note:* If you intend to revise and reuse this PowerPoint file and hand-out for a later presentation, click **Paste link**. Any updates to the PowerPoint file will be reflected in the Word file automatically.

5. Wait as your presentation is exported to Microsoft Office Word and format-ted into a three-column table. The notes you keyed in a previous activity will appear beside two slides. Refer to the Designer's Pointer on page 160 for tips on designing an appealing format for the notes appearing to the right of your slide thumbnails.

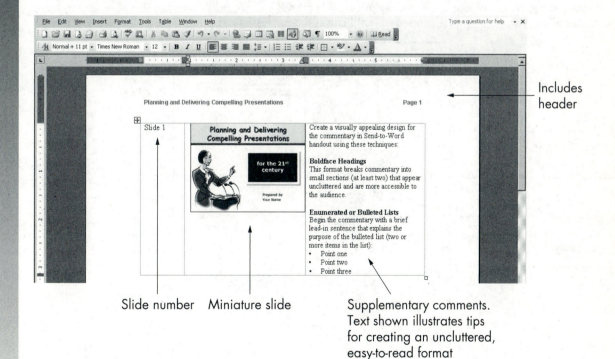

Slide number    Miniature slide

Includes header

Supplementary comments. Text shown illustrates tips for creating an uncluttered, easy-to-read format

6. Save this Microsoft Office Word document as **Present.doc**. Note that the file size is extremely large because of the graphic intensity of the content.

## Impressing Your Audience with a Superb "Take Home" Packet

Choosing the "Notes next to slides" Send-to-Microsoft Office Word format creates a highly professional handout. The handy column inserted automatically to the right of each slide can be used for adding supplementary notes related to the slide content or questions for audience consideration. The "take home package" is especially useful for an audience who will be responsible for the material covered in the presentation, such as seminar participants in required training programs. The commentary also will aid persons who cannot attend the presentation but who are responsible for or simply interested in the material. Follow these guidelines for developing content and format:

### Content

Include in a formal audience handout only the slides you anticipate the audience will need for later reference. For example, exclude dramatic opening or closing slides used to capture the audience's attention and any graphic-intensive slides that may not have meaning outside the presentation. By evaluating the usefulness of each slide carefully, you likely can avoid printing a lone slide on the final handout page and thus minimize reproduction and distribution costs.

When writing commentary to accompany your slides, avoid repeating information already shown on the slide. Instead include brief, precise statements that will help the audience immediately grasp the relevance of the slide and succinctly summarize further discussion and examples that are provided during the presentation but not included on the slide. A model for effective commentary is illustrated below.

### Format

Create a visually appealing format that will entice the audience to read rather than discard your handout. Use the design to help the audience quickly comprehend your content and highlight important information for maximum attention. Because of their brevity, the statements in the following model, keyed in paragraph format in a 10- or 11-point font, are visually appealing. For longer commentary that can appear cluttered and unorganized, apply the following visual enhancements:

- Add headings to partition the commentary into short sections the audience can access more easily.

- Use enumerated or bulleted lists to bring greater impact to items in a series. A brief lead-in sentence that clarifies the purpose of the bulleted list will help the audience find immediate meaning.

These formatting techniques are illustrated on page 159. Of course, add an appealing header and footer that provides valuable contact information and raises the professional appearance of the document.

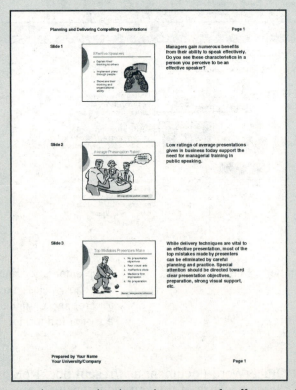

Take home packet created with Send-to-Microsoft Office Word feature

## Delete Unneeded Slides

7. Select the row containing the slide "A Speech Is a Gift" (or a slide of your choice) by clicking in the first column and dragging across to highlight the entire column.

8. Click **Table**, **Delete** and select **Rows**. The row is deleted and the other slides move up to fill the space. Alternatively, highlight the row, right-click, and click **Delete Cells**, **Delete entire row**.

9. Repeat the procedure to delete any other slides you believe should not be included in a formal handout.

## Inputting Supplementary Notes in the Send-to-Microsoft Office Word Handout

*Directions:* Follow the instructions to input supplementary notes to one slide.

1. Click in the Notes column (third column) to the right of a slide of your choice. Key notes that will allow an audience member unable to attend your presentation to grasp the intended meaning of the slide. Follow the format tips described in the Designer's Pointer on page 160 and shown in the illustration on page 159 to avoid dense, unappealing text.

2. Scroll to display the text for the two slides you added earlier. Change the format to match the format of the notes you input directly in the Word document if necessary.

3. Continue to the next section to complete the Send-to-Microsoft Office Word handout.

## Adding a Header and a Footer to a Send-to-Microsoft Office Word Handout

*Directions:* Follow the instructions to add a header and a footer to the presentation Present. Print a copy to present to your instructor if directed.

## Insert a Header

1. Click **View**, **Header and Footer**.

2. Click in the Header placeholder and input the title of the presentation: **Planning and Delivering Compelling Presentations**.

3. Press **Tab** until the cursor reaches the end of the placeholder. Key the text **Page** and space once.

4. Click **Insert Page Number** in the Header and Footer dialog box. The number *1* appears to the right of the word *Page*. This number will change as you move through the pages of the document. You can change the beginning page number to a value other than 1 by clicking the **Format Page Number** button.

5. Highlight all text in the Header placeholder. Format with a font face of your choice, a font size of 9 points, and boldface.

6. Click **Switch between Header and Footer** to move to the Footer placeholder at the bottom of the page.

Header

**Planning and Delivering Compelling Presentations**                                        **Page 1**

**Header and Footer**
Insert AutoText ▾

Insert Page     Format Page     Switch between
Number          Number          Header and Footer

## Insert a Footer

7. Click in the Footer placeholder and input the text: **Prepared by** *your name*.

8. Press **Enter** and key the text: *Name of your university/company*.

9. Press the **Tab** key until the cursor reaches the end of the placeholder. Key the current date.

10. Highlight all text in the Footer placeholder and format it to match the header text using the shortcut detailed in the Technology Tip on page 156.

Exit header and
footer box

**Header and Footer**
Insert AutoText ▾                                                           Close

Footer

**Prepared by Your Name**                                           **February 22, 2005**
**Your University/Company**

Key footer text

11. Click **Close** to exit the header and footer area and return to the document.

## Print the Send-to-Microsoft Office Word Handout

12. Click **File**, **Print** and then click **OK**.

## ■ REINFORCEMENT ACTIVITIES

Complete the following activities for added reinforcement of the PowerPoint features you learned in this project.

# Activity 1

Create the speaker's notes for a presentation you are currently developing using both techniques presented in this project: (1) adding notes as you complete an actual dry run of your presentation or (2) inserting notes in the Notes pane. Be prepared to share with your instructor your opinion of the specific usefulness of each method. Print the notes pages to submit to your instructor.

# Activity 2

Edit the Handout Master for a presentation you are currently developing to include complete identification of the presentation (title of presentation, date, preparer, and page number). Print the slides six to a page to submit to your instructor.

# Activity 3

Create a Send-to-Microsoft Office Word handout for a presentation you are currently developing. To the right of each slide, add precise commentary that will increase the usefulness of the handout following the presentation. Develop a visually appealing format for the commentary and include complete identification for the presentation in a header/footer. Print the file to submit to your instructor.

# Slide Order

Print and submit as directed by your instructor.

# Designing an Interactive Presentation

## LEARNING OBJECTIVES

- Hide a slide that can be accessed conveniently should the information be needed during a presentation.

- Create hyperlinks to the Internet and to slides within a presentation using the Mouse Click and Mouse Over techniques.

- Create a series of hyperlinks accessed from a summary slide to provide increased flexibility over the sequence in which the slides are displayed.

- Link a PowerPoint chart to a Microsoft Excel notebook to update data in the chart automatically when the notebook file is revised.

## ADDING INTERACTIVITY TO SLIDES

Experienced speakers recognize the importance of adapting a presentation in response to feedback received from an audience during an actual presentation. Hidden slides and hyperlinks build flexibility and convenience into an electronic presentation by allowing the speaker to move through a presentation in sequences other than the typical linear pattern (i.e., from the first slide to the last) and to launch other applications automatically and inconspicuously (e.g., a notebook file or an Internet browser).

### Hiding a Slide

A hidden slide allows you to customize a slide show for a particular audience. You simply mark slides you won't project unless the information on the slide is needed during a presentation. For example, you may include a hidden slide including detailed data in case an audience member asks for an in-depth explanation of this particular point.

*Directions:* Follow the instructions to hide specific slides and to project the hidden slides during the presentation.

1. Display the file Present in the Slide Sorter view.

## Hide a Slide

2. Select two slides of your choice and click the **Hide Slide** button on the Slide Sorter toolbar. A diagonal line appears over the slide number to indicate the slide is hidden.

3. Select the slide that immediately precedes the hidden slide.

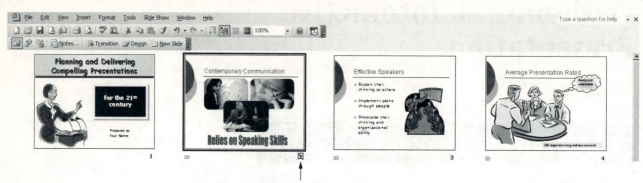

Denotes hidden slide

4. Click the **Slide Show View** button to begin running the presentation.

5. Click the mouse once. Note that the slide following the hidden slide is displayed, bypassing the hidden slide.

## View a Hidden Slide

6. Select the slide that immediately precedes the hidden slide.

7. Click the **Slide Show View** button to begin running the presentation.

8. Press the letter **H** to advance to the hidden slide.

### PRESENTER'S STRATEGY

#### Viewing a Hidden Slide

Another way to view a hidden slide is to right-click and click **Go, Slide Navigator**. The slide number of a hidden slide is enclosed in parentheses in the list of titles. Using the keyboard command presented in the previous activity (Steps 6–8) is preferable because of the seamless delivery. The effort spent completing these mouse clicks and the display of several unattractive drop-down menus draw attention away from the speaker and toward the technology.

| Next |
| --- |
| Previous |
| Last Viewed |
| Go to Slide ▶ |
| Custom Show ▶ |
| Screen ▶ |
| Pointer Options ▶ |
| Help |
| Pause |
| End Show |

| ✓ | 1 Slide 1 |
| --- | --- |
| | (2) Contemporary Communication |
| | 3 Effective Speakers |
| | 4 Average Presentation Rated |
| | 5 Crucial Presentation Components |
| | 6 Top Mistakes Presenters Make |
| | 7 Meeting the Demands of Today's |
| | 8 Adept Speakers Must . . . |
| | 9 Adapting Speaking Style to Toda |

Parentheses denote
a hidden slide

## Unhide a Slide

9. Select the hidden slide in the Slide Sorter view.

10. Click the **Hide Slide** button on the Slide Sorter toolbar (or click **Slide Show, Hide**). The diagonal line over the slide number is removed. Alternatively, right-click the **Slide** icon in the Outline pane and click **Hide Slide**.

# CREATING HYPERLINKS

A *hyperlink* is an area of the screen the speaker clicks to automatically advance the slide show to a variety of locations. A hyperlink can be created from any object on the slide—text, clip art, photograph, AutoShape, table, graph, and so on. In this project you will create hyperlinks to (1) access a Web site, (2) move to a specific slide within a presentation, and (3) open a Microsoft Excel notebook. Hyperlinks can also be added to move to a different PowerPoint presentation, other files, and numerous other locations.

## Adding a Hyperlink to a Web Site

*Directions:* Follow the instructions to create a hyperlink to a Web site.

## Insert Hyperlink

1. Display the "Top Mistakes Presenters Make" slide in Normal view.

2. Highlight the source note text: **http://www.presentersonline.com**.

3. Click **Insert, Hyperlink**.

4. Input the URL address for the source **http://www.presentersonline.com**. The text you highlighted in Step 2 is now displayed on the slide in a different color—the color of the hyperlink before it is accessed.

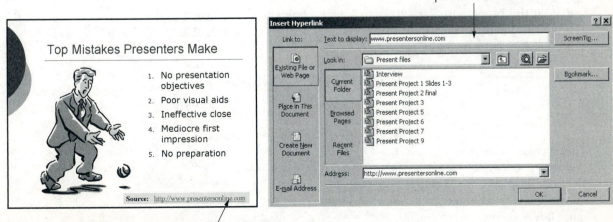

Input URL address

Add hyperlink to source note

## Access the Hyperlink to Verify Accuracy

5. Display the slide in Slide Show view.

6. Move the mouse over the hyperlinked text (words accented in a different color) until the hand pointer appears.

7. Click the text to access the hyperlink, which opens the default Internet browser and connects to the appropriate Web site.

8. Click the **Exit** or **Minimize** button in the Internet browser to return to the presentation still running in Slide Show view.

Source:    http://www.presentersonline.com

Click the hyperlink when
the hand pointer appears

Top Mistakes Presenters Make

1. No presentation objectives
2. Poor visual aids
3. Ineffective close
4. Mediocre first impression
5. No preparation

Source:  http://www.presentersonline.com

## *Editing the Color Scheme for the Hyperlink*

You will need to specify colors for the hyperlink before and after it has been accessed. Select colors with high contrast to the background to ensure that the audience can read the text. Review editing color schemes in Project 4 if necessary.

9. Click **Format**, **Slide Design**.

10. Click **Color Schemes** and **Edit Color Schemes**.

11. Change the color of the hyperlink before it is accessed.

    a) Select the color thumbnail for **Accent and hyperlink**.

    b) Click **Change Color** and select a color from the Standard or Custom tab.

12. Repeat the process in Steps 9–11 to select a color for the **Accent and followed hyperlink** color thumbnail, which controls the color of hyperlink after it has been accessed.

Select color for hyperlink
before it is accessed

Select color for hyperlink
after it is accessed

**Edit Color Scheme**

Standard | Custom

Scheme colors

Background
Text and lines
Shadows
Title text
Fills
Accent
Accent and hyperlink
Accent and followed hyperlink

Change Color...

Add As Standard Scheme

Apply
Cancel
Preview

Title of Slide
• Bullet text

## *Hyperlinking Using the Mouse Over Technique*

*Directions:* Follow the instructions to create a hyperlink to a specific slide that you will access by moving the mouse over the hyperlinked object rather than pointing to the object and clicking the mouse.

## Insert a Hyperlink

Adapting Speaking Style
to Today's Fast Pace

- Provide useful information quickly
- Direct to useful resources
- Include more visuals, ample "entertainment," and participation
- Connect experiences and feelings to the topic

1. Display the "Adapting Speaking Style to Today's Fast Pace" slide in Normal view.

2. Select the photograph and click **Slide Show**, **Action Settings**.

3. Select the Mouse Over tab. Note that the mouse click is the default method for accessing a hyperlink.

4. Click the **Hyperlink to** option.

5. Click the list arrow and select **Next Slide**.

## Access the Hyperlink

6. Display the slide in Slide Show view.

7. Move the mouse across the photo without clicking, and the slide advances to the next slide ("Today's Messages Are").

## *Creating Hyperlinks on a Summary Slide*

Hyperlink buttons created with AutoShapes create a subtle, virtually transparent design. Attention remains directed toward the speaker and the message—unlike with the obvious underlined hyperlinks illustrated in the original slide. Hyperlink buttons are dynamic and appealing, and the audience is unaware of the presence of a hyperlink until the speaker accesses it to jump to specific slides in the file Present. You will create (1) a hyperlink from each button to a specific slide in the presentation and (2) return hyperlinks to jump back to the summary slide, where you can draw attention to the summary list before transitioning into the discussion of the next hyperlinked point.

Types of Presentation Visuals

o Multimedia

o Still projection options

o Boards and flipcharts

o Hard copy visuals

Original summary slide
with hyperlinked text

Types of Presentation Visuals

| Multimedia | Still projection options |
| Boards and flipcharts | Hard copy visuals |

Enhanced summary slide
with hyperlinked buttons

Multimedia

**Advantages**
o Meet audience expectations of visual standards
o Enhance professionalism and credibility of a speaker
o Provide special effects to enhance retention, appeal, flexibility, and reuse

**Disadvantages**
o Can lead to poor delivery
o Require highly developed skills
o Can be expensive
o Pose technology failure and cross-portability challenges

*Recommendation*
Used for maximum formal presentations

Still Projection Options

**Advantages**
o Are simple to prepare and use
o Allow versatile use: prepare beforehand or as you speak
o Are inexpensive and readily available

**Disadvantages**
o Are not easily updated
o Pose potential for equipment failure
o Are cumbersome to use
o Must have a special detailed needs and markers unless using a document camera

*Recommendation*
Used for a dark room or as a stop mid-stream

Boards and Flipcharts

**Advantages**
o Encourage discussion because of informality
o Are easy to use
o Are inexpensive if traditional units are used

**Disadvantages**
o Are cumbersome to transport; can be messy
o Require turning back to audience
o Are not reusable, provide no hard copy, and must be developed on site if traditional units are used

*Recommendation*
Used for small and informal presentations

Hard Copy Visuals

**Advantages**
o Provide detailed information that audience can examine closely
o Extend a presentation by providing additional resources for later use
o Are a reference tool

**Disadvantages**
o Divert audience's attention from the speaker
o Can be expensive

*Recommendation*
Used when ideas' analysis is needed

1. Display the "Types of Presentation Visuals" slide in Normal view.

2. Delete the bulleted list placeholder.

# Create a Master Design for the Hyperlink Buttons

3. Click **AutoShapes**, **Basic Shapes**, **Bevel**.

4. Hold the left mouse button and drag to draw the beveled button.

5. Release the mouse and key the text describing the first hyperlink in the text box in front of the button **Multimedia**.

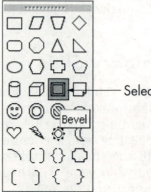

Select bevel

Bevel

**TECHNOLOGY TIP**

## Editing AutoShapes the Easy Way

A shortcut for editing an AutoShape is to right-click and click **Format**, **AutoShape**. The tabs allow you to conveniently edit (1) colors and lines, (2) size, and (3) position. Specific techniques that can be applied from these menus follow:

## Size Tab

1. Input an exact dimension and then compare these values with other AutoShapes to ensure consistency.

2. Input a percentage in the scale section. Click **Lock aspect ratio** to change the height and width proportionally.

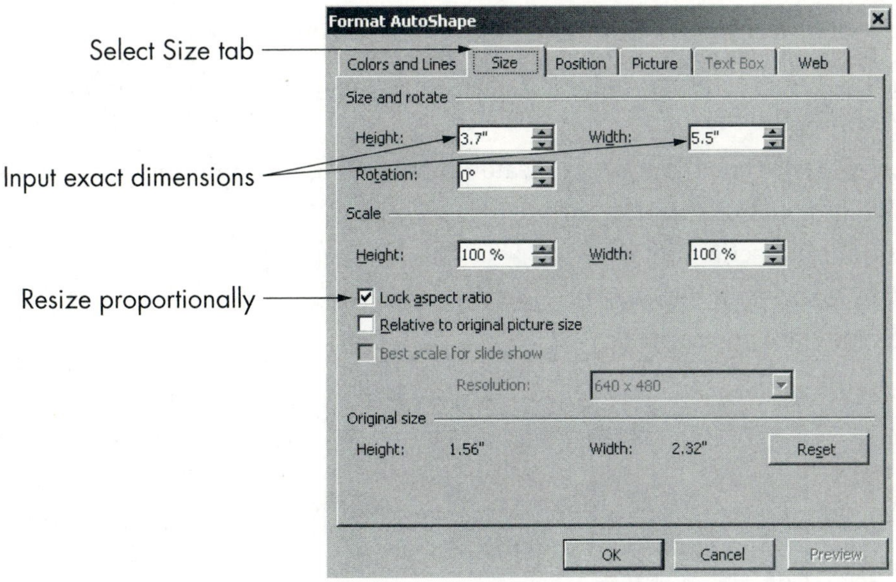

Select Size tab ——

Input exact dimensions ——

Resize proportionally ——

**Format AutoShape**

| Colors and Lines | Size | Position | Picture | Text Box | Web |

Size and rotate

Height: 3.7"    Width: 5.5"

Rotation: 0°

Scale

Height: 100 %    Width: 100 %

☑ Lock aspect ratio
☐ Relative to original picture size
☐ Best scale for slide show

Resolution: 640 x 480

Original size

Height:    1.56"        Width:    2.32"        Reset

OK    Cancel    Preview

## Position Tab

Increase or decrease the horizontal or vertical placement to align an object in a precise location.

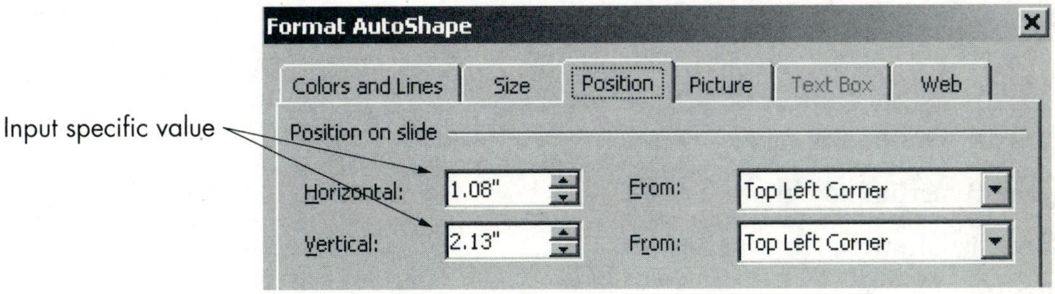

Input specific value ——

**Format AutoShape**

| Colors and Lines | Size | Position | Picture | Text Box | Web |

Position on slide

Horizontal: 1.08"    From: Top Left Corner

Vertical: 2.13"    From: Top Left Corner

6. Format the button and the text, allowing space for the four buttons to appear attractively on the slide as shown in the model.

   a) Center the text in the button. (Click **Format**, **AutoShape**. Select the Text Box tab and select "Middle Centered" as the text anchor point.)

   b) Select an appealing font face and size that fits in the button but is large enough to be read easily. Add effects such as boldface or a shadow to create the appearance of your choice.

## Create the Remaining Buttons Using the Copy Feature to Ensure Consistency

7. Select the completed button and hold down the **Ctrl** key as you drag the button. An icon with a plus sign appears as you drag the slide, indicating an object is being moved.

8. Release the mouse to drop the button in a new location on the slide.

9. Repeat Steps 7–8 to create two additional buttons. Position the four buttons attractively on the slide.

10. Edit the text in each copied button to create the following four buttons:

    • **Top left:** Multimedia (already keyed).

    • **Top right:** Still projection options.

    • **Bottom left:** Boards and flipcharts.

    • **Bottom right:** Hard copy visuals.

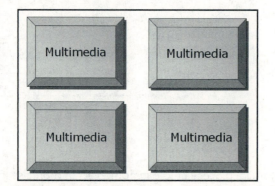

## Insert the Hyperlinks

11. Click to select the first button (**Multimedia**).

12. Click **Slide Show**, **Action Settings**.

13. Be sure the Mouse Click tab is selected.

14. Click the **Hyperlink to** option.

15. Click the list arrow and select **Slide**.

16. Scroll down and select the "Multimedia" slide as the destination of the hyperlink—the slide where the hyperlink will jump when it is accessed.

17. Repeat Steps 12–16 to insert the hyperlinks from each of the other three buttons on the summary slide to its related slide describing the advantages and disadvantages of each visual type.

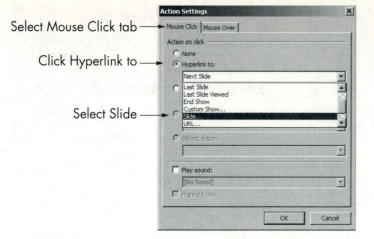

## Create the Return Hyperlinks

18. Display the "Multimedia" slide in Slide view.

19. Click **Slide Show**, **Action Buttons** (or click **AutoShapes**, **Action Buttons**).

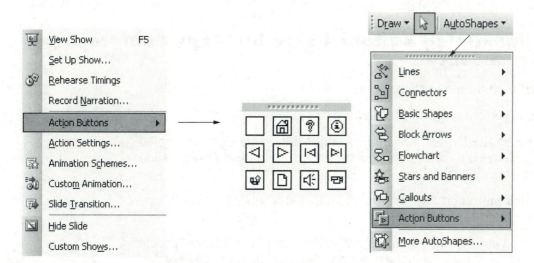

20. Note the variety of return buttons available. You can use ready-made action buttons that depict commonly understood symbols (arrows that refer to next, previous, first, and last slides; information, help; sound; and movies) or create a custom button using your own text or graphics.

21. Select the return arrow [ ∪ ] or create a custom button [ Menu ] that will remind you to go back to the summary slide "Types of Presentation Visuals."

22. Drag to draw the button and release the mouse to display the Action Settings dialog box.

23. Be sure the Mouse Click tab is selected.

24. Click the **Hyperlink to** option.

25. Click the list arrow and select **Slide**.

26. Scroll down and select the "Types of Presentation Visuals" slide as the destination of the hyperlink—the slide where the hyperlink will jump when it is accessed.

Select Mouse Click tab ⟶

Click Hyperlink to ⟶

Select Slide ⟶

Select slide

## Edit the AutoShape (the Button)

27. Select a fill color, line color, and line style. Consider using a design similar to the button on the summary slide as a reminder of the destination.

28. Size the button to achieve a subtle look that's large enough to click conveniently while running the presentation.

## Create the Remaining Buttons Using the Copy Feature to Ensure Consistency

29. Select the hyperlink button and click **Copy**.

30. Display the "Still Projection Options" slide in Normal view.

31. Click **Paste** to insert the hyperlink button on this slide. Note that the copied button already includes the correct action setting to jump to the summary slide "Types of Presentation Visuals."

32. Paste the hyperlink button on the "Boards and Flipcharts" and the "Hard Copy Visuals" slides.

*Note:* A return hyperlink can be omitted on the last slide ("Hard Copy Visuals") if the speaker plans to access the hyperlinks in the order presented on the slide. The speaker advances to the next slide rather than returning to the summary slide ("Types of Presentation Visuals"). However, adding the hyperlink to each button gives the speaker flexibility to adapt the presentation order to meet the audience's needs or to omit sections, if necessary, to fit the time slot. Also, an individual viewing a presentation posted on the Web or a CD/DVD could access the hyperlinks in any order and return conveniently to the summary slide, as you will see in Project 10.

## Access the Hyperlinks to Verify Accuracy

33. Display the "Types of Presentation Visuals" slide in the Slide Show view.

34. Click the first hyperlink button (**Multimedia**) and verify that the slide show advances to the "Multimedia" slide.

35. Click the return hyperlink on the "Multimedia" slide and verify that the slide returns to the summary slide "Types of Presentation Visuals."

36. Verify the accuracy of the other three hyperlink buttons on the summary slide and each return hyperlink to the summary slide.

37. Follow this procedure for editing an action setting if the hyperlink does not jump to the correct slide:

a) Right-click and click **Edit Hyperlink**.

b) Edit the Action Setting Box by selecting the correct slide from the list of slide titles.

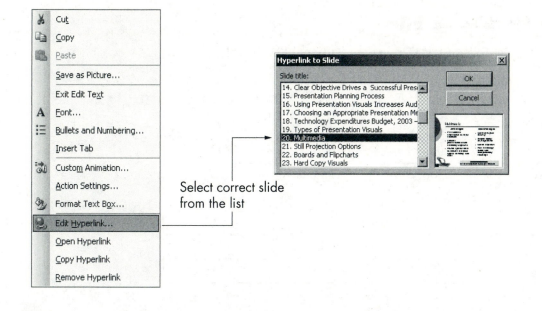

Select correct slide from the list

# LINKING A CHART CREATED IN EXCEL TO A POWERPOINT SLIDE

Linking documents allows managers to update timely information in a source document with automatic updates to any linked object. For example, current values input into a notebook file are reflected in other documents linked to this notebook file (e.g., charts in a written report prepared in word processing software and slides prepared in PowerPoint). In addition, a speaker can use the linking feature to facilitate an audience's analysis of various viable solutions to a problem. Using a spreadsheet linked to a chart in PowerPoint, the speaker inputs the values for a specific "what if" analysis and then switches to project the results on a PowerPoint slide.

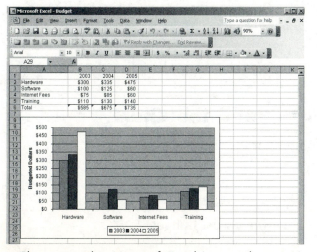

Chart created in Microsoft Excel (source document)

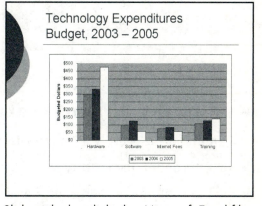

Slide with chart linked to Microsoft Excel file

## *Creating a Notebook File*

*Directions:* To complete this project, you will create a column chart using Microsoft Excel, link the Excel chart to a slide in the PowerPoint file Present, and revise the source document noting the automatic update of the chart on the PowerPoint slide.

## Create the Notebook File

1. Open Microsoft Excel (click **Start**, **Programs**, **Office 2003**, **Excel**).

2. Enter the labels and amounts (including the $ signs) shown for each cell.

|   | A | B | C | D |
|---|---|---|---|---|
| 1 |   | 2003 | 2004 | 2005 |
| 2 | Hardware | $300 | $335 | $475 |
| 3 | Software | $100 | $125 | $60 |
| 4 | Internet Fees | $75 | $85 | $60 |
| 5 | Training | $110 | $130 | $140 |
| 6 | Total | $585 | $675 | $735 |

3. Increase the width of column A:

   a) Position the cell pointer on any cell in column A.

   b) Click **Format**, **Column**, **Width**. Enter **18** and press **Enter**.

4. Highlight cells B5 to D5 and click the **Borders** button on the Formatting toolbar to insert a line above the total row.

## Create the Chart

5. Highlight cells A1 to D5. Note that this range does not include the column totals.

6. Click the **Chart Wizard** button on the Standard toolbar.

Chart Wizard button

## Respond to the Wizard Prompts to Build the Chart

7. Click **Column** for the chart type and **Clustered Column** for the chart subtype.

8. Click **Next** to confirm the chart type.

9. Click **Next** to confirm the chart source data.

10. Be sure the Titles tab is selected and input the label for the y-axis: **Budgeted Dollars**.

*Note:* Because the items in the x-axis are self-explanatory, an x-axis label is omitted for a simple, uncluttered design.

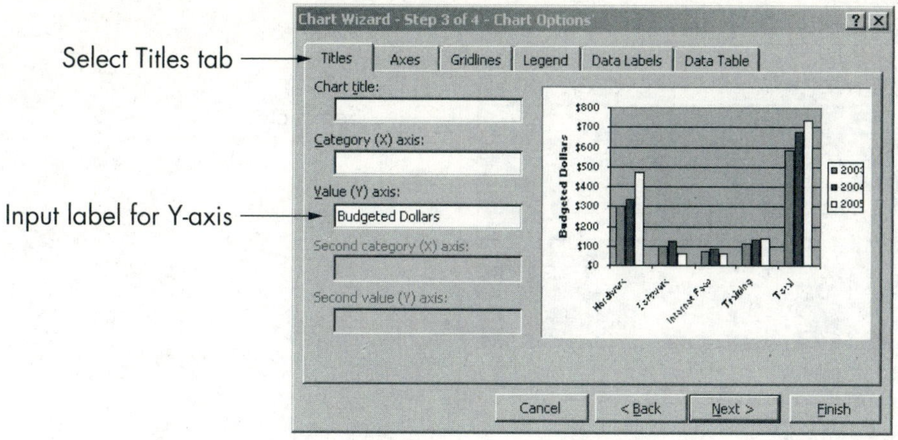

Select Titles tab ———

Input label for Y-axis ———

11. Make sure the **As object in** button is selected and click **Finish**.

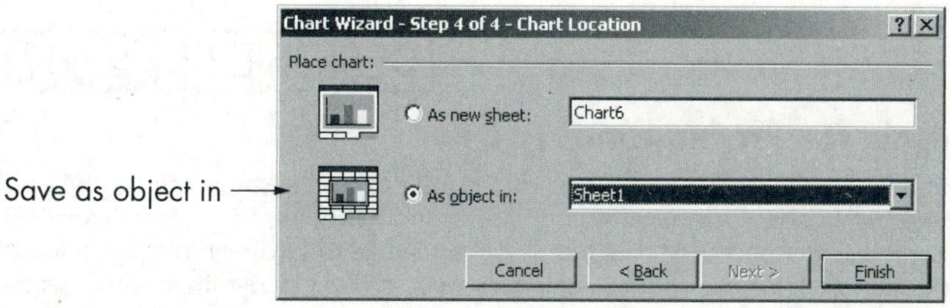

Save as object in ———

## Format the Chart

12. Make the following format changes to the chart. Refer to Project 7 to review detailed instructions for formatting charts if necessary. You can format a chart created in Excel by right-clicking on a specific area of the chart just as you do in PowerPoint.

   a) Move the legend below the column chart.

   b) Change the font size for the category axis to 8 points bold so that the expense categories (hardware, software, Internet fees, and training) will fit horizontally across the x-axis. Format the y-axis in the same manner for consistency with the x-axis.

   c) Save the notebook using the file name **Budget**.

## Link the Chart to the Slide

13. Select the column chart by pointing and clicking to the outside border of the chart. Handles appear on the outside border of the chart when the chart area is selected.

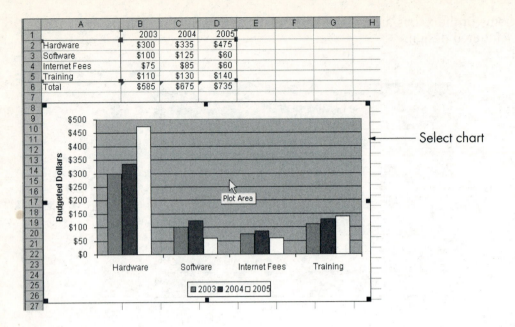

Select chart

14. Click **Copy**.

15. Minimize Excel and make PowerPoint your active application.

---

**DESIGNER'S POINTER**

## Using Special Symbols for Professional Polish

Special symbols often help create highly professional slides and handouts and ensure accuracy when phonetic spelling is needed. Some keystrokes, such as quotation marks and fractions, are automatically replaced with such special symbols. To insert a symbol that is not on the keyboard or replaced automatically, click **Insert**, **Symbol**, then click the appropriate category and scroll to locate the desired symbol. Following are some special symbols and their appropriate uses.

### En Dash

Use the en dash (–) instead of a hyphen (-) to separate words indicating a duration (May–June or 2004–2005).

### Em dash

Use the em dash (—) instead of a dash (- -) to indicate an abrupt change in thought or a title (Project 9—Designing an Interactive Presentation).

### Feet/Inches or Hours/Minutes

Use the prime mark (') instead of a single quotation mark (') for feet or hours and the double prime mark (") instead of a quotation mark (") for inches or minutes.

### Fractions

Create common fractions ($\frac{1}{4}$, $\frac{1}{2}$, and $\frac{3}{4}$) rather than key the numbers separated by a slash if the software does not replace them automatically with the symbol. Special symbols are available for common fractions only.

### Phonetic Spelling

Key José rather than Jose and résumé rather than resume for accuracy.

### Other Symbols

Use the symbols for ©, ®, ™, ÷, ¶, and so on.

16. Create a new slide using the Title and Chart layout from the Other Layouts category.

17. Read the instructions for formatting special symbols in the Designer's Pointer on page 178 and then key the chart title in the slide Title placeholder: **Technology Expenditures Budget, 2003–2005.**

## *Linking the Notebook File to the PowerPoint Slide*

18. Click one time to select the Chart placeholder.

19. Click **Edit**, **Paste Special** and select **Paste link**.

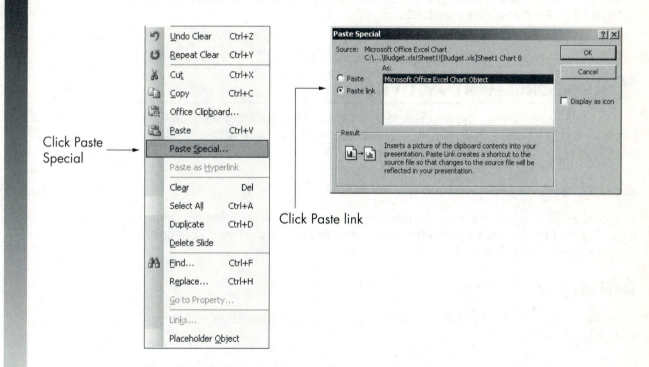

Click Paste Special

Click Paste link

Note that the chart is inserted in the presentation and linked to the Excel file Budget (source file). Linking these files ensures that changes to the Excel file will be reflected in the chart on the slide.

## Update the Linked Notebook

20. Click one time to select the chart on the PowerPoint slide.

21. Right-click and click **Linked Worksheet Object**.

22. Select **Edit**. The notebook file (source document) is displayed for revisions.

23. Change the cost of training in 2005 to **$500**. Press **Enter**.

24. Save the file and return to the PowerPoint slide. Note that the revised value is reflected in the chart.

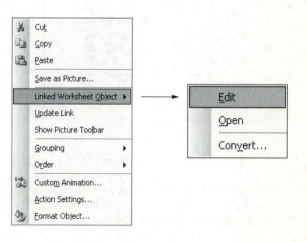

*Note:* If the link to the notebook file is broken, just select the chart placeholder, right-click, and click **Update Link**.

# ■ INSERTING SLIDE TRANSITIONS

*Directions:* Follow the instructions to add slide transitions to the slides created in this project.

1. Display the presentation in Slide Sorter view and select slides without slide transitions.

2. Click the **Slide Transition** button on the Slide Sorter toolbar and select the **Wipe from Left** effect at a **Fast** speed setting.

3. Click **Apply**.

# ■ REINFORCEMENT ACTIVITIES

Add the following slides to the file Present for added reinforcement of the PowerPoint features you learned in this project. Position the slides as shown in the table on page 214–216 at the end of the book.

## Activity 1

Add a hyperlink to your personal home page or your college/university's home page that will be accessed by clicking your name or the name of your college/university on the "Title" slide.

## Activity 2

Copy the "Types of Presentation Visuals" slide and create the enhanced design as shown in the model.

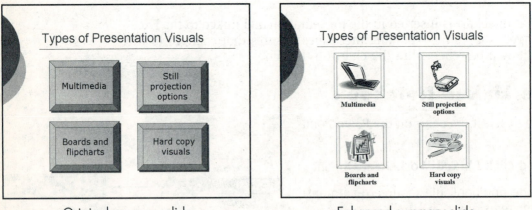

Original summary slide          Enhanced summary slide

1. Reposition the text box beneath the hyperlink button.

2. Copy and paste the clip art of the laptop from the "Multimedia" slide in front of the button. If the image falls behind the button, select the button and click **Draw**, **Order**, **Send to Back**.

3. Reformat the AutoShape button to create a subtle backdrop for the image as illustrated in the model or create an effect of your own:

a) Eliminate the fill color by selecting **No Fill** as the fill color.

b) Select a .75-point line slightly darker than the background color.

c) Decrease the angle of the bevel by dragging the yellow rectangle away from the center of the bevel.

d) Reformat the remaining three buttons using the Format Painter. Refer to the Technology Tip on page 171 for instructions for using this time-saving technique.

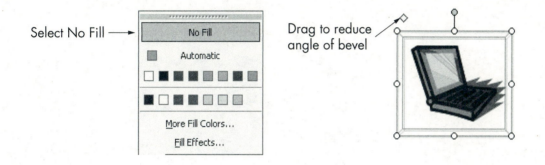

4. Group the clip art and the "Multimedia" text box.

5. Animate the grouped object to start with the hyperlink button directly above it (e.g., laptop button and text "Multimedia") and add animation effects of your choice.

   You can bypass the grouping process; simply animate the text box and the image to be displayed with the button (use the **Start with Previous** animation). The grouping process is recommended because it reduces the number of objects you must manage in the Custom Animation list.

6. Insert a hyperlink on the button *and* the text box to jump to the related slide just as you did in the project.

# Activity 3

As manager of the Human Resources Department at Becker Enterprises, you must submit a periodic written report and presentation depicting the relative attendance of the company's executive training programs. The number of managers attending the programs offered in 2004 includes the following: Electronic Presentations, 152; Internet Commerce, 142; Leadership Skills, 84; Public Speaking, 75; Conflict Resolution, 64; and Customer Service, 44.

1. Use the Chart Wizard to construct a pie chart in Microsoft Excel showing the percentage of managers participating in each program. Input the raw data; Excel will compute the percentages when the pie chart is built. Save the file as Training.

2. Create a new slide in the file Present using the Title and Chart layout from the Other Layouts category.

3. Input a slide title: **Management Executive Training Attendance, 2005**.

4. Link the pie chart from Excel to the PowerPoint slide.

5. Return to the Excel file Training (source document) and input revised values for 2005: Electronic Presentations, 168; Internet Commerce, 145; Leadership Skills, 96; Public Speaking, 82; Conflict Resolution, 58; and Customer Service, 84.

6. Save the Excel file and return to the PowerPoint slide to verify the changes and to revise the date in the slide title.

## Slide Order

Sequence slides in the files Present according to the table on pages 214–216. Print and submit as directed by your instructor.

# Designing Presentations to Reach Remote Audiences

## LEARNING OBJECTIVES

- Adapt PowerPoint slide design for optimal delivery by videoconference.

- Design an interactive Web presentation using the PowerPoint Web Wizard.

- Publish a PowerPoint presentation as a Web page and view the Web version on an Internet browser.

- Create a streaming media presentation using Microsoft Producer.

More than ever, presenters must be prepared to adapt their presentation style and PowerPoint support to adjust to constant changes in the business environment. From live presentations in conference rooms or board meetings, in a videoconference to audiences across time zones, or in a published presentation distributed by e-mail or CD/DVD, business presenters are challenged to meet audience's needs and expectations. Even more challenging are live Web presentations that link hundreds of viewers who are watching presentation visuals on their Internet browsers to a live speaker on a conference call or through Internet conferencing software such as Microsoft NetMeeting.

As the dominant presentation design tool, PowerPoint slides provide the primary content for all these delivery methods. You will need to be prepared to adapt your PowerPoint presentations for any of these live or distance presentation setups. In this project, you'll focus on reaching audiences through videoconferencing and published presentations, also referred to as *on-demand,* viewed at the audience's convenience.

## ADAPTING SLIDES FOR VIDEOCONFERENCE

Even more than in a live presentation, you will need strong visual aids to engage and maintain participants' attention during a videoconference. Graphics are a welcome break to the "talking head" displayed on the monitor for long periods. Readability of text will be a critical issue because text becomes fuzzy when transmitted through compressed video. Thus, select a large, sturdy sans serif font only and a color scheme that provides high contrast between the background and the text. Stay with a tested color scheme such as dark blue background, yellow title text, and white bulleted list text to ensure readability; avoid busy background effects that may diminish readability. Plan animation that focuses the audience's attention on specific ideas on the slides, but avoid unnecessary switching between the visual and the speaker during the discussion of one visual. Projecting your visual ahead of time so that you can adjust the color scheme and fonts and practice the balance between display of the visual and the speaker is important for presentations delivered by videoconference.

***Directions:*** Follow the instructions to create the slide shown at the right in the model. Note the differences in the same slide designed for delivery to a live audience and delivery by videoconference.

Slide designed for live presentation setup        Slide designed for videoconference

1. Select a tested color scheme and large sturdy fonts and bullets that can be read easily:
   - Background: Solid dark blue.
   - Title text: Yellow; Arial, 48 point.
   - Text for Level 1 bulleted list: White; Arial, 44 point.
   - Bullets: Choose a filled rather than open bullet and change size to at least 125% (e.g., choose ●, ■ not ❏, ○).

2. Select a simple, high-quality graphic that conveys ideas effectively and that the audience can see easily through this medium. Enlarge as much as possible without overcrowding the slide.

3. Animate as follows:
   a) Unanimated: Slide title.
   b) First: Clip art—Start .2 seconds after previous event with a dramatic effect such as Curve Up.
   c) Second: Bullet list—Start with a subtle effect such as Wipe from Left; no build effect.

4. Add a subtle slide transition effect.

5. Save the file as **Videoconference**.

6. Project in a classroom connected to a distant location if possible so that you can evaluate the effectiveness of your design.

# ■ DESIGNING A WEB PRESENTATION USING THE POWERPOINT WIZARD

Publishing a PowerPoint presentation to a Web site using the PowerPoint wizard is simple. The wizard converts the slides to a series of Web pages that can be viewed by anyone with access to the Web site. You may require assistance from a systems administrator to actually post the presentation file to a Web server after you have considered the options for accessing your presentation. For example, will you give anyone on the Web access to your presentation or restrict access to employees at various company locations or to business partners (e.g., vendors, suppliers, or customers)?

Creating effective Web presentations is challenging because of the multitude of technical issues that affect the way a presentation loads on a viewer's monitor. These issues are explored in greater detail in the Designer's Pointer on page 187.

## *Creating the Web Pages*

*Directions:* Follow the instructions to create a presentation to be posted to the company intranet to inform employees about the company's wellness program—complete with text and engaging photographs illustrating the benefits of this company-sponsored program.

Opening screen (main menu)

The Web presentation consists of (1) an Opening screen that identifies the company, reveals the purpose of the page, and provides a legend for navigating through the presentation, and (2) a series of pages related to the three components of the wellness program accessed from the legend on the Opening screen. Your instructor may require you to customize the design for a company of your choice.

## Create the Opening Screen

1. Open a new presentation using the default (blank) presentation design. Select a color scheme following the guidelines presented in the Designer's Pointer.

2. Create a new slide using the Title Only layout in the Text Layouts category.

3. Input the title in the Title placeholder using a 32-point Arial Black font. Position as shown on the model.

4. Insert and format the company's name and address attractively: **American Insurance Agency, 7346 Executive Park Drive, Chicago, IL 74957.**

5. Insert an image or company logo that portrays the company's corporate identity and professional image.

6. Create the legend viewers will use to navigate through the presentation:

   a) Create the buttons for the three items in the legend using the bevel AutoShape or an image of your choice.

   b) Add the text identifying each item in the legend.

PRESENTER'S **STRATEGY**

## Making Your Stage Presence Picture Perfect

A speaker's stage presence plays an important role in capturing attention, establishing rapport and credibility, and earning the trust of the audience—regardless of the presentation setup. Delivering by videoconference or producing a video presentation for distribution to a broad audience poses greater challenges for the speaker's delivery skills. Even the most confident speaker can become unnerved by the presence of a camera that doesn't miss anything and the increased difficulty of communicating to a distant, less personal audience.

Thorough preparation and practice will minimize your intimidation with this delivery. As you would in a live presentation, remain focused on the contribution you are making to your audience—only now remember to smile at the camera and follow these guidelines for perfecting your stage presence on camera:

- **Concentrate on projecting positive nonverbal messages.** Keep a natural, friendly expression; relax and smile. Avoid the tendency to stare into the lens of the camera. Instead of this glassy-eyed stare, look naturally at the entire audience as you would in a live presentation. Speak clearly with as much energy as you can. If a lag occurs between the video and audio transmission, adjust your timing to avoid interrupting other speakers. Use gestures to reinforce your points and to add needed energy to your talking head on a flat screen. However, avoid fast or excessive motion that will appear blurry or large gestures or head movements outside the camera angle. Avoid side conversations and coughing and throat clearing that could trigger voice-activated microphones. Be aware of noisy shuffling of notes pages, overly aggressive keyboard strokes or mouse clicks to advance slides, or nervous tapping on the lectern that will be amplified when transmitted through a microphone. Pay close attention to other presenters to guard against easy distraction in a distance environment and to capture subtle nonverbal cues. In short, for a polished, personal camera style, your goal is to maximize your energy while minimizing your activity—a daunting and often overwhelming challenge.

- **Select clothing and accessories that are camera-friendly and that communicate a professional, polished look.** Choose solid colors in wrinkle-free fabrics with moderate shaping and padding. Avoid shiny or sheer fabrics; jewelry that reflects light back to the camera; or close patterns such as plaids, stripes, dots, and checks that create annoying vibration effects. Any shade of blue works well on camera, from light blue to navy; avoid pure white, black, and bright shades of red, pink, yellow, or green. Women should avoid large buttons or jewelry, dangling earrings, noisy bracelets, or anything that may take attention away from their face. Select ties and scarves with small prints. Your attire should be a contemporary conservative style that reflects current fashion trends but avoids untasteful passing fads.

- **Adjust camera settings to enhance communication.** Generally, adjust the camera so that all participants can be seen, but zoom in more closely on participants when you wish to observe nonverbal language. Project a wide-angle shot of yourself during rapport-building comments at the presentation's beginning and zoom in to signal the start of the agenda or to emphasize an important point during the presentation. You will want to be conscious in switching the camera between a view of you and your presentation visuals, depending on what is needed at the time.

- **Develop high-quality graphics appropriate for the videoconference.** You will apply these guidelines as you design a slide for distance delivery in this project.

To refine your stage presence, set up a video camera or a Webcam and begin "performing"; then immediately critique the effectiveness of your stage presence as well as your speaking and writing skills. The result of your dedicated practice will be increased personal credibility and persuasiveness that your audience and your supervisor will value.

---

   c) Format the hyperlink button and the text box attractively using colors complementary to your color scheme.

7. Position relevant photos in front of each button. If the image falls behind the button, select the button and click **Draw**, **Order**, **Send to Back**.

8. Save the file as **Wellness Program**.

## DESIGNER'S POINTER

### Mastering Effective Web Design Principles

Giving a presentation on the Web gives you access to many more people than you could gather in a conference room, especially when many of these people are located in numerous remote locations. Simply posting an existing presentation is an ineffective practice that could sabotage your success in achieving the goals for the presentation. Rather, follow these basic guidelines for designing a presentation specifically for the Web:

- **Design a unified look and feel for the presentation.** Begin with a tightly organized Opening screen that clearly identifies the company and reveals the purpose of the presentation. Consider repeating certain elements from the Opening screen to other pages within the presentation to tie the sections of the presentation together.

- **Design your presentation for easy navigation.** Give viewers control over the order in which they will view the presentation. The Opening screen may include a simple legend that lays out the viewers' options for creating their own experiences within your presentation.

- **Consider selecting a Web template until you gain experience designing Web content.** A Web template will assist you in selecting simple light backgrounds with spots of color using a Web-safe palette of colors. You can be confident that these presentation slides will be clear and easy to read and that they will load on the screen with a minimal amount of wait time. Likewise, attempt to keep animation and sound effects to a minimum. Although these effects may be dazzling on your laptop computer, not all viewers may be able to download them because of vast differences in technical setups.

- **Use graphics effectively.** Include only graphics that serve a specific function in the presentation and limit the total size of the graphic to reduce the time it takes for the image to download.

Now note how these guidelines are illustrated in the Web presentation you will build for this project.

## Create Linked Pages from the Legend—Health Testing

You will create two pages that provide more specific information about the health testing component of the wellness program. Employees access the first of these two pages by clicking the **Health Testing** button on the Opening screen.

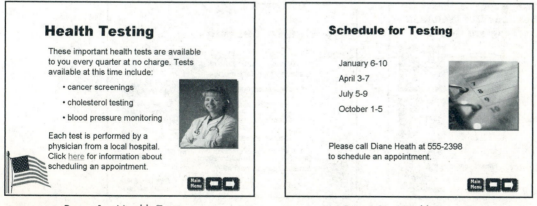

Page 1—Health Testing                    Page 2—Health Testing

9. Create page 1 as shown in the model on page 187.

   a) Create a new slide using the Title & Text layout in the Text Layouts category.

   b) Input the title in the Title placeholder using a 40-point Arial Black font.

   c) Key the text using a 24-point Arial font; use a bulleted list to highlight the types of tests.

   d) Copy the company image/logo and the photo associated with the **Health Testing Legend** button from the Opening screen. Resize and reposition for appeal. Adding these elements on the link pages creates unity with the Opening screen and assures users they have not inadvertently followed a link out of the presentation.

10. Create page 2 as shown in the model.

   a) Create a new slide using the Title & Text layout in the Text Layouts category.

   b) Input the title in the Title placeholder using a 28-point Arial Black font.

   c) Key the text using a 24-point Arial font and position as shown on the model.

   d) Insert a photo that conveys the key idea of scheduling an appointment and has a tone consistent with the other photos in the Web presentation.

## Link the Legend and Related Pages

11. Insert a hyperlink from the **Legend** button on the Opening screen to page 1 (Health Testing). Review the process of creating hyperlinked text and objects in Project 9 if necessary.

   a) Select the photo *and* the AutoShape. Sizing handles will appear on both the photo and the AutoShape if both objects are selected.

   b) Click **Slide Show**, **Action Settings**.

   c) Choose the Mouse Click tab to require viewers to click the hyperlink to access the first link page.

   d) Click **Hyperlink to** and select **Next Slide** (or click **Slide** and select the desired slide title).

12. Insert a hyperlink from the text box (Health Testing) on the Opening screen to page 1 (Health Testing).

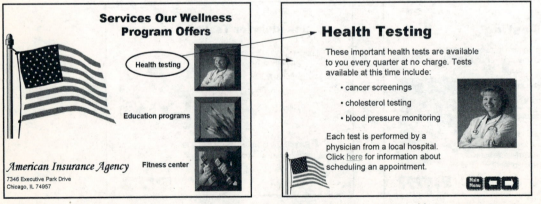

Page 1—Opening screen (main menu)          Page 1—Health Testing

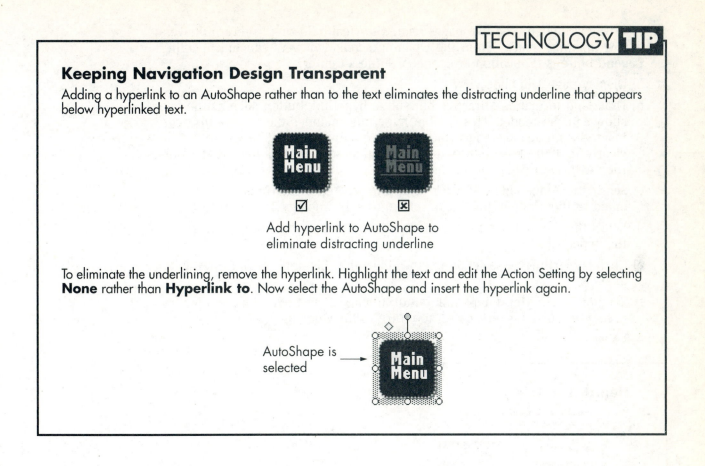

**TECHNOLOGY TIP**

## Keeping Navigation Design Transparent

Adding a hyperlink to an AutoShape rather than to the text eliminates the distracting underline that appears below hyperlinked text.

☑            ☒

Add hyperlink to AutoShape to
eliminate distracting underline

To eliminate the underlining, remove the hyperlink. Highlight the text and edit the Action Setting by selecting **None** rather than **Hyperlink to**. Now select the AutoShape and insert the hyperlink again.

AutoShape is
selected →

13. Insert a hyperlink from the word *here* on page 1 to additional information provided on page 2.

    a)  Display page 1 (Health Testing) in Slide view.

    b)  Select the Mouse Click tab to require viewers to use a mouse click to access the hyperlink.

    c)  Highlight the word *here*, click **Insert**, **Hyperlink**, and select page 2 (Schedule for Testing).

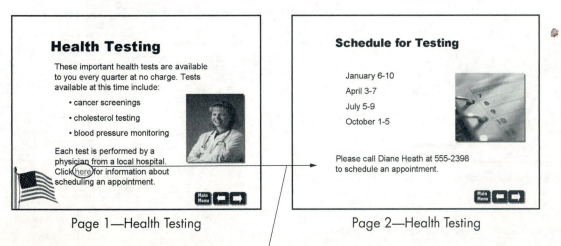

**Health Testing**

These important health tests are available to you every quarter at no charge. Tests available at this time include:

  • cancer screenings

  • cholesterol testing

  • blood pressure monitoring

Each test is performed by a physician from a local hospital. Click here for information about scheduling an appointment.

**Schedule for Testing**

January 6-10

April 3-7

July 5-9

October 1-5

Please call Diane Heath at 555-2398 to schedule an appointment.

Page 1—Health Testing                    Page 2—Health Testing

Link *here* on page 1 to access page 2

14. Insert hyperlinks on the two pages related to Health Testing to return viewers to the Opening screen. From the Opening screen, viewers can link to other **Legend** buttons (Education Programs or Fitness Center).

a) Display page 1 in Slide view.

b) Draw and format an attractive but subtle hyperlink button such as the one shown in the model. This custom hyperlink includes the text *Main Menu* inside a Rounded Rectangle (found in **AutoShapes**, **Basic Shapes**) to denote clearly that the link returns to the Opening screen. A dotted border surrounds the AutoShape for added appeal.

c) Select the AutoShape and click **Slide Show**, **Action Settings**. If this command results in underlined text, refer to the Technology Tip on page 189.

d) Select the Mouse Click tab to require viewers to use a mouse click to access the hyperlink.

e) Click **Hyperlink to**, select **Slide**, and select the Opening screen from the list of slides.

f) Copy the **Main Menu** hyperlink button to page 2. The hyperlink requires no editing because it is already set to return to the Opening screen.

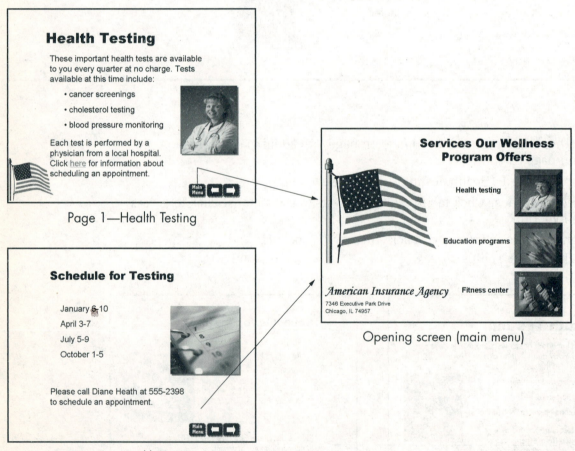

Page 1—Health Testing

Page 2—Health Testing

Opening screen (main menu)

15. Create a hyperlink on page 2 to return to page 1.

a) Display page 2 in Slide view.

b) Create an attractive, subtle hyperlink button using the left arrow from **AutoShapes**, **Block Arrows**. The arrow pointing to the left communicates clearly that the hyperlink will move backward in the presentation. A custom hyperlink with the text *Previous* would achieve the same results.

c) Select the Mouse Click tab to require the viewer to use a mouse click to access the hyperlink.

d) Click **Hyperlink to**, select **Previous** (or select **Slide** and the desired slide title from the list of slides).

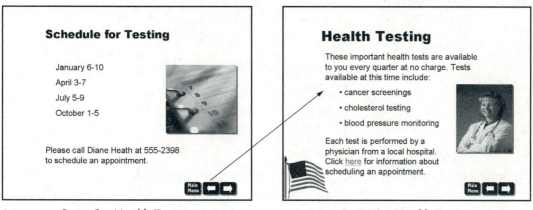

Page 2—Health Testing                    Page 1—Health Testing

16. Run the presentation in Slide Show view to check the accuracy of all hyperlinks.

17. Continue to Reinforcement Activity 1 to build the remaining slides in this Web presentation.

## Adding Voice Narration to a Presentation

Adding voice narration to a PowerPoint presentation can enhance your Web-based PowerPoint presentation or self-running slide show presentation at a kiosk or exhibit booth. Also, recording audience comments, notes, and actions taken during a presentation can allow you to create a record of the presentation for later review. To record a voice narration, you need a sound card, microphone, and speakers. To ensure accessibility, you may choose to provide a handout containing your slides and the narration for the benefit of anyone who might have difficulty hearing and those without the appropriate computer equipment. Any notes keyed in the Notes pane of the PowerPoint window will appear beneath the slide as it is displayed as a Web page.

1. Display the Opening screen of the Wellness Program file in Normal view.

## Create Narration Notes

2. Click in the Notes pane and key a couple of sentences you will later record to introduce employees to the company's corporate wellness center. This text will appear below the slide when it is displayed in the browser.

3. Key brief notes for both pages of the Health Testing component.

## Prepare Narration Settings

4. Click **Slide Show**, **Record Narration**.

| | |
|---|---|
| ⬚ | <u>V</u>iew Show |  F5 |
| | <u>S</u>et Up Show... |
| 🔁 | <u>R</u>ehearse Timings |
| | Record <u>N</u>arration... | ◄── Select Record Narration |
| | Ac<u>t</u>ion Buttons | ▶ |
| | Action Se<u>t</u>tings... |
| 🔲 | Animation S<u>c</u>hemes... |
| 🔳 | C<u>u</u>stom Animation... |
| 🔲 | Slide <u>T</u>ransition... |
| ▨ | <u>H</u>ide Slide |
| | Custom Sho<u>w</u>s... |

5. Click **Set Microphone Level** and follow the directions to set your microphone level; then click **OK**.

6. Click **OK** to begin recording the narration and to embed the narration sound so that it becomes a part of the presentation and travels with the presentation.

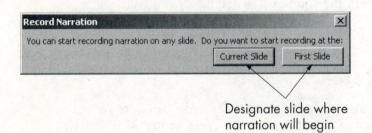

Link to another location rather than embed in the presentation

Set microphone level and click to begin narration

7. Designate the slide where the recording will begin. If you begin recording on a slide other than the first slide, you will receive the following prompt.

Designate slide where narration will begin

Click **Current Slide** to start the designing the narration on the currently selected slide. Click **First Slide** to start the narration on the first slide in the presentation.

## Record the Narration

8. Display the Opening screen in Slide Show view and speak the narrative text for the first slide into the microphone. Click to advance to the next slide and speak the narrative text for that slide, advance to the next slide, and so on. To pause and resume the narration, right-click the slide and, on the shortcut menu, click **Pause Narration** or **Resume Narration**.

9. Click **Exit** when you are ready to stop recording and save the narration.

10. Determine the timings you will use to advance the show. Click **Save** to save the timings resulting from the narration or click **Don't Save** to set timings separately. Refer to using rehearsal timings in Project 5, page 102, if necessary.

Designate whether timings will be set separately

11. Run the Wellness Program file in Slide Show view and listen to the narration.

## Publishing a PowerPoint Presentation to a Web Site

Rather than saving your presentation in the default format as a PowerPoint presentation, you will convert the presentation to an HTML (hypertext markup language) document using a PowerPoint wizard. Your Web browser (such as Internet Explorer or Netscape) interprets instructions and taglines written in HTML and displays the page on the viewer's screen. You will view your Web presentation in your browser to see how it looks as a series of Web pages, but you will post the presentation to an actual Web server only if directed by your instructor.

## Create the Web Pages

1. Be sure that the file Wellness Program is open.

2. Click **File**, **Save as Web Page** and click **Publish**.

Save as Web page

3. Edit the Publish dialog box as follows:

   a) Click **Complete presentation** to publish all slides in the file.

   b) Specify support for both Netscape and Internet Explorer by selecting **All browsers listed above** to ensure greater support to your viewers.

   c) Specify the drive location you want to use for saving your Web files.

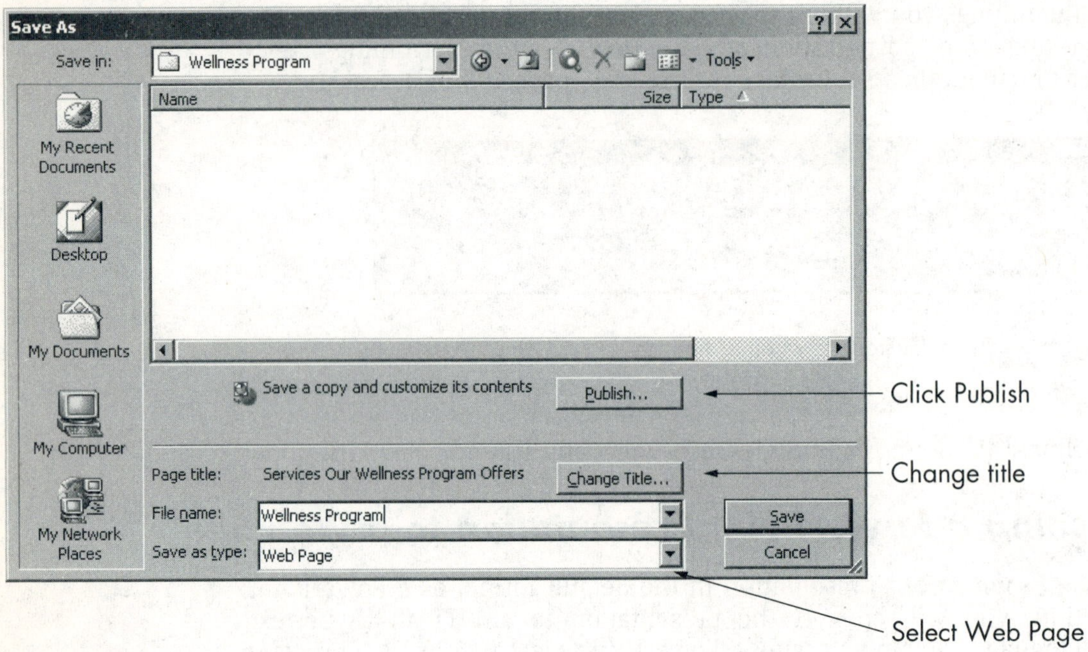

Click Publish

Change title

Select Web Page

4. Click **Publish**. PowerPoint creates an HTML, or Web page, version of your presentation and saves it in the specified location.

## View the PowerPoint Web Pages

You will open the page or HTML document that you created in your Internet browser so that you can see exactly how it will look after it has been published as a Web page.

1. Open your Internet browser.

2. Click **File**, **Open** and browse to locate the Web file.

Note the browser window shown in the model is divided into two vertical frames, similar to the Normal view in PowerPoint. You can navigate through the presentation by clicking (1) the title of each slide displayed in the left frame, (2) the **Previous** and **Next Slide** buttons at the bottom of the slide, or (3) the **Legend** buttons on the slide that you designed earlier. The address in the browser indicates that the presentation is stored on a local drive and not a Web server.

3. Consult your instructor for directions related to publishing the Web presentation to a Web server for others to view.

Address indicates presentation is saved on a local drive not a Web server

Select a slide to view from the hyperlink list

Click legend buttons to view linked Web pages

Click to move through the presentation

## *Creating a Streaming Media Presentation with Microsoft Producer*

Microsoft Producer, a free add-in with PowerPoint 2002 and higher, offers many features that transform a standard PowerPoint presentation into an engaging streaming media format that can be easily published for distribution to large audiences. Producer allows you to (1) capture media or import files (images, audio, video, slides, and HTML); (2) synchronize any audio or video to match still images; and (3) publish the presentation to your computer, a network drive, or a Web server.

*Directions:* Follow the instructions to produce the media presentation shown in the model using Microsoft Producer. Your instructor may vary the requirements based on available video and audio equipment.

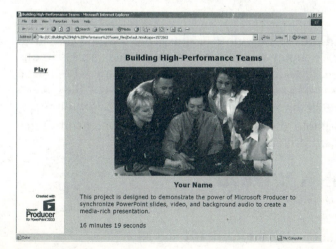

# Download and Install Software

1. Download and install the free download of Microsoft Producer at **http://www.microsoft.com.** Input "Producer" as the search term and select the link to **Download Producer for PowerPoint 2003**.

# Prepare Content Files

2. Compile all project files to be imported into Microsoft Producer for the video presentation:

   a) **PowerPoint file:** Create the following PowerPoint slides and save as **Team Building**. Add custom animation and slide transitions that will be retained when the PowerPoint slides are imported into Microsoft Producer. Your instructor may ask you to create a video presentation using slides you have already created.

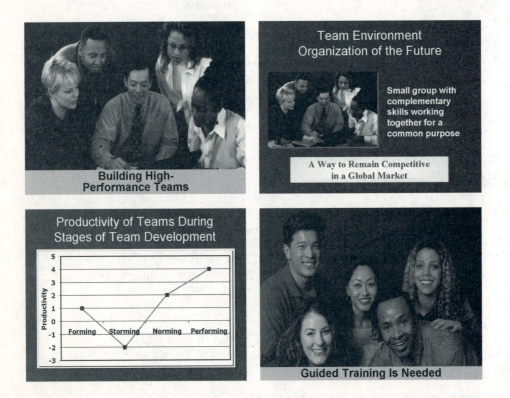

   b) **Audio file for background music:** Download a music file in .mp3 format to your hard drive from **http://freeplaymusic.com**, which provides access to one of the world's largest "free" broadcast music production libraries, or from a library of your choice. Choose a feel such as "motivational." Preview the choices and download a short clip ranging from .10 seconds to just over 2 minutes.

   c) **Still image:** Download a photo of an effective team from Microsoft Office Online and save to your hard drive as **Effective Team**.

# Create a Presentation Wizard

3. Open Microsoft Producer.

4. Select **Use the New Presentation Wizard**. Click **OK** and **Next**. Take a moment to review the steps in the wizard, beginning with selecting a template, importing

project files, capturing new media files such as video and voice narration, synchronizing the slides to the video and audio, and previewing the presentation.

Use the New
Presentation
Wizard

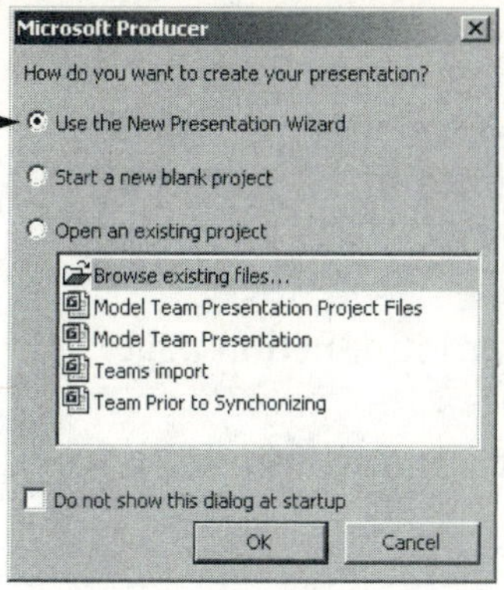

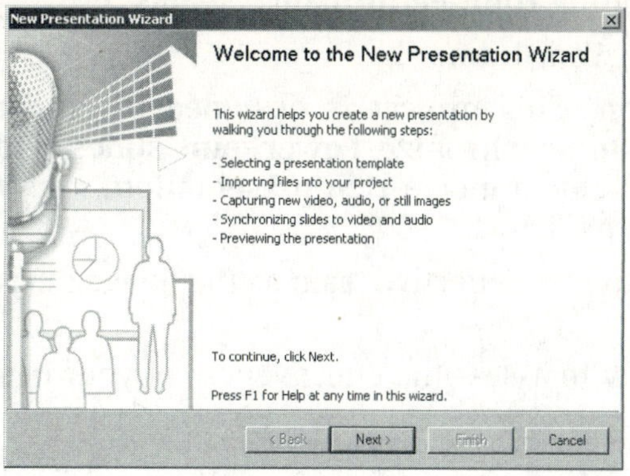

5. Follow the prompts to designate design elements and import the project files:

a) **Choose a Presentation Template:** Scroll to view available options, including combinations of video, audio, slides, and HTML text. Select **Standard Audio-Resizable Slides** for this project. You can change the template after exiting the wizard if, for example, you decide to add video. Click **Next**.

Choose Standard
Audio - Resizable
Slides

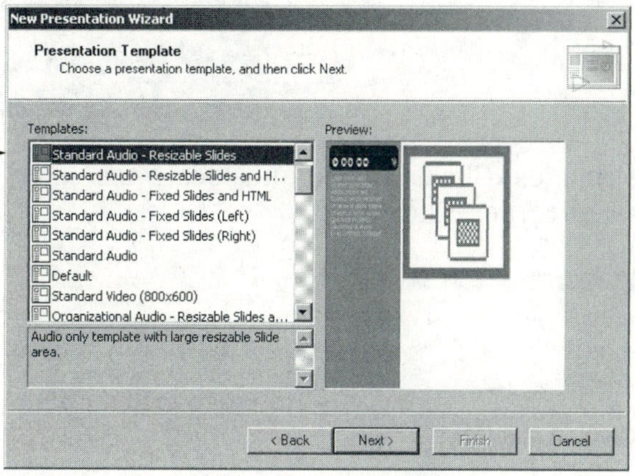

b) **Choose a Presentation Scheme:** Retain the default settings of the introduction page and click **Next**. Changes can be made to the font face, size, and color and to the background color of this page. Refer to the model to review the format.

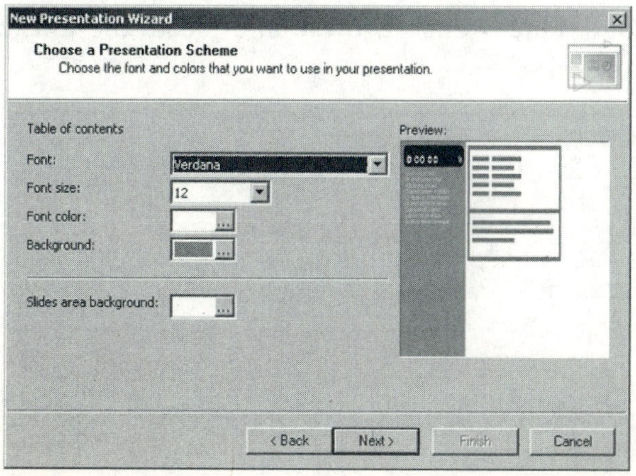

c) **Provide Presentation Information:**

  – Input the following information that will appear on the introduction page:

  **Title: Building High-Performance Teams**

  **Presenter: Your Name**

  **Description: This project is designed to demonstrate the power of Producer to synchronize PowerPoint slides, video, and background audio to create a media-rich presentation.** *(You may include your own text if you wish.)*

  – Select a photo of an effective team as the image for your introduction page. Click **Next**.

  – Click **Preview** to assess the effectiveness of your design and wording.

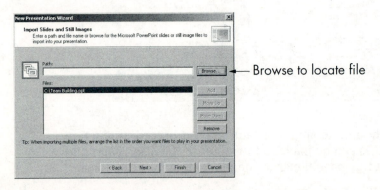

Provide information and an image to appear on the introduction page

Preview the introduction page

d) **Import slides and still images:** Click **Browse** and locate the Team Building PowerPoint file you created earlier. Click **Next**.

Browse to locate file

e) **Import and Capture Audio and Video:** Click **Browse** and locate the music file you created earlier.

Browse to locate audio file

f) **Synchronize:** Click **Yes**.

g) **Complete Presentation:** Click **Finish**.

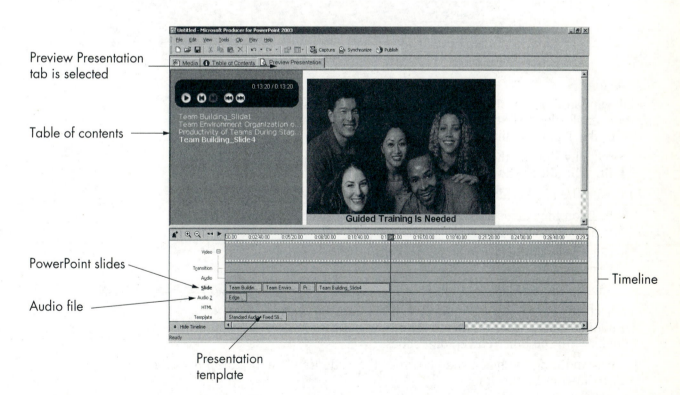

h) Save your presentation as **Team Building Video**.

6. Click **No** to bypass the synchronization process for now and display the video timeline. The PowerPoint slides and the audio file the wizard automatically imported into Producer are displayed on the timeline as shown in the following model. Study the various elements of the Producer presentation window before proceeding to edit and add other media to the timeline.

7. Edit the Table of Contents:

   a) Select the Table of Contents tab.

   b) Select the first slide, click **Change**, and key the word: **Introduction**.

c) Repeat for the remaining slides to create the following text for the Table of Contents:

**Introduction**

**Value of Teams**

**Productivity Levels**

**Solution**

d) Select the Preview Presentation tab to view the project and the revised Table of Contents.

Table of Contents tab is selected

Click Change

Input revised slide title

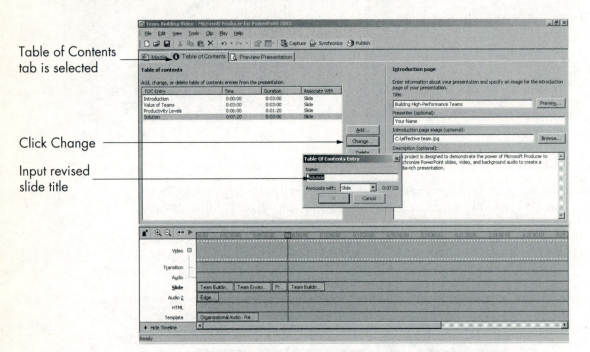

8. Make updates to PowerPoint slides quickly and easily within Producer. To illustrate this feature, add a black slide at the end of the Team Building PowerPoint file:

a) Select any slide on the Slide track of the timeline and click **Edit, Edit Slide**. The PowerPoint file opens automatically.

b) Create the black slide:

– Position the cursor after the last slide in the PowerPoint file.

– Click **New Slide, Format, Background, More Colors**; select black.

– Save to update the file.

c) Select the Media tab in Producer and click on the Team Building folder. Note the black slide now appears in the folder with the other PowerPoint slides.

d) Click and drag the black slide down to the Slide timeline and drop it as the last slide on the timeline.

Select Edit Slide

*Note:* The object will naturally want to snap to the left of the previous slide on the timeline. Click the **Zoom Timeline In** and **Zoom Timeline Out** buttons to allow you to see individual media items more easily.

e) Select the Table of Contents tab and change the name of the final slide to "The End."

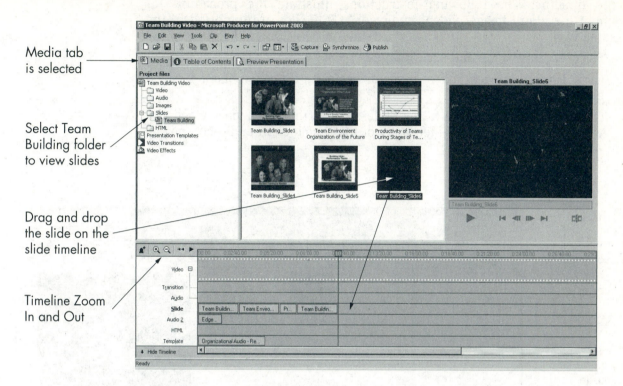

9. Review these additional useful commands for editing and importing media. Incorporate new media as you wish or as directed by your instructor.

a) To delete slides, select the slide to be deleted from the timeline or the Table of Contents and press the **Delete key**.

b) To rearrange slides, click **Tools**, **Rearrange Items On**, **Slide Track**. Select a slide and click **move up** or **down** as desired. (The changes made to the Table of Contents earlier are not reflected in this slide track menu, so identifying the slides can be tricky.)

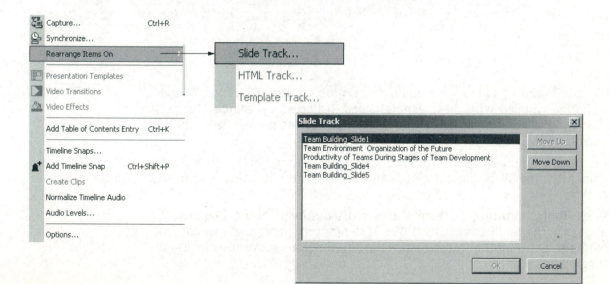

c) To import media files into the video after exiting the wizard, simply insert the media file in the appropriate project folder and drag the desired file to the timeline. The following instructions illustrate the procedure for importing a still image; video, audio, or HTML files are imported in the same way.

- Select the Media tab and click **Images**.

- Click **Import Images** and browse to locate the Effective Team file you downloaded earlier.

- Click and drag the image to the Slide track of the timeline. A video clip would be placed on the Video track of the timeline; an audio clip on the Audio2 track, and so on.

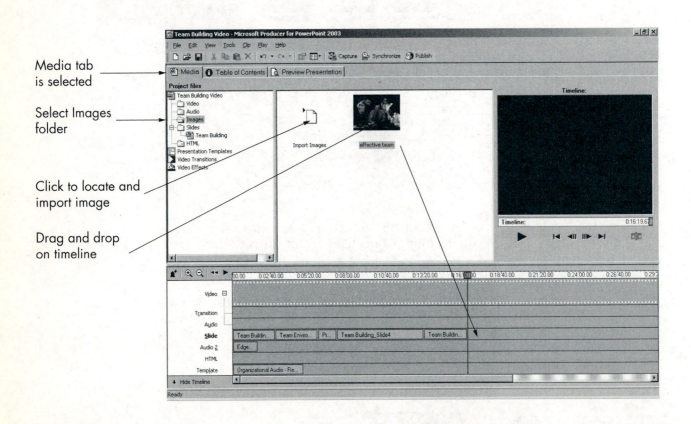

Media tab is selected

Select Images folder

Click to locate and import image

Drag and drop on timeline

d) To create audio or video with audio to accompany the PowerPoint slides, familiarize yourself with these general steps. If necessary, search Microsoft Office Help using the key term "narration" and select the needed subtopic to learn more.

- Connect a microphone if you are capturing audio only and a digital camcorder or Web camera (Webcam) if you are capturing video and audio.

- Click **Tools**, **Capture**, **Narrate slides with audio**. If audio files already appear in the Audio2 track, click **Yes** at the prompt to remove this content. Now the narration file can be placed in the timeline above the corresponding slide.

Select Narrate
slides with audio

– Complete the wizard that requires you to select the connection speed and method your intended audience will use to watch your final presentation (e.g., modem versus DSL) and the input source (microphone). Select **Microphone** as the input source and adjust the input level setting to achieve the desired volume. Select **Mute speakers** if you do not wish to hear the audio playing through the speakers as you record the narration.

– Click **Capture** and begin recording the narration. Click or press the **spacebar** to display the next slide or animation effect.

– Click **Stop** to end capturing when you have completed the narration.

– Input a file name for your captured audio file. The audio is saved as a Windows Media Audio/Video file (.wmv). The .wmv file is automatically added to the timeline above the corresponding slide.

e) To capture a video clip from footage recorded with a digital camcorder, follow these steps (in this project, for example, you might add a short clip of business workers participating in a team building exercise such as a trust fall):

– Connect a digital camcorder to the firewire port of your computer using a firewire cable.

– Click **Tools**, **Capture**, **Video with audio**. (This feature is active only when the camera is connected.)

– Choose **Medium 320 × 240** as the video display size.

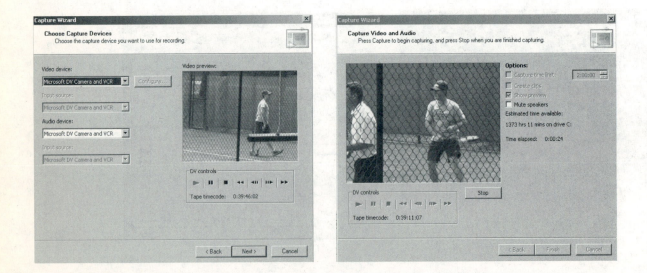

– Click **Play** to begin the video. Click **Capture** when you reach a segment you wish to capture.

– Click **Stop** to end the recording. Save the video clip in the Video project folder for this project. The file is saved as a .wmv file.

– Repeat Step 10c to import the video file; drag and drop the file in the Video track of the timeline.

10. Synchronize the media elements so that any audio and video match the slides.

*Note:* If you did not add narration to the PowerPoint presentation, assume the audio/video files have been added to the timeline. When synchronizing, estimate the amount of time a speaker would want to remain on each slide.

a) Select the Preview Presentation tab.

b) Position the cursor at the beginning of the project by clicking on the "Introduction" slide in the Table of Contents or click the **Rewind Timeline** button.

c) Click **Tools**, **Synchronize**.

d) Click **Set slide timing**.

e) Click **Play** to start the video presentation. Click **Next Effect** to advance to the next animation or **Next Slide** to advance to the next slide.

f) Click **Finish** when all slides have been displayed.

g) Play the video and make manual adjustments on the timeline as needed. For example, you might:

– Select the black slide file and shorten the time duration. To select a file, point to the center of the image until the hand appears and then drag.

– Select the .mp3 audio file and lengthen it to end at the same time as the black slide.

11. Publish the presentation to a network drive, Web server, or your computer or CD/DVD so that it can be viewed by your intended audience.

a) Click **File**, **Publish Presentation**, **My Computer**. Click **Next**. (Other options include saving to a network to be shared with others or posting to the Web.)

b) Complete the wizard to publish the file. The following introduction page appears. Click **Play** to view your video presentation.

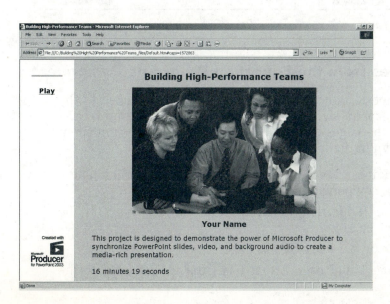

## ■ REINFORCEMENT ACTIVITIES

Add the following slides to the file Wellness Program for added reinforcement of the PowerPoint features you learned in this project. Position the slides as shown in the table on page 216.

## Activity 1

Adapt a presentation that you are currently developing for delivery by videoconference. Be prepared to share with your instructor and the class the rationale for your design choices. Print the slides as an audience handout. If you are not working on a presentation at this time, develop two to three additional slides that present basic principles for adapting presentation visuals and delivering by videoconference using information contained in the Presenter's Strategy on page 186 or from online articles you locate from the library or an online database.

## Activity 2

Create the remaining slides in the Web presentation related to the corporate wellness program: (1) two linked pages from the **Education Programs** button, (2) one linked page from the **Fitness Center** button, and (3) slides of your own design to complete the Fitness Center component of the Web presentation.

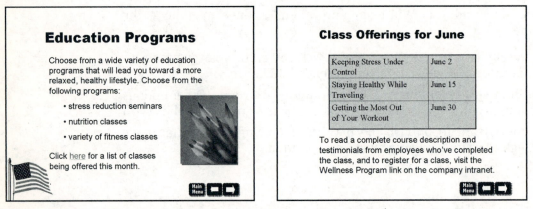

Page 1—Education Programs                Page 2—Education Programs

### Create the Linked Pages from the Education Programs Component

1. Create the two pages related to Education Programs that will be linked to the legend on the Opening screen. To increase your efficiency and to ensure consistency in the design, copy the pages created for the Health Testing component (page 187). Revise as shown in the models.

2. Insert the hyperlinks to link these pages. Refer to the instructions for linking the pages in the Health Testing component if necessary.

   a) Link the **Legend** button (Education Programs) and the text box on the Opening screen to access page 1.

   b) Hyperlink the word *here* on page 1 to access page 2.

   c) Add a hyperlink on page 1 and page 2 that takes the viewer back to the Opening screen.

   d) Add a hyperlink on page 2 that takes the viewer back to page 1.

## Create the Linked Pages from the Fitness Center Component

3. Create a page related to the Fitness Center that will be linked to the legend on the Opening screen. Edit a copy of another first page for optimal efficiency, just as you did in Step 1 of this activity.

4. Insert the hyperlinks to link these pages.

   a) Link the **Legend** button (Fitness Center) and the text box on the Opening screen to access page 1.

   b) Add the hyperlink on page 1 to return the viewer to the Opening screen.

5. Design the linked page containing the Fitness Center's hours of operation using your own information. Add a hyperlink to the word *here* on page 1 to access your page (Hours of Operations) and add a hyperlink on your page to return the viewer to page 1.

6. Design a page of your own for the links to the three areas in the Fitness Center (Main Exercise Room, Indoor Track, and Aquatic Center). Add a photograph depicting each of these areas and brief information describing what the employee could expect to experience there. Add the hyperlinks needed to (1) move from Fitness Center, page 1 to your three pages and (2) return from each of your pages to Fitness Center, page 1.

7. Run the presentation in Slide Show view to check the accuracy of all hyperlinks.

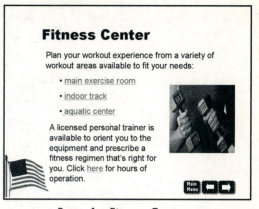

Page 1—Fitness Center

# Activity 3

Add voice narration to the new slides you created in Reinforcement Activity 2 for the Wellness Program slide show.

# Activity 4

Publish the updated Wellness Program file as a Web page and view the Web version of your presentation in your Internet browser. Publish the Web presentation to a Web server if directed by your instructor.

# Activity 5

Prepare a 2- to 3-minute media presentation using Microsoft Producer on a topic approved by your instructor. Plan a variety of compelling media, including PowerPoint slides with animation effects, a still image, and background audio. If directed by your instructor, add narration with video or audio and a dynamic video clip that reinforces an important point. This short video presentation may emerge naturally from a longer presentation you've already developed for a live audience (e.g., a welcome video announcing the first meeting to members of a committee recently formed to develop a new corporate policy, orientation video outlining the implementation of a new policy with general guidelines and reference to future training or intranet bulletins, video persuading an audience to participate in a program of your choice). Your instructor may direct you to prepare a video résumé highlighting your qualifications for a position.

# Slide Order

Print the slides in the file Wellness Program according to the table on page 216. Print and submit as directed by your instructor.

# Slide Sequence

Slides completed for the file Present should appear in the following sequence. New or revised slides are shown in bold print.

## Project 1

1. Title Slide
2. Effective Speakers
3. Crucial Presentation Components
4. Benefits of Designing Visuals In-House
5. Guidelines for Effective Delivery

## Project 2

1. Title Slide
2. **Effective Speakers** *(revised)*
3. **Top Mistakes Presenters Make** *(revised)*
4. **Adept Speakers Must...**
5. **Crucial Presentation Components** *(revised)*
6. Choosing an Appropriate Presentation Media
7. **Multimedia**
8. **Still Projection Options**
9. **Boards and Flipcharts**
10. **Hard Copy Visuals**
11. **Benefits of Designing Visuals In-House** *(revised)*
12. **An Effective Slide Show...**
13. Guidelines for Effective Delivery

## Project 3

1. **Title Slide** *(revised)*
2. **Contemporary Communication**
3. **Effective Speakers** *(revised)*
4. **Average Presentation Rated**

5. Top Mistakes Presenters Make

6. **Meeting the Demands of Today's Audiences**

7. Adept Speakers Must...

8. **Adapting Speaking Style to Today's Fast Pace**

9. **Today's Messages Are...**

10. **Personal Connection a Must**

11. Crucial Presentation Components

12. **Clear Objective Drives a Successful Presentation**

13. **Choosing an Appropriate Presentation Media** *(revised)*

14. Multimedia

15. Still Projection Options

16. Boards and Flipcharts

17. Hard Copy Visuals

18. **Process for Converting Slides to Overheads**

19. **Benefits of Designing Visuals In-House**

20. **A Speech Is a Gift**

21. **An Effective Slide Show**... *(revised)*

22. Guidelines for Effective Delivery

23. **Additional Resources**

24. **Consultant on Call**

25. **Project 3, Activity 4** *(position in file will vary)*

# Project 4

Print as directed by your instructor.

# Project 5

## Present File

1. Title Slide

2. Contemporary Communication

3. **Effective Speakers** *(revised)*

4. Average Presentation Rated

5. **Agenda**

6. **Challenges Facing Today's Speakers** *(divider slide 1)*

7. Top Mistakes Presenters Make

8. Meeting the Demands of Today's Audiences

9. Adept Speakers Must...

10. Adapting Speaking Style to Today's Fast Pace

11. Today's Messages Are...

12. Personal Connection a Must

13. **Presentation Planning Process** *(divider slide 2)*

14. Clear Objective Drives a Successful Presentation

15. **Presentation Planning Process** *(divider slide 3)*

16. Choosing an Appropriate Presentation Media

17. **Types of Presentation Visuals**

18. Multimedia

19. Still Projection Options

20. Boards and Flipcharts

21. Hard Copy Visuals

22. Process for Converting Slides to Overheads

23. **Benefits of Designing Visuals In-House**

24. A Speech Is a Gift

25. An Effective Slide Show...

26. **Presentation Planning Process** *(divider slide 4)*

27. Guidelines for Effective Delivery

28. Additional Resources

29. Consultant on Call

30. Project 3, Activity 4 *(position in file will vary)*

31. **Crucial Presentation Components** *(Divider Slide 1, Activity 1)*

32. **Crucial Presentation Components** *(Divider Slide 2, Activity 1)*

33. **Crucial Presentation Components** *(Divider Slide 3, Activity 1)*

## Interview File (Activity 2)

1. Enhanced Agenda Slide

2. Attention-Getter Slide: Real-Life Bloopers

3. Divider Slide—Feature Presentation: Act 1

4. Divider Slide—Feature Presentation: Act 2

5. Divider Slide—Feature Presentation: Act 3

6. Summary Slide: Make Your First Take...

# Project 6

1. Title Slide

2. Contemporary Communication

3. Effective Speakers

4. Average Presentation Rated

5. Agenda

6. Challenges Facing Today's Speakers *(divider slide 1)*

7. Top Mistakes Presenters Make

8. Meeting the Demands of Today's Audiences

9. Adept Speakers Must...

10. Adapting Speaking Style to Today's Fast Pace

11. Today's Messages Are...

12. Personal Connection a Must

13. Presentation Planning Process *(divider slide 2)*

14. Clear Objective Drives a Successful Presentation

15. Presentation Planning Process *(divider slide 3)*

16. Choosing an Appropriate Presentation Media

17. Types of Presentation Visuals

18. Multimedia

19. Still Projection Options

20. Boards and Flipcharts

21. Hard Copy Visuals

22. Process for Converting Slides to Overheads

23. Benefits of Designing Visuals In-House

24. A Speech Is a Gift

25. An Effective Slide Show...

26. **Common Problems with Visuals**

27. **The Speaker Is the Star**

28. Presentation Planning Process *(divider slide 4)*

29. Guidelines for Effective Delivery

30. **Harnessing the Power of Your Voice**

31. **Communicate Warmth and Confidence with Body Language**

32. **Avoid Confusing Expressions**

33. Additional Resources

34. Consultant on Call

35. Project 3, Activity 4 *(position in file will vary)*

36. Crucial Presentation Components *(Divider Slide 1, Activity 1)*

37. Crucial Presentation Components *(Divider Slide 2, Activity 1)*

38. Crucial Presentation Components *(Divider Slide 3, Activity 1)*

# Project 7

1. Title Slide

2. Contemporary Communication

3. Effective Speakers

4. Average Presentation Rated

5. Agenda

6. Challenges Facing Today's Speakers *(divider slide 1)*

7. Top Mistakes Presenters Make

8. Meeting the Demands of Today's Audiences

9. Adept Speakers Must...

10. Adapting Speaking Style to Today's Fast Pace

11. Today's Messages Are...

12. Personal Connection a Must

13. Presentation Planning Process *(divider slide 2)*

14. Clear Objective Drives a Successful Presentation

15. Presentation Planning Process *(divider slide 3)*

16. **Using Presentation Visuals Increases Audience Retention**

17. Choosing an Appropriate Presentation Media

18. Types of Presentation Visuals

19. Multimedia

20. Still Projection Options

21. Boards and Flipcharts

22. Hard Copy Visuals

23. Process for Converting Slides to Overheads

24. Benefits of Designing Visuals In-House

25. Common Problems with Visuals

26. **Annoying PowerPoint Usage**

27. A Speech Is a Gift

28. An Effective Slide Show...

29. The Speaker Is the Star

30. Presentation Planning Process *(divider slide 4)*

31. **Public Speaking Tops List of People's Greatest Fears**

32. **Preparation Is the Key to Reducing Speech Anxiety**

33. Guidelines for Effective Delivery

34. Harnessing the Power of Your Voice

35. Communicate Warmth and Confidence with Body Language

36. Avoid Confusing Expressions

37. Additional Resources

38. Consultant on Call

39. Project 3, Activity 4 *(position in file will vary)*

40. Crucial Presentation Components *(Divider Slide 1, Activity 1)*

41. Crucial Presentation Components *(Divider Slide 2, Activity 1)*

42. Crucial Presentation Components *(Divider Slide 3, Activity 1)*

43. **Percentage Increase in Audience Retention When Visuals Are Used** *(simplified chart)*

44. **Percentage Increase in Audience Retention When Visuals Are Used** *(photo background)*

## Project 8

Print as directed by your instructor.

## Project 9

1. Title Slide *(revised Project 9, Activity 1)*

2. Contemporary Communication

3. Effective Speakers

4. Average Presentation Rated

5. Agenda

6. Challenges Facing Today's Speakers *(divider slide 1)*

7. **Top Mistakes Presenters Make** *(revised)*

8. Meeting the Demands of Today's Audiences

9. Adept Audiences Must...

10. **Adapting Speaking Style to Today's Fast Pace** *(revised)*

11. Today's Messages Are...

12. Personal Connection a Must

13. Presentation Planning Process *(divider slide 2)*

14. Clear Objective Drives a Successful Presentation

15. Presentation Planning Process *(divider slide 3)*

16. Using Presentation Visuals Increases Audience Retention

17. **Technology Expenditure Budget 2003–2005**

18. Choosing an Appropriate Presentation Media

19. **Types of Presentation Visuals** *(revised)*

20. **Multimedia** *(revised)*

21. **Still Projection Options** *(revised)*

22. **Boards and Flipcharts** *(revised)*

23. **Hard Copy Visuals** *(revised)*

24. Process for Converting Slides to Overheads

25. Benefits of Designing Visuals In-House

26. Common Problems with Visuals

27. Annoying PowerPoint Usage

28. A Speech Is a Gift

29. An Effective Slide Show...

30. The Speaker Is the Star

31. Presentation Planning Process *(divider slide 4)*

32. Public Speaking Tops List of People's Greatest Fears

33. Preparation Is the Key to Reducing Speech Anxiety

34. Guidelines for Effective Delivery

35. Harnessing the Power of Your Voice

36. Communicate Warmth and Confidence with Body Language

37. Avoid Confusing Expressions

38. Additional Resources

39. Consultant on Call

40. Project 3, Activity 4 *(position in file will vary)*

41. Crucial Presentation Components *(Divider Slide 1, Project 5, Activity 1)*

42. Crucial Presentation Components *(Divider Slide 2, Project 5, Activity 1)*

43. Crucial Presentation Components *(Divider Slide 3, Project 5, Activity 1)*

44. Percentage Increase in Audience Retention When Visuals Are Used *(simplified chart)*

45. Percentage Increase in Audience Retention When Visuals Are Used *(photo background)*

46. **Types of Presentation Visuals *(Project 9, Activity 2)***

47. **Management Executive Training Attendance, 2005 *(Project 9, Activity 3)***

# Project 10
## Wellness Program file

1. Services Our Wellness Program Offers (Opening Screen)

2. Health Testing

3. Schedule for Health Testing

4. Education Programs

5. Scheduled Classes

6. Fitness Center

7. Main Exercise Room (student's design)

8. Indoor Track (student's design)

9. Aquatic Center (student's design)

## Effective Team

1. Introduction

2. Value of Teams

3. Productivity Levels

4. Solution

5. The End

# Index to Feature Boxes